The New
Institutionalism
in Education

THE NEW INSTITUTIONALISM IN EDUCATION

Edited by

HEINZ-DIETER MEYER
BRIAN ROWAN

STATE UNIVERSITY OF NEW YORK PRESS

Published by
State University of New York Press, Albany

© 2006 State University of New York

For information, contact State University of New York Press, Albany, NY
www.sunypress.edu

Production by Christine L. Hamel
Marketing by Susan M. Petrie

Library of Congress Cataloging-in-Publication Data

The new institutionalism in education / edited by Heinz-Dieter Meyer,
Brian Rowan.
     p. cm.
Includes bibliographical references and index.
   ISBN: 978-0-7914-6905-7 (hardcover : alk. paper)
   ISBN: 978-0-7914-6906-4 (pbk. : alk. paper)
1. School management and organization—Philosophy. 2. Educational sociology.
3. Institutions (Philosophy) I. Meyer, Heinz-Dieter. II. Rowan, Brian.

LB2805.N489 2006
306.43—dc22

                                                          2005033518

               10 9 8 7 6 5 4 3 2 1

Contents

Illustrations

Acknowledgments

This volume began with a generous grant by the RGK Foundation in support of a scholarly conference to explore the implications of the "new institutionalism" for education research and analysis. The conference was attended by sociologists and scholars in the fields of education, education policy, and organization studies and generated the drafts for the majority of the chapters in this book. It is a reasonable guess that without such small, more sharply focused conferences many themes and topics in the social sciences would remain unexplored. Thus our sincere thanks to the people at RGK who generously and unbureaucratically supported this undertaking. Thanks, too, to the University at Albany, for the hospitality extended to the conference participants and the support to the organizers. Finally, warm thanks to Lisa Chesnel at State University of New York Press who remained a cheerful supporter of this book from proposal to final version.

ONE

Institutional Analysis and the Study of Education

HEINZ-DIETER MEYER
BRIAN ROWAN

SINCE THE 1990s, a theoretical perspective known as the "new institutionalism" has captured the imagination of scholars working in academic fields that contribute to educational research and policy analysis, including sociology, political science, economics, and organization theory. The rise of this theoretical perspective has been due, in part, to a widespread disenchantment of social scientists with models of social and organizational action in which relatively autonomous actors are seen as operating with unbounded rationality in order to pursue their self-interests. It also has been due to advances in theory and research, reflected in the publication of several influential volumes showing how a "new" institutionalism could be applied to research in particular areas of study. March and Olsen (1989), for example, applied institutional theory to the study of politics broadly, and North (1990), DiMaggio (1998), Powell and DiMaggio (1991), Scott (1995), and Brinton and Nees (1998) applied it to the study of economic change and development, organization theory, and the sociological study of institutions respectively. The emergence of a new institutionalism across the social sciences signals the possibility of a new unity in these often fragmented disciplines, and it promises to provide researchers with a more universal language to describe and conceptualize research problems that are common to many fields.

Despite its promise, applications of the new institutionalism to the study of education have been scattered and diffuse (Bacharach, Masters, and

1

Mundell 1995; Crowson, Boyd, and Mawhinney 1996). With the exception of Rowan and Miskel's (1999) survey of the new institutionalism in education, comprehensive efforts at describing and interpreting the new landscape of institutional theory have been missing in the field. Instead, many education theorists have tended to treat institutional theory as if the theoretical models and predictions that emerged out of work by John W. Meyer, W. Richard Scott, Brian Rowan, and others during the late 1970s and early 1980s represented its final form (e.g., Meyer and Rowan 1977, 1978; Meyer and Scott 1983). This slow recognition of new developments in the ways educational institutions might be studied stands in sharp contrast to the actual changes in educational institutions occurring on the ground. New social developments, we argue, have produced novel institutional practices with which institutional theory and research in education have yet to catch up. In the United States, for example, we are experiencing enormous and (as we show in this book) consequential changes in education that are bringing about an increased level of centralization and pragmentation, an increased demand for accountability, and a heightened concern with educational productivity. New forms of educational organizations ranging from home schooling, through charter schools, to privately held firms that provide tutoring and other forms of instructional services have arisen outside public education and are on the way to becoming firmly institutionalized. At the same time there are changes in higher education, too. The emergence of a small but growing for-profit higher education sector in the United States and abroad is introducing a new element of competition and forcing established institutions to become more market minded and entrepreneurial. Three changes in particular have altered the institutional reality of education in both the K–12 and the higher education arena:

1. *Greater provider pluralism:* while basic schooling and much of higher education around the world used to be provided almost exclusively by states, rapid growth in the private provision of educational services has dramatically altered this situation; no longer a monopoly of government, education providers now come from the third sector and civil society and include private, market-oriented organizations.
2. *More tight coupling:* widespread calls for more accountability have led to a shift to more tightly coupled and narrowly controlled practices in organizations that were once exemplars of "loose coupling."
3. *More central role of educational institution in society:* in an increasingly knowledge-dependent economy, schools and colleges take on a more central role in society's institutional fabric, and their performance has definite repercussions throughout society. As a result, families, entrepreneurs, voluntary organizations, and corporate ventures take a stronger role in the governance of education, and the institutional landscape changes from a monistic to a pluralistic world.

These new institutional realities present a challenge to the reigning institutional theories in education, especially those developed by John W. Meyer and colleagues in the late 1970s and early 1980s. The institutional analyses of education developed at that time have had an enormous impact on the field—both in the social sciences generally and in education in particular. But the view of educational institutions that emerged out of that work now seems oddly out of step with current events in the field. The institutional analyses of Meyer and colleagues say the American educational system is "loosely coupled," largely because the formal structure of schools and colleges were derived less from demands for technical efficiency than from needs to maintain their legitimacy in society. In this view, education was seen as being fully controlled by government and the professions and thus beyond the grip of market forces. Moreover, in this early version of institutional theory, change in educational organizations was seen almost exclusively as a process of evergrowing "isomorphism" of educational forms brought into conformity with the norms, values, and technical lore institutionalized by the state and the professions. Educational organizations were thus seen as "captive" (i.e., nonmarket) organizations, passively conforming to broader (and already institutionalized) forces, securing success through processes of institutional conformity as opposed to technical efficiency.

As the chapters of this book will show, however, many of these early ideas about educational organizations are undercut by changes in the field of education over the past fifteen years. Schools, it seems, are no longer shielded from the pressures of accountability and efficiency; the once airtight government monopoly of schooling has been invaded by private providers; the dominant institutional forms of schooling no longer serve as unrivalled models for emulation. Against this backdrop, this book is an attempt to reflect on, redefine, and reposition institutional analysis. It is also an attempt to catch up with some of the significant new developments occurring in education in order to develop a keener sense of institutional continuity and change in this important sector of our society.

In the remainder of this chapter, we will characterize older and newer lines of institutional analysis in greater detail and offer an overview of the book's chapters.

THE INSTITUTIONAL PERSPECTIVE
IN EDUCATION RESEARCH

A basic assumption of institutional thinking (old or new) is that large institutional complexes such as education, and the practices they give rise to, are contingent and contested. That is, social institutions can assume a large number of different shapes and forms, some of which appeal more to a particular

group of collective actors than others. A school, for example, can be a hand-
ful of children sitting under a tree listening to a story, a group of youngsters
learning to throw a discus in a gymnasium, or a group of adolescents in a
chemistry lab huddled around a Bunsen burner. The purpose of an institutional analysis is to tell us why—out of this stupendous variety of feasible
forms—this or that particular one is actually "selected" and whose interests
might be best served by that selected arrangement. Institutionalists want to
understand the trade-offs involved in using one form of institution to the
exclusion of other possible ones. They want to know what alternatives a society and its policy makers might have; which social group might be favored or
disadvantaged by a particular arrangement; whose vested interests might be
tied up with a given institutional form and practice. Through institutional
analysis we learn something about how education connects with other vital
institutions in society; what the constraints are under which this important
part of our social life takes place; and what the latitude and the limits are that
we confront if we attempted to change the existing institutional order.

Given formal education's central importance within modern societies, it
is not surprising that institutional analyses of education have been present in
the social sciences for more than a century. From the pioneering studies of
sociological founders such as Durkheim (1956) and Weber (1947), to early
critics such as Veblen (1918) and Waller (1932), to contemporary sociologists
such as Bidwell (1965), Archer (1984), Bourdieu and Passeron (1977), and
Collins (1979), social scientists have recognized the importance of education
and its institutional configurations. For this vein of research, Durkheim's char-
acterization of educational institutions in society is still valid:

> Education has varied infinitely in time and place. . . . Today, it tries to make
> of the individual an autonomous personality. In Athens, they sought to form
> cultivated souls, informed, subtle, full of measure and harmony, capable of
> enjoying beauty and the joys of pure speculation; in Rome, they wanted
> above all for children to become men of action, devoted to military glory,
> indifferent to letters and the arts. In the Middle Ages, education was above
> all Christian; in the Renaissance it assumes a more lay and literary charac-
> ter; today science tends to assume the place in education formerly occupied
> by the arts. (Durkheim 1956, 64)

In the United States, this sociological and comparative perspective has
been markedly enriched by work on the nature and functioning of American
education by institutional historians such as Bowles and Gintis (1976), Brint
and Karabel (1989), Callahan (1962), Kaestle and Vinvoskis (1980), Katz
(1968), Katznelson and Weir (1985), Lagemann-Condliff (2000), Tyack
(1974), Tyack, James, and Benevot (1987), and Ravitch (1974), to name a few.
Tyack (1974) showed how many American educators believed the march of

history was leading (through various fits and starts) to the unrivaled triumph of today's education system—a heavily bureaucratized "one best system" of state-supplied schooling, complete with an all-powerful and highly professionalized administration.

Starting in the 1970s, however, this older tradition of institutional analysis received strong innovative impulses from organizational scholars at Stanford who noted that educational organizations did not seem to conform to key tenets of organizational theory. For example, while bureaucratic hierarchies are almost always assumed to be held together by tight relations between top and bottom levels, scholars from the Stanford school found in the late 1970s that higher and lower levels of hierarchy in schools and colleges often were "loosely coupled" (Meyer and Rowan 1978, Weick 1976, March 1980). Moreover, where organization theory predicted that these loosely integrated organizations would be unstable, loosely coupled educational hierarchies in fact proved remarkably stable over long periods of time. Finally, although organization theorists at the time saw the structure of organizations as strongly determined by conditions in the technical core, the Stanford theorists noted that the links between the technical core of educational institutions—teaching and learning in classrooms—and the formal structure of schools seemed highly tenuous.

The key to explaining these anomalies was to view educational organizations as institutionalized organizations, that is, as organizations whose most important constraint was not efficiency but rather legitimacy (Meyer and Rowan 1977; Meyer 1977; Meyer and Scott 1983; March 1980). Organizations such as schools and colleges, the Stanford argument went, are held together more by shared beliefs—"myths"—than by technical exigencies or a logic of efficiency. Thus, the key constraint for educational institutions in this view is the need to maintain the trust and confidence of the public at large—in short, to maintain legitimacy by conforming to institutionalized norms, values, and technical lore.

WHAT IS THE NEW INSTITUTIONALISM?

The arguments just reviewed are often seen as constituting the new institutionalism in the field of education. But as Rowan (1995) and Rowan and Miskel (1999, 359) point out, during the 1990s there was a renaissance of institutional scholarship in the social sciences generally. An important feature of this renaissance was that it encouraged researchers across the social sciences to move beyond the narrow confines of their specialized expertise in order to explore a common set of theoretical concepts and ideas about the structure and operations of major societal sectors in nations around the world. Though diverse and sometimes inconsistent in their goals and assumptions, these researchers shared a number of ideas that distinguished their approach to institutional analysis from more traditional (or "older") forms of institutional scholarship.

This book takes up three important themes that mark the difference between this newer institutionalism and the older forms of institutional analysis it seeks to replace. In the following sections we discuss these themes briefly and signal to the reader the chapters in this book that develop these themes in the context of education.

Cognition and the Social Construction of Institutions

Much of the "older" institutional analysis was focused on formal legal structures as they developed over long historic periods. This type of institutional analysis tended to view institutions as objective structures that exist independent of human action. The new institutionalism, by contrast, sees man-made rules and procedures as the basic building blocks of institutions. In this view, institutions gain an independent existence "out there" by being socially constructed "in here"—that is, in the minds of individual actors who have a stake in them. Before institutions can gain authority as objective social structures they must be endowed with meaning by cognitive acts of individuals. New institutionalists locate the origin of institutions in taken-for-granted classifications, scripts, and schemata that humans use to make sense of a disorderly world. "Compliance occurs in many circumstances because other types of behavior are inconceivable; routines are followed because they are taken for granted as the way we do these things. Institutions are thus repositories of taken-for-granted cognitive schemata that shape people's understandings of the world they live in and provide scripts to guide their action. The emphasis in the new institutionalism, then, is on how people actively construct meaning within institutionalized settings through language and other symbolic representations.

Several chapters in this volume emphasize the role that shared beliefs and cognitions play in institution building. Ramirez, for example, discusses the role that an evolving conception of the "modern" university is playing in shaping higher educational institutions worldwide. He describes how this cognitive schema has been shaped by the uniquely American image of the modern university and how the global diffusion of this variant of higher education often comes into conflict with local traditions of culture, language, and a uniquely national narrative of "our" university system. Ramirez argues that the relative strength of national versus global models of education in the evolution of higher education differs across nations. In nations with weak indigenous academic traditions, the global pressures to rally around a singular "world" model of universities are felt more strongly than in countries that have long academic histories of their own.

Interestingly, Ramirez' attention to a dominant "world" model of higher education stands in marked contrast to Levy's discussion (in this volume) of the tendency in many nations around the world toward diversity in higher education. In fact, Levy presents considerable evidence that divergent forms of higher education are emerging all over the world, largely in the private education sector, and that many of these forms are sharply at odds with the established university models in these nations. Levy's chapter thus questions a central tenet of early institutional theory—the notion that educational forms will tend toward structural isomorphism.

H. D. Meyer looks at how shared beliefs and cognitive schemata have helped stabilize the conception of American public education as the common school. Noting that the widespread support for public education in the United States has depended to a large extent on the legitimacy of the common school ideal and the associated ideas that schools can level socioeconomic differences and bridge religious-moral divides, he argues that to the extent that the legitimacy of these ideas is waning, American's historic faith in the redemptive and equalizing role of public schooling will erode, too.

Institutions, States, and Markets

A second theme of the new institutionalism involves the changing ties among the polity, the economy, and civil society. In particular, the new institutionalists view economic markets as institutionally embedded and thus affected by institutionalized forms of property, security, modes of enforcing contracts that are developed by states and enacted in civil society. Depending on the specific institutional arrangements, the relative efficiency and distributional consequences of economic behavior may vary widely. Like traditional economic actors, the parties to economic transactions are seen as motivated by the potential costs and benefits of an exchange. But unlike rational choice notions of economic behavior, the new institutionalism does not see individuals as autonomous authors of their preferences. Rather, their preference formation takes place within the constraints of the "preferences" imposed by the institutional settings (Immergut 1998; Ingram and Clay 2000).

In this view, then, economic actors are not indifferent to the institutional arrangements (and the concomitant cost/benefit ratios) under which they barter. Therefore, they will bargain over not only a given exchange, but also over the institutional framework for their action. This makes bargaining, conflict and power ubiquitous facts in the world of institutions. It also leads to a view of institutional change as interest-based struggle that rational actors use to obtain favorable institutional arrangements. Self-interest is always constructed in the context of specific institutional and historical parameters. Rational actor models in the new institutionalism thus explicitly recognize the futility of trying to explain human behavior without reference to history, tradition, culture, and idiosyncratic institutional configurations—all manner of social contexts that lend human behavior its characteristic complexity. As Powell (1991, 187) put it: "institutional processes help shape the very structure of economic arrangements." The fact that institutional processes penetrate and shape economic relations further implies the obsolescence of the identification of "institutional with non-profit and technical with for-profit" (Powell and DiMaggio 1991, 33). Finally, when highly rationalized actions such as market transactions are seen as shaped by institutions, "the notion that institutional and technical imperatives are inconsistent" seems out of date (Powell and DiMaggio 1991, 32).

Several chapters in this volume take off from these insights about markets as institutions, about the ways in which governance and market forces combine in institutional affairs to produce unique pressures on educational organizations for both conformity and efficiency, and about the deeply institutionalized nature of even the most rational of actions. The tightening control of government over the core technology of schooling inevitably invites a discussion about the emergence of market supply of education in K–12 and higher education sectors around the world. Institutional theories of the 1970s and 1980s (e.g., Meyer and Rowan 1978) largely ignored this problem, but discussions of education "markets" now seem central to education reform, not only in the United States, but in many other nations of the world as well. Indeed public attention to marketlike forms of education is growing, as shown in the United States by the growth of charter schools, voucher schemes, privately managed school systems, home schooling, and so on.

Three chapters in this book examine this problem through the lens of institutional theory. One is Levy's analysis of growth in private-sector higher education; another is Davies, Quirke, and Aurin's chapter on the structure and operations of private K–12 education in Toronto, Canada. Both chapters ask whether education markets work against the trend toward structural isomorphism that early institutional theorists saw as a central trend of educational organization in the modern world. The authors find that, under certain conditions, markets do indeed appear to produce more diverse forms of educational organization than institutional theory heretofore predicted. Finally, Bernasconi's study of higher education reform in Chile (chapter 11) focuses on a case in which a government effectively broke the mold of government-controlled higher education by introducing market-based reforms. He shows that as market ideologies penetrated Chilean society during the Pinochet era, the Chilean government introduced a performance measurement system into higher education that opened this system up to increased competitiveness and entrepreneurialism.

The expanding reach of institutionalized markets also becomes obvious in the chapters by Rowan and Baker. Brian Rowan (in both his chapters in this volume) calls attention to the fact that a variety of organizations serve as key actors in the larger institutional environment of education—including for-profit organizations such as textbook manufacturers, nonprofit research and advocacy groups, trades unions, and so on. Similarly, David Baker's chapter in this volume points to the growing complexity of forces shaping education in modern societies, including parental pressures that are apparently giving rise to an entire "shadow education" system of private organizations that seems to be emerging alongside the usual state-sponsored, mass education system.

Other chapters in this volume address the relation between institutional and technical imperatives. Rowan (chapter 2), for example, shows how government regulations targeting the institutionalization of new accountability schemes have real effects on the inner ("technical") workings of schools. Spillane and Burch also look at this issue and demonstrate that government controls can take on different forms, especially in the regulation of different subject areas within the school curriculum. Their analysis suggests that math and language arts instruction in schools tend to be far more tightly coupled to government policy than science or history instruction. Together, these analyses suggest a need to revisit one of the master themes in institutional analyses of schooling—the argument that institutional controls necessarily lead to loose coupling and "nonrational" action in education systems.

History, Power, and Change

A final theme in the new institutionalism is the notion that we need to pay more attention to the concrete historical actors who built a particular institution. These actors are motivated by self-interest, but also by their values and cultural beliefs, which arise in a context of existing institutions. Whereas older forms of institutional analysis built around simple descriptive data or guided by structural functionalism sometimes neglected issues of power and conflict in institution building, new institutionalists try to address "head on issues of change, power, and efficiency" (DiMaggio and Powell 1991, 27). They "place interests and power on the institutional agenda" and "deepen the conversation about the form that a theory of institutional change might take" (ibid.). Institutionalists make no assumption that institutional arrangements garnering the support of the most powerful coalitions necessarily produce the most efficient institutional arrangements. In fact, dominant coalitions may precisely act to delay or prevent institutional change toward more optimal solutions. This also means that institutional change will often require political change—a redistribution of power that issues in greater societal emphasis on heretofore neglected or suppressed ideas and the groups that hold them.

Whereas older forms of institutional theory were satisfied with giving descriptive accounts of institutional change, the new institutionalism aspires to greater levels of analytical precision. At present, the most frequently invoked model of institutional change relies on notions of institutional equilibrium that can be upset by "exogenous shocks" that disrupt existing institutional equilibriums, or by internal contradictions in existing institutional logics. As actors confront these conditions, historical institutionalism locates many different mechanisms that structure institutional change, including not only interest-based conflict and power struggles but also mechanisms of social learning and experimentation. As these mechanisms of change unfold, the emphasis in historical institutionalism is on how existing institutional arrangements both exclude actions from the "feasible set" of proposed changes and how these arrangements facilitate or enable particular new actions. Institutional arrangements are seen as path dependent, that is, emerging as a result of preexisting institutional formations and the affordances and constraints provided therein.

Several chapters in this volume examine issues of power and change in the process of institutional change. The chapter by Charles Bidwell, for example, argues that to understand institutional change in education, we have to understand the role of power in society. As Bidwell sees it, issues of power and conflict have been largely absent from many newer institutional theories of education, particularly versions of institutional theory that emphasize the stable and consensual nature of educational institutions and the ways in which this stimulates isomorphism within organizational fields. Bidwell's emphasis on the centrality of power in institutional analysis does not negate a view of institutions as forces of order and stability in society, but it does call attention to how such stable and orderly institutions are built in the first place. His account of the creation of the University of Paris is a fascinating illustration of the political dimension of institution building.

H. D. Meyer's study of the emergence and decline of the myth of the common school also deals with power in American public education. Meyer argues that the common school ideal was created in American society by an idiosyncratic coalition of New England patricians and urban reformers who united for a brief historical moment to avoid civil unrest and instability in the days of mass immigration. A slightly different course of history might not have resulted in the formation of this unlikely coalition of aristocratic patricians and idealistic urban reformers. Moreover, his comparison of the common school ideal to the German educational master-myth of *Bildung* underscores the distinctiveness of the common school myth.

LOOKING TO THE FUTURE

The empirical trends documented in this book suggest a complex picture of increasing institutional diversity and of conflicting trends that defy easy categorization. The chapters describe the strong growth of decentralized, private-sector education around the world, which—in the United States at least—stands opposite a growing government capacity to manage and control established educational organizations. While the growth of private education—both full-time and auxiliary (tutoring)—is giving a degree of control and choice back to the parents and students who can afford it, it may also signal new educational inequality in the form of unequal power to purchase private educational services. The partial retreat of the state, which harbors the possibility for a growing plurality of independent providers, has also eased the emergence of corporate giants in the field of education, especially firms that control textbook, test, and educational media production. Just as the call for accountability became the leading mantra of education reform, the private interests directing the mammoth corporations are not accountable to the public but only to their shareholders. This concentration of power over the minds of the young in the hands of a small group of corporate investors not only makes the government call for accountability sound hollow. It may also counteract the increase in individual autonomy and choice that otherwise might result from the partial retreat of the state and the growth of education markets.

While it is too early to declare any of these emerging trends as settled reality, neither is it likely that the chain of these ongoing changes will lead back to the status quo ante. In this volatile situation, the new institutionalism has a unique contribution to make in analyzing complex and contradictory patterns of institutional change. By casting a wider net to capture developments outside of, yet influential for, the educational arena proper, by comparing developments in different societies, and by fresh efforts to fit institutional theory to new conditions and circumstances, we believe institutional analysis can continue to make exciting and useful contributions to understanding the changes in an important part of our institutional fabric.

REFERENCES

Archer, Margaret S. 1984 [1979]. *Social origins of educational systems.* Beverly Hills: Sage.

Bacharach, Samuel B., W. Frank Masters, and Bryan Mundell. 1995. Institutional theory and the politics of institutionalization: Logics of action in school reform. In *Advances in research and theories of school management and educational policy,* ed. Rodney T. Ogawa, 3: 83–122. Greenwich, CN: JAI.

Bidwell, Charles. 1965. The school as formal organization. In *Handbook of Organizations,* ed. J. G. March, 972–1019. New York: Rand McNally.

Bourdieu, Pierre, and Jean-Claude Passeron. 1977. *Reproduction in education, society, and culture.* London: Sage.

Bowles, Samuel, and Herbert Gintis. 1976. *Schooling in capitalist America.* New York: Basic Books.

Brint, Steven and Jerome Karabel. 1989. *The diverted dream: Community colleges and the promise of educational opportunity in America, 1900–1985.* New York: Oxford University Press.

Brinton, Mary, and Victor Nee. 2000 [1998]. *The new institutionalism in sociology*. Stanford: Stanford University Press.

Callahan, Raymond E. 1962. *Education and the cult of efficiency*. Chicago: University of Chicago Press.

Campbell, John L., and Ove K. Pedersen. 2001. The rise of neoliberalism and institutional analysis. In *The rise of neoliberalism and institutional analysis*, ed. John L. Campbell and Ove K. Pedersen. Princeton, NJ: Princeton University Press.

Collins, Randall. 1979. *The credential society*. New York: Academic.

Crowson, Robert L., William L. Boyd, and Hanne B. Mawhinney, eds. 1996. *The politics of education and the new institutionalism: Reinventing the American school*. Washington, DC: Falmer.

DiMaggio, Paul. 1998. The new institutionalism: Avenues for collaboration. *Journal of Institutional and Theoretical Economics* 154(4): 696–705.

Durkheim, Émile. 1956. *Education and sociology*. Trans. Sherwood D. Fox. Glencoe, IL: Free Press of Glencoe.

Immergut, Ellen M. 1998. The theoretical core of the new institutionalism. *Politics and Society* 26(1): 5–35.

Ingram, Paul, and Karen Clay. 2000. The choice-within-constraints new institutionalism and implications for sociology. *Annual Review of Sociology* 26(1): 525–47.

Kaestle, Carl F., and Maris Vinovskis. 1980. *Education and change in nineteenth century Massachusetts*. Cambridge: Cambridge University Press.

Katz, Michael. 1968. *The irony of early school reform: Educational innovation in mid-nineteenth century Massachusetts*. Cambridge MA: Harvard University Press.

Katznelson, Ira, and Margaret Weir. 1985. *Schooling for all: Race, class, and the decline of the democratic ideal*. New York: Basic Books.

Lagemann-Condliffe, Ellen. 2000. *An Elusive Science: The Troubling History of American Education Research*. Chicago: University of Chicago Press.

March, James 1980. *Ambiguity and choice in organizations*. Oxford: Oxford University Press.

March, James G., and Johan P. Olsen. 1989. *Rediscovering institutions: The organizational basis of politics*. New York: Free Press.

Meyer, Heinz-Dieter. 2002. From loose coupling to tight management? Making sense of the changing landscape in organization and management. *Journal of Education Administration* 40(6): 515–20.

———. 2003. Tocqueville's cultural institutionalism. *Journal of Classical Sociology* 3(2): 197–220.

Meyer, John W. 1977. The effects of education as an institution. *American Journal of Sociology* 83(1): 55–77.

Meyer, John W., and Brian Rowan. 1977. Institutional organizations: Formal structure as myth and ceremony. *American Journal of Sociology* 83: 340–63.

———. 1978. The structure of educational organizations. In *Environments and organizations*, ed. Marshall W. Meyer, 78–109. San Francisco: Jossey-Bass.

Meyer, John W., and W. Richard Scott. 1983. *Organizational environments: Ritual and rationality*. Beverly Hills: Sage.

North, Douglass C. 1990. *Institutions, institutional change, and economic performance.* Cambridge: Cambridge University Press.

Powell, Walter. 1991. Expanding the scope of institutional analysis. In *The new institutionalism in organizational analysis,* ed. Walter Powell and Paul J. DiMaggio, 183–203. Chicago: Chicago University Press.

Powell, Walter. W., Jr., and Paul DiMaggio, eds. 1991. *The new institutionalism in organizational analysis.* Chicago: University of Chicago Press.

Ravitch, Diane. 1974. *The great school wars: A history of the New York City public schools.* New York: Basic Books.

Rowan, Brian. 1995. Institutional analysis of educational organizations: Lines of theory and directions for research. In *Advances in research and theories of school management and educational policy,* ed. Rodney T. Ogawa, 3: 1–20. Greenwich, CN: JAI.

Rowan, Brian, and Cecil G. Miskel. 1999. Institutional theory and the study of educational organizations. In *Handbook of research on educational administration,* ed. J. Murphy and K. Seashore-Louis. San Francisco: Jossey-Bass.

Scott, W. Richard. 1995. *Institutions and organizations.* Thousand Oaks, CA: Sage.

Tyack, David. 1974. *The one best system.* Cambridge, MA: Harvard University Press.

Tyack, David, Thomas James, and Aaron Benavot. 1987. *Law and the shaping of public education, 1785–1954.* Cambridge, MA: Harvard University Press.

Waller, Willard. 1932. *The sociology of teaching.* New York: Wiley.

Veblen, Thorstein. 1971. *The higher learning in America.* New York: Augustus Kelley (first published: 1918).

Weber, Max. 1947. *The theory of social and economic organization.* Ed. A. H. Henderson and Talcott Parsons. Glencoe, IL: Free Press.

Weick, Karl A. 1976. Educational organizations as loosely coupled systems. *Administrative Science Quarterly* 21: 1–19.

TWO

The New Institutionalism and the Study of Educational Organizations: Changing Ideas for Changing Times

BRIAN ROWAN

THIS CHAPTER IS ABOUT the "new" institutionalism in the social sciences and how it can be used to analyze contemporary trends in American education. It is not a systematic review of this constellation of theoretical perspectives on institutions or how they have developed in the social sciences over the past decade (for reviews on this topic, see Brinton and Nee 1998; DiMaggio and Powell 1991; March and Olsen 1989; Rowan and Miskel 1999; Scott and Meyer 1991; Scott 1995; Scott and Christensen 1995). Instead, this chapter focuses on new developments in the field of organizational studies and on how these new developments can be used to study K–12 educational organizations in the United States.

A fundamental premise of the chapter is that both the new institutionalism and American education have evolved considerably since the 1970s, when the new institutionalism first burst on the scene. Early contributions to institutional theory tended to focus on public organizations, especially on public organizations such as schools that operate ill-defined technologies within fragmented and pluralistic policy environments (e.g., Meyer and Rowan 1978,

Meyer, Scott, and Deal 1983). The primary contribution of early institutional theory was the argument that such organizations were built largely around a logic of institutional conformity rather than a logic of technical efficiency and that they were characterized by a pattern of management in which the institutional and technical levels of administration were only loosely coupled (e.g., Parsons 1960).

Since these early arguments were first advanced, however, the scope of institutional theory has expanded. For example, institutional theorists now study both public *and* private organizations, as these operate in institutional environments emphasizing both institutional conformity and technical efficiency. In addition, new ideas have emerged in institutional theory about who the key actors in institutional environments are, about how institutional environments are organized, and about the kinds of pressures that institutional environments bring to bear on organizations. Whereas institutional theorists once viewed the state and the professions as the dominant actors in institutional environments, once saw politics as the main animating force of institutional change, and once postulated ceremonial conformity as the main way organizations gained support and resources, institutional theorist today give attention to a great many agencies and actors in the social environment (including private firms, political interest groups, and primordial groups such as families), study both markets and politics as animating forces in institutional environments, and analyze how institutional environments can promote both efficiency and conformity.

American education also has changed since the new institutionalism burst on the scene in the 1970s and 1980s. For more than two decades, school finance laws and federal policy initiatives have been altering longstanding patterns of educational governance in the United States, shifting power and authority in education more clearly into the hands of state governments and bringing about a small measure of "systemic" reform to the fragmented system of educational governance in American education. In addition, a more elaborate "technical theory" of schooling has emerged, as large testing companies, state education agencies, and various segments of the education profession coalesced in support of policy instruments designed to more clearly specify standards for curricular content in schools, allow student achievement outcomes to be inspected more closely, and hold schools more accountable for student performance. All of this, it appears, has worked to decrease Americans' historic confidence in public schools and as a consequence, unleashed at least a measure of market competition into the K–12 education sector.

These changes lead to the main theme of this chapter. I argue that a "new" institutional analysis is needed to understand the changing landscape of American education. Such an analysis, I argue, will build on developments in institutional theory over the past two decades to take fuller account of the diversity of actors in the institutional environment of American schools; it will better describe the role these actors play in shaping both governance and market arrangements in education; it will explain how pressures for technical efficiencies emerged alongside pressures for political conformity in contemporary American education; and it will aim to study the effects of these factors on the populations of organizations that provide instructional services directly to students.

SOCIETAL SECTORS: THE STARTING POINT FOR A "NEW" INSTITUTIONAL ANALYSIS

My preferred starting point for a new institutional analysis of K–12 education is Scott and Meyer's (1991) work on the organization of societal sectors and the role sectoral analysis plays in institutional theory. Scott and Meyer defined a societal sector as: (1) that set of organizations directly supplying particular kinds of goods and services to consumers, as well as (2) the organizations and agencies that regularly interact with, support, or attempt to govern these organizations (DiMaggio and Powell 1983; Scott and Meyer 1991). In Scott and Meyer's view, the key tasks of institutional theory are to carefully chart the actors making up a societal sector, to analyze how these actors come to be organized into networks of governance and exchange, and to build theories about how sectoral configurations affect the structure and functioning of organizations composing the sector.

Following Scott and Meyer's (1991) lead suggests several new directions for institutional analyses of educational organizations. First, their definition of institutional sectors encourages us to take an expansive view of the organizations composing the K–12 education sector in American society. For example, there is tremendous diversity among the organizations directly providing instructional services in the sector, including not only the eighty-eight thousand or so public and private schools providing K–12 "schooling" but also a variety of other organizations that provide tutoring, test preparation, and other educational services outside of school hours. In my view, an important goal of any new institutional analysis of American education would be to examine how all of these organizations function—both as separate populations of organizations and in relation to one another.[1]

But a new institutional analysis of education should examine more than the sets of organizations that directly provide services in the education sector, for another obvious feature of K–12 education in America is the centrality of politics to educational organization. The political control of education, its provision as a public good, and the large place education assumes in public budgets makes educational organizations a frequent target of government policy. Thus, the activities of government agencies in the field of education are also an important part of any institutional analysis. But elected officials and their administrative agencies are not the only political actors in the sector. There are also political elites and their party organizations, experts and their think tanks and advocacy groups, professionalized and unionized employee groups in myriad diversity, and a host of organized interest groups, all of whom not only lobby politicians but also seek judicial protection of their interests.[2]

Finally, education in the United States is more than big politics; it is also "big" business. Indeed, many different private and/or quasipublic organizations arise in the K–12 education sector to supply a vast array of goods and services to schools through economic exchange. In the United States, for example, more than 80 percent of all K–12 education agencies contract with business establishments for the provision of "back office" business and technical services, generating a $3.7 billion per year market catered to by thirty-seven hundred separate business organizations in the United States. The business of education also includes the supply of goods and services that are directly relevant to the main function of schooling—instruction. For example, more than four hundred establishments offer research and evaluation services in the U.S. education sector, earning over $500 million per year, while another one thousand to two thousand private organizations provide schools and their employees with training and information. Finally, in the K–12 sector alone, the purchase of textbooks by local school systems is a $1.85 billion per year business. Thus, education in the United States (and in most other advanced capitalist societies) is both "big" politics and "big" business.[3]

GOVERNANCE AND EXCHANGE
IN SOCIETAL SECTORS

One implication of this last observation is that any "new" institutional analysis of American education will examine not only *governance* relations in the K–12 education sector but also *exchange* relations.[4] In fact, there is a great deal of interest in exchange relationships in the broader field of institutional analysis (e.g., Brinton and Nee 1998), but institutional analyses of K–12 education have not followed suit, tending to emphasize problems of governance while underplaying problems of exchange. In educational analysis, for example, the "problems" of K–12 education in the United States are often examined in reference to relationships among schools and their governing agencies. In the United States, especially, the fragmented centralization of K–12 education governance is seen as a major explanation for why schools exist as "loosely coupled" organizations and as a major target of educational reform.

To be sure, political analyses of education will remain important to institutional analysis in education in the coming years. However, I would like to build a case in this chapter about the need to expand institutional analyses in education beyond an exclusive concern with political governance to include also a concern with issues of market exchange. I do this for several reasons. One is that problems of exchange loom large in many areas of education. They figure centrally in such mundane problems as whether or not K–12 schools should contract with Pepsico or other major food companies to supply school cafeterias. But they also figure prominently in issues that are central to the core mission of educational organizations, for example, in debates about whether private education management organizations (EMOs) such as Edison schools can provide better and more effective management services to K–12 schools, in debates about the wisdom of allowing Channel 1 (with its commercial advertising) into classrooms in exchange for televisions and educational programming, and in debates about the role of comprehensive school reform program providers in stimulating instructional improvement in schools. More to the point, economic exchange has also been central to the very construction of the "technical core" of schools, which is built around textbooks, tests, and other instructional supplies manufactured outside K–12 schools. Indeed, as I tried to argue in my discussion of the nature of the K–12 education sector in American society, economic exchange is a central element of educational affairs and, as such, worthy of attention in its own right.

Exchange and Governance

One way to study exchange problems in the K–12 education sector would be to draw on neo-institutional approaches in economics. Here, for example, one might examine the classic "make or buy" problem of transaction cost economics, or use principal-agent theory, and in this way study how to rationalize the contracts governing a wide array of internal and cross-boundary exchange relationships in education. Along these lines, one might analyze the contracts among teachers and school systems using principal-agent theory, asking how such contracts developed, whether they provide the most cost-efficient and rational employment relation possible, and so on. Similar analyses could be performed for many other exchanges using the transaction cost perspective, including purchases of food, management services, textbooks, professional development services, and so on. The goal, of course, would be to arrive at the most "rationalized" and economizing forms of contractual governance for these exchanges.

However, strictly economic thinking will not take us very far in understanding economic exchanges for several reasons. One problem is that exchange relationships emerge in and are constrained by unique institutional configurations, configurations that result as much from path-dependent historical circumstances and deliberate political choices as from pure considerations of economic efficiency. Indeed, in many circumstances, networks of exchange relationships and the contractual forms that govern them are highly constrained by extraeconomic considerations. Thus, in contemporary times, schools might be able to provide food to students at a lower cost by contracting with Pepsico, but they also meet parent resistance. Or, historically, consider how an exchange decision about the supply of textbooks was structured by institutional forces. Around the time of the First World War, the Lutheran schools decided to abandon their own textbook publishing efforts and to purchase textbooks on the open market—a classic make or buy decision. However, this decision appears to have been driven not simply by considerations of economic efficiency but also by a powerful need to demonstrate the legitimacy of the Lutheran school system in a German-hating era, mainly by switching the language of textbooks and instruction from German to English inside the system (Verseman 1998). These examples show that exchange networks in education are structured as much by institutional considerations as by considerations of economic efficiency and the ways in which this happens, as a result of both government regulation and procurement policies or as a result of considerations of legitimacy, is worthy of study.

Exchange and Productivity

An understanding of exchange relations in institutional sectors is all the more pressing since networks of economic exchange can have lasting functional consequences for educational organizations. Consider, as one example, the often observed "failure" of educational reform in the United States to produce lasting effects on the instructional core of K–12 schools. Many observers argue that the K–12 schooling in the United States is characterized by a peculiar pattern of instructional reform—one in which wave after wave of innovation occurs (all of it promising fundamental reform of instruction), with little real or lasting change in the ways teachers work or how much students learn (e.g., Cuban 1993; Tyack and Cuban 1995). Institutional theorists have often explained this phenomenon by reference to patterns of fragmented centralization in educational governance. Here, the pluralistic and decentralized nature of American educational governance is seen to promote multiple and incoherent instructional reforms that are adopted ceremonially (i.e., without much impact) at the local level (e.g., Meyer and Rowan 1978).

In fact, there is a great deal of evidence (discussed later) showing that governance processes in education can positively or negatively influence the likelihood that educational reforms will be adopted and worked into the technical core of schools. But for now, let us also consider a single example of how exchange relationships in K–12 education also can affect how much impact educational reform ideas have on instructional practices.[5] In almost all societies, instructional activities inside K–12 schools are built around the extensive use of texts and tests obtained *outside* of schools. In the United States, however, economic conditions in the publishing industry force schools looking for reform-oriented textbooks to engage in market exchanges with publishing firms that exist in a highly concentrated industry, where firms succeed in capital markets by achieving high sales volume derived from a national marketing strategy. In this environment, textbook firms in the United States operate as classic "k-strategists."[6] They invest heavily in new product launches, are quite slow to innovate, and respond to unique local demands for curriculum reform, not by producing locally tailored products, but rather by developing textbooks that respond to diverse curricular concerns within a single text that is "a mile wide and an inch deep." In this way, local efforts at instructional change bump up against inertial forces in the textbook industry, producing the pattern of stability so often observed in the instructional core of schools.

The example shows that in explaining educational reform, it is possible to place governance in the background and to highlight instead the constraints on reform that result from patterns of economic exchange in an institutional sector. As a result, it would seem that fundamental reform of a societal sector requires reform not only of governance arrangements but also of exchange networks. Perhaps this is well known by institutional theorists and policy analysts concerned with American education. But my reading of the literature on K–12 education suggests that the study of exchange networks inside the K–12 education sector is not much emphasized in educational analysis. Thus, opening up institutional analyses of American education to a consideration of governance *and* exchange within institutional environments seems to hold promise for explaining the structure and functioning of K–12 educational organizations.

MOVING BEYOND THE BLURRY DISTINCTION BETWEEN INSTITUTIONAL AND TECHNICAL ENVIRONMENTS

A related point concerns new ideas about what Scott and Meyer (1991) discussed as "technical" and "institutional" environments within societal sectors. In Scott and Meyer's presentation, institutional environments were seen largely as governance arrangements functioning mostly to ensure conformity, while technical environments involved networks of economic transactions affecting organizational efficiency. The distinction probably originates from a concern for differentiating processes of political control from processes of market control and from Weber's distinction between substantive and formal rationality. But, as much subsequent analysis in institutional theory demonstrates, the dichotomy between institutional and technical environments is difficult to maintain analytically, especially because governance (in the expanded definition in note 2) and conformity turn out to be central in the construction of technical environments.[7]

I believe this blurry distinction between institutional and technical environments has obscured the role that institutional theory can play in explaining one of the most important new trends in American education—the increasing definition of a "technical" theory of education and the associated trend toward test-based accountability systems in the K–12 education sector. As a result, in this section I turn to how a new institutional analysis of American schooling can be used to explain these developments.

The Institutional Construction of Technical Environments

Consider how researchers studying industrial organizations have studied the emergence of "technical" environments in industrial sectors. Suchman's (1995) discussion of venture capital financing suggests that institution-building processes can crucially affect technical developments in a given industrial sector. In his view, institution building of the technical core usually begins with the discovery of a "technical" (e.g., a performance) problem by agents in one or more locations within a sector. This problem is then named and defined as recurrent, after which potential responses are generated, categorized, and theorized about. But—and here is the crucial point—the degree to which a socially agreed-upon theory of the problem emerges depends on a variety of structural conditions in an institutional sector. For example, Suchman proposes that sectors involved in many diverse activities and characterized by fragmented governance are less likely than focused and centralized sectors to arrive at consensual "technical" theories. Moreover, he argues that local units are more likely to adopt the technologies implied by technical theories as these theories become institutionalized at higher levels.

A variant of these ideas was presented in Garud and Kumarswamy's (1995) analysis of developments in the market for computer workstations. Initially, multiple technical theories and forms existed in this domain to resolve the problems of workstation computing, each with its own distinctive technical architecture. Moreover, distinctive institutional environments (groups of producers, suppliers, and support organizations) arose around these technologies. This had several consequences. First, each of the institutional environments worked to "cement in" various technical forms so that technical choices and standards for judging performance became limited. In this way, the very survival of producers in one of these microenvironments also became dependent on adoption in the marketplace of the particular technical architecture around which the microenvironment was formed. This led firms and their support groups to lobby for industrial standards that favored their architecture and their methods of performance evaluation over others, often in cooperation with the architects of related (but not competing) technical forms. But, as the authors point out, these processes can unfold differently depending on the nature of the larger industrial sectors in which they occur. In some environments, the market for different architectures is weak and few architectures are available, but in other sectors, there is a high demand and multiple, competing possibilities.

Technical Environments in Education

These are important contributions to institutional theory generally. But, more important for our purposes, they also have direct application to the study of contemporary events in American education. There is obviously an evolving technical environment in the K–12 sector of American education, and this trend warrants more description and analysis. But a related question is why this trend is more apparent in K–12 education and less so in tertiary or pre-K sectors of American education. With respect to the former problem, it is fairly easy to reconstruct events leading to the "discovery" of the academic achievement problem in K–12 education and its trajectory toward current forms of test-based accountability. The story is more elaborate than I can present here but involves the ready availability of a technical architecture of achievement testing in K–12 education from at least the 1920s onward, the post-Coleman era redefinition of education quality by both scholars and policy makers in terms of achievement as measured by these tests (rather than competing conceptions), and the recent centralization of education governance into the hands of states, which were, in turn, being coerced by federal agencies to act on the "achievement" problem. All groups in the environment lacked alternatives to the architecture of achievement testing as a means to theorize about, and measure, educational outcomes. And as a result, several states developed early versions of test-based accountability systems, which diffused still more rapidly to other states during the 1990s.

An interesting question, however, is why similar events have not occurred in other sectors of the American education system—especially the tertiary sector. To be sure, there is discussion in higher education circles about the "learning" problem. But, for a variety of historical reasons, government control over the tertiary sector in U.S. society is even more fragmented than in the K–12 sector, and the entire sector is far less focused on the production of student learning as a single output, producing in addition such "products" as research, service, and sports and entertainment. In this environment, many different architectures for performance evaluation are available—in the form of ubiquitous rankings of research dollars won, patents created, papers authored, league championships won, and on and on. Thus, in higher education, achievement testing is just one of many potential architectures for performance evaluation, and learning is just one of many technical problems. Lacking any center to elevate and define "learning" as the central, technical problem of higher education, and faced with competing architectures of evaluation, the problem of accountability in tertiary education continues to be defined in ways that are far more fragmented, specialized, and localized than they are in K–12 education.

GOVERNANCE AS MORE
THAN MYTH AND CEREMONY

It follows from this discussion that another way the new institutionalism can contribute to the study of K–12 education is in its recognition that institutional governance (in the expanded definition I presented in note 2) can, in fact, result in more than ceremonial conformity and loose coupling, even in regulated organizations such as schools. Indeed, I take this to be a major point of Scott and Meyer's (1991) discussion of societal sectors, as well as Meyer's (1983) discussion of fragmented centralization and Scott's (1995) later synthesis of ideas about institutional analysis. In all of these analyses, and in many more recent contributions to institutional analysis, the institutional rules governing social action (whether these are conceptualized as regulatory, normative, or cognitive in form) have been found to vary in the degree to which they lead either to ceremonial conformity and loose coupling or to real conformity and tight coupling.[8] All of this should be especially comforting to education analysts interested in problems of policy implementation in K–12 education, especially reformers intent on overcoming historic patterns of loose coupling in American education. But as we shall see, the problems of conformity and governance are more complex than a simple analysis of overt regulatory regimes might suggest.

To illustrate this point, let me take as a point of departure Meyer and Rowan's (1978) analysis of schools as loosely coupled systems. Here, you will recall, institutionalized rules were seen as producing tight conformity in terms of organizing and managing the ritual classifications of schooling—the presence of registered students being taught standardized curricula by certified teachers in accredited schools—but as having few if any substantive consequences for the instructional activities or learning outcomes occurring within this framework. Again, the argument was predicated on the location of American schools in a particular kind of institutional sector and on the kinds of rules and regulations developed by governing agencies in that sector. In particular, the sector itself was seen to be politically fragmented, and as a consequence, providing dissonant guidance about the technical activities of instruction, based on "theories" generated by multiple social agencies, largely in the form of vaguely specified platitudes rather than detailed and substantive rules backed by tight inspection, agreed-upon measures of performance, and sanctions based on these measures.

Subsequent research, however, has confirmed that this is far from a universal property of institutional environments in education. Indeed, the degree of centralization and consistency in instructional guidance in the education sector varies, across nations in the world, across states in the American system, and within states in the American system over time. Moreover, evidence is growing that there is more conformity to technical rules and guidance when such rules are developed in centralized education systems offering consistent and clear guidance, rather than in decentralized and inconsistent institutional sectors that formulate unclear rules (Stevenson and Baker 1991; Cohen and Spillane 1992). It also seems to be the case—as organization theory generally predicts—that the imposition of clear standards of performance, when coupled with the presence of sanctions, produces real conformity, as many qualitative studies of the consequences of state accountability systems are demonstrating. Thus, it is a real mistake to assume that institutional theory sees only myth, ceremony, and loose coupling in the relationship of governance to action, for it does not. Instead, it simply calls analysts' attention to the many different ways control systems can be organized, for example, variation in the number agencies exercising control, the consistency of these controls, the extent to which the controls are clearly specified, and the presence or absence of sanctions for deviance.

That is not the end of the story. For, in institutional theory, it is very possible to have tight conformity to institutional governance even when governance is not provided by regulatory agencies acting with the coercive power of the state. Take the matter of "governance" conceived as deeply institutionalized cognitive schemata. In the past ten years, educational researchers have developed a growing body of evidence about the effects of academic disciplines—seen as deeply institutionalized epistemologies—on instructional organization and activity in schools. Stodolsky (1988), Stodolsky and Grossman (1995) and Rowan and colleagues (Rowan, Raudenbush, and Cheong 1993; Rowan 2002) have shown, for example, that conceptions of knowledge, patterns of instructional practice, and modal patterns of instructional coordination vary greatly across disciplines in American schools. Moreover, all of this appears to happen even in the absence of overt efforts at socialization or control in the form of government regulation or workplace norms. Instead, the controlling influence of disciplinary cultures seems to result from taken-for-granted assumptions about the knowledge being taught, about how it can be taught, and about how it should be coordinated through time—ideas that inhere in disciplinary knowledge structures and socialization practices.[9]

The point, of course, is that the new institutionalism has come a long way in its assumptions about the effects of governance on conformity. It is a mistake to assume that institutionalized rules necessarily have only the weakest consequences for action—even technical action. Instead, institutional theorists have increasingly described a multitude of conditions under which government regulation of education can have real consequences for educational activities—even in the instructional core of schools. Moreover, they discovered along the way that activities can also be powerfully organized by other forms of institutionalized control—especially deeply institutionalized cognitive schemata.

INSTITUTIONAL PROCESSES
AND MARKET ACTIVITIES

The final place where I think the new institutionalism can contribute to the analysis of current trends in education has to do with the role of institutional processes in governing market activities. By now, it should be clear that I see markets as pervasive in education, even in the K–12 sector, which is typically assumed to be dominated by a pattern of bureaucratic supply. In this sector, there is a limited (but expanding) market for instructional services, ranging from public to private schools, but also including provision of instructional services by for-profit, tutorial and test-preparation firms. Equally important, however, are the host of other markets in the K–12 education sector, including labor markets for professional staff, markets for instructional supplies and services, markets for back office services, and on and on. The question for this chapter is how insights from the new institutionalism can be used to analyze how these markets arise in education sectors, how market structures and functions vary, and the consequences markets have, both for the emergence of different populations of education service providers and for the operations of specific educational organizations.

Markets, Politics, and the Supply of Instructional Services

I shall focus here only on the direct supply of instructional services to the public, having discussed other markets (at least in part) in the section on exchange relationships. Perhaps the most dominant form of "policy talk" about the market for K–12 schooling emerges out of the literature on welfare economics, where the extremes of bureaucratic versus market supply of public goods are compared for their effects on net social benefit where market mechanisms are proposed as a means of shoring up failures in political supply, and where political mechanisms are proposed as means of shoring up market failures. From the standpoint of debates about educational governance, such discussions are useful, for they show the host of ways in which markets and politics mix in the supply of public goods. Here, for example, we see such common institutional forms as professional certification and licensing, the development of accountability schemes, the creation of tax incentives, subsidies, and so on being proposed as means of shoring up market failures, while policy instruments such as vouchers and other means are proposed as methods for rectifying problems in the political supply of goods. This literature also includes an elaborate methodology for assessing the net social benefit of different policy or market arrangements and also a rhetoric that sees this form of analysis as a reflection of natural laws of economics that improve the efficiency with which public goods are supplied to society.

There is a sense, however, in which this kind of policy talk functions in society as an elaborate "theory" (or ideology) of efficiency that ultimately shapes the structure of education markets. Dobbin (1995), for example, has developed this viewpoint in his discussion of the market theories governing the railroad industry in nineteenth-century American society. His basic argument is that economic ideas were socially constructed on the basis of experience and learning, formalized as government policies regulating railroad investment and commerce, and then acted upon by railroaders who developed business strategies to cope with resultant market conditions. In fact, Dobbin identifies several such market theories, shows how these led to new industrial policies, and shows that unique business strategies arose in response to such policies. His analysis demonstrates that markets are institutionally created and then constrain organizational operations and strategies, with real consequences for the structure and functioning of the population so regulated.

I am not aware of a similar treatment of the emergence of "markets" in American education, but the pieces of such an argument are in view in the K–12 sector, originating in debates about compulsory school laws, running through court decisions legalizing religious forms of schooling, and culminating in the current "economized" logic of markets versus bureaucratic supply and the invention of new forms of market regulation and supply. While this history is murky, it seems clear that education was not always conceptualized as some kind of market commodity, but that legislative and judicial decisions did affect both the socially permissible forms of supply, and along with other social forces also shaped demand, thus creating "de facto" markets in education. But how all of this transpired in K–12 education, and with what consequences for population dynamics and educational outcomes, especially compared to the trajectories found in pre-K and tertiary sectors, seems like a useful area of study.

Isomorphism and Market Differentiation in Educational Populations

The existence of markets in education, and the strategic responses of organizations to these markets, raises other interesting problems for institutional theorists. One of these questions is how market conditions shape the kinds of organizational forms that arise to provide instructional services in education, and with what consequences for performance. Sociological perspectives on the new institutionalism have tended to see the development of societal sectors as generally leading to isomorphism in organizational populations, typically as a result of coercive, normative, and mimetic processes. But the literature on strategic groups arising in the business literature seems less certain about the generality of these phenomena, stressing that different strategic groups of organizations typically form, even within the same industry, as part of a process of market differentiation. Here, organizations in an institutional sector take on different forms—they adopt different structures, pursue different clients, market marginally different product mixes, and so on, largely as a result of their shared positions within the sector. Examining these different perspectives is important—not only for the development of institutional theory but also for an analysis of the possible consequences of decreasing regulation and increasing market choice in the supply of instructional services in the K–12 education sector.

Once again, I know of no readily identifiable research base in education investigating this problem, so I can only piece together a minimal outline of how such research might proceed. In the K–12 sector of American education, there is at least some support for the principle of isomorphism. For example, Versemann's (1998) analysis of the Lutheran schools and Baker's (1992) discussion of Catholic schools both provide evidence of mimetic isomorphism—or what those who study corporate strategy often call "emulation." That is, both the Catholic and Lutheran systems of private schooling deliberately emulated their public counterparts, both as a matter of deliberate strategic choice and as a result of a facing many of the same demographic, labor market, and consumer pressures as the public schools. In this sense, the differences between public and private schools in terms of "business" strategy are only marginal. The religious schools continue to emphasize the religious aspect of their educational program, they are forced to rely on a different set of resources as a result of legal decisions, they offer a somewhat less differentiated curriculum (perhaps more as a function of size and resource scarcity than deliberate choice), but they otherwise resemble public schools in the most obvious ways. A similar set of findings is emerging from research on magnet and charter schools, which, although freed from a great deal of regulation, end up looking quite a lot like regular public schools.

There is evidence, however, that there are limits to isomorphism, especially where centralizing controls are extremely weak, technical environments are heterogeneous, or information on organizational performance is introduced into the marketplace. For example, Kraatz and Zajac (1996) examined variation in the organizational structures of liberal arts colleges in the United States between 1971 and 1986. They found that instead of converging in structure over time, the colleges became more diverse and that this was driven to a considerable extent by responses to both global and local consumer preferences, demographics, and economic trends. Moreover, many of these colleges made "downward" rather than "upward" emulation decisions—that is, they chose to model less rather more prestigious variants. Contrary to most theories of institutional isomorphism, however, these decisions often resulted in increased market success (cf. Labianca et al. 2001 for contrasting evidence). There is also some evidence from England and Wales on the ways in which the introduction of school choice has had differentiating consequences for the population schools. Adnett, Bougheas, and Davies (2002), for example, note that the introduction of league tables that group schools according to unadjusted student outcomes has affected consumer choice in ways that lead schools to become more socioeconomically segregated, with the consequence that school performance has become more heterogeneous over time, rather than rising uniformly across all schools.

All of this raises some new ways of thinking about school choice and some possible lines of research. It suggests, first of all, that markets for educational services are socially constructed as a result of deliberate institutional theorizing. How this happens is worth studying. It also suggests that the consequences of market reforms will vary and that such variation will depend on the larger structure of the institutional sector in which market reforms are introduced, on the types of information provided to consumers and managers about market performance, and on the strategic decisions of organizations operating in the market. The evidence just reviewed— although sketchy—seems to suggest, for example, that the more centralized and uniform are the institutional environments in which markets arise, and the less information about performance is available to consumers and managers, the more the market system will be characterized by isomorphism (other things being equal). But to the extent that institutional environments are fragmented, market locations are heterogeneous, and performance information is available to suggest differences in product quality, the more producers will form into distinctive strategic groups, consumers will make discriminating market choices, and diversification in form and outcomes will occur. None of this is well documented, however, and further studies are warranted.

CONCLUSION

I have developed a set of arguments intended to illustrate how changing ideas in institutional theory can be used to address changing circumstances in K–12 education in the United States. Overall, these arguments were intended to signal the capacity of institutional theory to adequately explain these changing circumstances, but only by taking into account new ideas about the organization of societal sectors, the role of institutional environments in shaping both markets and politics, and the ways in which institutions govern both political and technical processes in an institutional sector. Using these ideas, I have argued that institutional theorists studying K–12 education in the

United States could move well beyond historic concerns in education policy analysis with the fragmented nature of political controls in American education and help organization theorists move well beyond a narrow view of institutionalized rules as promoting only ceremonial conformity and loose coupling within schools. Overall, I am fairly confident that the ideas I introduced in this chapter constitute some worthwhile directions for a new institutional analysis of American education, and I am confident that future analyses along these lines can contribute to better explanations of emerging trends in American education. But none of this will be possible if education scholars fail to produce more careful studies of the problems laid out in this chapter or if they ignore the insights of the new institutionalism as these have emerged in the social sciences over the past decade.

NOTES

1. As an example, see Baker (this volume).

2. For some interesting "institutional" analyses of politics in sectors other education, see the collection of papers in Campbell and Pedersen (2001), which discuss the emergence of neoliberal policies in recent decades.

3. For a discussion of these issues and documentation on the statistics cited here, see Rowan (this volume).

4. I am defining *governance* quite broadly here to include not only what Scott (1995) labels as regulatory regimes backed by the coercive power of the state but also the more informal normative and cognitive aspects of institutions that also govern social action. Thus, for now, let us consider governance to involve the coordination of social action through regulatory agreements and exchange to involve coordination of action through material transactions.

5. For a fuller treatment of the argument presented here, see Rowan (this volume).

6. The notions of "k-strategists" in a business setting and the contrasting "r-strategy" discussed in the next paragraph are explained in Hannan and Freeman's (1989) classic work on organizational ecology.

7. Indeed, this is the crucial idea in transaction cost analysis and principal agent theory and also figures centrally in a number of recent arguments about the construction of markets and technologies found in various essays in Scott and Christensen (1995).

8. See, especially, the analysis of this problem by Spillane (this volume).

9. Other studies show the subtle power of national culture in organizing instruction—again without overt regulatory regimes or obvious patterns of workplace control. Thus, in the recent TIMSS video studies, patterns of classroom instruction were seen to vary across nations, and teaching was argued to involve more than a set of technical rules, but rather to be "fundamentally embedded in culture in both its conception and execution" (Schmidt et al. 1996, 6).

REFERENCES

Adnett, Nick, Spiros Bougheas, and Peter Davies. 2002. Market-based reforms of public schooling: Some unpleasant dynamics. *Economics of Education Review* 21 (4): 323–30.

Baker, David P. 1992. The politics of American Catholic school expansion, 1870–1930. In *The political construction of education: The state, school expansion, and economics change*, ed. Bruce Fuller and Richard Rubinson, 189–206. New York: Praeger.

Brinton, Mary, and Victor Nee. 2000 [1998]. *The new institutionalism in sociology.* Stanford, CA: Stanford University Press.

Cohen, David K., and James P. Spillane. 1992. Policy and practice: The relations between governance and instruction. In *Review of research in education*, ed. Gerald Grant. Washington, DC: American Educational Research Association.

Cuban, Larry. 1984. *How teachers taught: Constancy and change in American classrooms, 1880–1980.* New York: Longman.

DiMaggio, Paul J., and Walter W. Powell. 1983. The iron cage revisited: Isomorphism and collective rationality in organizational fields. *American Sociological Review* 48: 147–60.

Dobbin, Frank R. 1995. *Forging industrial policy: The United States, Britain, and France in the railway age.* New York: Cambridge University Press.

Garud, R., and A. Kumarswamy. 1995. Coupling the technical and institutional faces of Janus in network industries. In *The institutional construction of organizations*, ed. W. R. Scott and S. Christensen. Thousand Oaks, CA: Sage.

Hannan, M. T., and J. H. Freeman. 1989. *Organizational ecology.* Cambridge, MA: Harvard University Press.

Kraatz, M. S., and E. J. Zajac. 1996. Exploring the limits of the new institutionalism: The causes and consequences of illegitimate organizational change. *American Sociological Review* 61 (5): 812–36.

Labianca, Ginseppe, James F. Fairbank, James B. Thomas, Dennis A. Gioia, and Elizabeth E. Umphiess. 2001. Emulation in academia: Balancing structure and identity. *Organization Science* 12 (3): 312–30.

March, James G., and Johan P. Olsen. 1989. *Rediscovering institutions: The organizational basis of politics.* New York: Free Press.

Meyer, John W. 1983. Centralization of funding and control in educational governance. In *Organizational environments: Ritual and rationality*, ed. John W. Meyer and W. Richard Scott, 179–98. Beverly Hills: Sage.

Meyer, John W., David Kamens, and Aaron Benavot. 1992. *School knowledge for the masses: World models and national primary curriculum categories in the twentieth century.* London: Falmer.

Meyer, John W., and Brian Rowan. 1978. The structure of educational organizations. In *Environments and organizations*, ed. Marshall W. Meyer, 78–109. San Francisco: Jossey Bass.

Meyer, John W., and W. Richard Scott. 1983. *Organizational environments: Ritual and rationality.* Beverly Hills: Sage.

Rowan, Brian. 2002. Teachers' work and instructional management, part 1: Alternative views of the task of teaching. In *Theory and research in educational administration*, ed. W. K. Hoy and C. G. Miskel, 1: 129–49. Greenwich, CT: Information Age.

———. in press. The ecology of school improvement: Notes on the school improvement industry in the United States. *Journal of Educational Change.*

Rowan, Brian, and Cecil G. Miskel. 1999. Institutional theory and the study of educational organizations. In *Handbook of Research on Educational Administration*, ed. J. Murphy and K. Seashore-Louis. San Francisco: Jossey-Bass.

Rowan, Brian, Stephen W. Raudenbush, and Yuk Fai. Cheong. 1993. Teaching as a nonroutine task: Implications for the management of schools. *Educational Administration Quarterly* 29: 479–500.

Schmidt, William et al. 1996. *A summary characterizing pedagogical flow: An investigation of science teaching in six countries.* London: Kluwer.

Scott, W. R., and S. Christensen, eds. 1995. *The institutional construction of organizations.* Thousand Oaks, CA: Sage.

Scott, W. Richard. 1995. *Institutions and organizations.* Thousand Oaks, CA: Sage.

Scott, W. Richard, and John W. Meyer. 1991. The organization of societal sectors. In *The New Institutionalism in Organizational Analysis*, ed. Paul J. DiMaggio and Walter W. Powell, 108–140. Chicago: University of Chicago Press.

Stevenson, David, and David Baker. 1991. State control of the curriculum and classroom instruction. *Sociology of Education* 64: 1–10.

Stodolsky, Susan S. 1988. *The subject matters: Classroom activity in math and social studies.* Chicago: University of Chicago Press.

Stodolsky, Susan S., and Pamela L. Grossman. 1995. The impact of subject matter on curricular activity: An analysis of five academic subjects. *American Educational Research Journal* 32: 227–49.

Suchman, M. C. 1995. Localism and globasm in institutional analysis: The emergence of contractual norms in venture finance. In *The institutional construction of organizations*, ed. W. R. Scott and S. Christensen. Thousand Oaks, CA: Sage.

Tyack, D., and L. Cuban. 1995. *Tinkering toward utopia: A century of public school reform.* Cambridge, MA: Harvard University Press.

Verseman, D. 1998. The distinctive mission of a private religious school system: The role of the teaching force in the schools the Lutheran Church-Missouri Synod. Ph.D. dissertation, University of Michigan.

THREE

Varieties of Institutional Theory: Traditions and Prospects for Educational Research

CHARLES E. BIDWELL

In this chapter, I review some principal strands of institutional theory in sociology and explore its uses in research on education.[1] My review is selective. It is governed by my judgment that there are biases in current versions of institutional theory that direct attention away from the process of institutionalization and, hence, have led to a neglect of historical analysis. They also direct attention away from the mechanisms of institutionalization, in particular, power and its uses, and away from its effects on behavior. I argue that institutional theory becomes useful in educational research when it attends to institutionalization as a political process, when it specifies the mechanisms that drive this process, and when it considers how institutionalization affects both the organization and the conduct of schooling.

Early groundwork for the analysis of social institutions was laid by the European founding fathers, including Montesquieu, Tocqueville, Marx, Weber, and, in particular, Emile Durkheim (see also Meyer 2003). However, the greater part of the theoretical action has transpired in the United States, so most, though not all, of my attention centers on forebears and contemporaries in American sociology. Following the review of theory, I draw out implications for new research.

33

THE PROCESS OF INSTITUTIONALIZATION

The varied definitional history of *institution* reflects the capacious nature of the concept. Virtually all of social science can be viewed through an institutional lens. The trick is to understand what this lens does that other theoretical lenses do not do as well and then to make fruitful empirical applications. Despite the varying definitions, two elements are found throughout—symbols (in particular, believed-in symbols) and structures of social relationships. The differences arise when these elements are specified and when theoretical weight is assigned to each of the pair.

For Durkheim (1901, 1912) institutions arise out of joint human activity and are constituted of sets of symbols, both cognitive (knowledge and belief) and moral ("moral authority"), that fix action into patterns that extend beyond the behavior of any individual. Thus, he treats institutions as emergent, taking form in the round of life of human groups. Once formed, institutions are profound external sources for the regulation of human conduct and the stabilization of social structures.

William Graham Sumner, writing in *Folkways* (1906, 53–54) at about the same time as Durkheim, says that "[a]n institution consists of a concept (idea, notion, doctrine, interest) and a structure. . . . The structure holds the concept and furnishes instrumentalities for bringing it into the world of facts and action in a way to serve the interests of men [sic] in society." His emphasis is on relationships more as a means for realizing what is symbolized than as a matrix out of which the symbols emerge. When Sumner went on to develop his ideas about social institutions, interests—particularly the interests of powerful actors—were brought to the fore among the symbols that motivate the action that, in turn, drives the institutionalization of relationships.

Thus, although Sumner says that institutions can be either "crescive" (i.e., emergent) or enacted, his emphasis, unlike Durkheim's, is on enactment. In fact, he argues that no social structure, whether crescive or enacted, can survive to full institutionalization unless it serves the interests of a powerful elite. At the same time, he is careful to stress that institutional formation is subject to the discipline of cultural selection. That is, the interests that are pursued by powerful actors must accord with the society's core values and normative specification (in Sumner's words, "the mores") if they are to find institutional expression. Thus, institutionalization is a matter of legitimacy as well as power.

Arthur Stinchcombe, writing over a half century later, echoed Sumner's elaborated definition. Stinchcombe (1968, 107) says that an institution is "a structure in which powerful people are committed to some value or interest." One could not state more clearly the idea that institutions are instruments of politics.

Other definitions derive from the American pragmatists. Charles H. Cooley, like Durkheim, defines institutions as symbol systems that arise out of human interaction, writing (1902, 314) that "[t]he individual is always the cause as well as effect of the institution." Everett Hughes, like Sumner, views structural elements of institutions as instruments for the realization of something symbolized. Thus, he (Hughes 1936, 180) identifies two elements of institutions, mores, or formal rules that, to use Sumner's words, can be translated into the "world of fact" only through the collective action of persons in complementary roles. At the same time, Cooley, Hughes, and Hughes' Chicago predecessors, Robert Park and Ernest Burgess (1921, 785–86), understand individual identity and modes of conduct to be constituted of institutionalized values, beliefs, and rules. In this way, institutions regulate human conduct, but indirectly via the membership of individual agents in a common, institutionalized realm of discourse, rather than directly via external norms.

The foregoing definitions are stated in process terms—institutionalization and the formation of persons and patterns of conduct through participation in social institutions. Talcott Parsons, early in his writings (Parsons 1934) and later in his action theory (Parsons 1951), bypasses the issues of institutionalization to elaborate Durkheim's notion of external regulation and stabilization. He defines social institutions as coordinated systems of human interaction that are consequences of the moral authority of values and rules of conduct. Moral authority renders values and norms, at least in subjective terms, external to the person and makes them objects of a common and, therefore, coordinated orientation of individual action. What is external is internalized so that stable structures of social relationships are consequences of institutionalization.

This conception of institutions as regulatory and stabilizing is equally clear in W. Richard Scott's (1995, 33) more recent definition of social institutions as "cognitive, normative, and regulative structures and activities that provide stability and meaning to social behavior." Scott goes on to make explicit an idea taken for granted by most of the analysts of social institutions—that they occur at all levels of social aggregation from small-scale systems of human interaction to entire societies.

This definitional variety sometimes is treated as if it were the product of theoretical conflict.[2] It may be more productive to think of the variety as posing three sets of questions, more complementary than conflicting, that direct our attention to various aspects of institutional analysis:

1. How are we to understand the process of institutionalization, more precisely, the mechanisms involved in institutional formation? To what extent are these mechanisms of deliberate acts of power or of emergence?

2. How are we to understand the role of social institutions in the regulation of conduct? What are the mechanisms through which such regulation occurs? What is the place of individual agency in institutional fields of conduct?
3. In what ways are social institutions constitutive of individual identity and conduct?

As I discuss these questions, I will also touch on the place of natural histories in institutional analysis.

POWER, LEGITIMACY, AND ACTORS IN INSTITUTIONALIZATION: TWO EXAMPLES

Two works on the institutionalization of formal organizations illustrate my ideas about the political nature of institutionalization, namely, Durkheim on the University of Paris and Philip Selznick on the Tennessee Valley Authority (TVA). I must preface these illustrations with Sumner. In *Folkways*, Sumner (1906, 75–118) argues, with numerous historical examples, that for institutionalization to take place, the concept and structure not only must serve the interests of a powerful elite but also must be fitted to the environmental conditions of the particular time and place. That is, institutions are subject to the discipline of environmental selection. They must accord with material conditions and with the mores or, as Park and Burgess (1921, 786) preferred it, with public opinion. Efforts by the powerful, to reinforce or weaken existing institutions are subject no less to this discipline than are the mechanisms of crescive institutional formation.

Durkheim on the University of Paris

In *L'Evolution Pédagogique en France* (translated in the English language version as *The Evolution of Educational Thought*), Durkheim (1911) analyzes the mechanisms that brought the University of Paris into being. Although he defines institutions in the terms of emergence, in these lectures he analyzes institutionalization as a matter of enactment and, in a way that should have pleased Sumner, as a matter of power.

He begins by enumerating the economic, demographic, and political preconditions for the emergence of universities in the cities of medieval Europe. The growth of commercial classes and improvements in transportation and in public safety following upon a strengthened secular political authority created demand for advanced education. The rise of guilds provided a structural format that could be appropriated by groups of teachers that came together in response to this demand.

Durkheim next offers an essentially political analysis of the events that operated under these conditions to yield an autonomous university. In Paris, the teachers, drawn from cathedral schools across Europe, set up shop under the eaves of Notre Dame, clustered together on a bridge between the Isle St. Louis and the Left Bank. Proximity and a resulting dynamic density made the teachers aware of a distinctive and common interest in cutting loose from the ecclesiastical control of Notre Dame and in providing the essentially secular curriculum that their students demanded.

Capitalizing on papal efforts to constrain the power of the cathedrals and forming something of a coalition with the papacy, the teachers were able to secure a guildlike charter, establish their own organizational government, and fix the rules and ceremonies for inducting teachers, regulating their teaching, and judging and graduating students. As their work continued, they developed a conventional division of labor, which was regularized first in separate faculties and then in residential colleges where a myriad of conventional understandings and more formal rules and ceremonies governed and stabilized the daily life of the university.

Three aspects of Durkheim's analysis are particularly noteworthy. First, the institutionalization of the university was set in motion by the action of both individual and group interests, for example, the interests of students, on the one hand, and of the group of teachers and of the papacy, on the other. Both material and ideal interests were at stake, interacting to direct and propel what these actors did. For example, the teachers wanted to safeguard their collective welfare so that their immediate interests were material. However, the group of teachers formed around a shared belief in the worthiness of the secular knowledge that they were prepared to teach. Their group action and collective welfare were thus grounded on a central ideal interest. These ideal and material interests, which were complementary and reinforcing, were pursued through political action in which the more powerful prevailed and thereby created a stable situation for the further structural and normative development of the university.

Second, structural and normative development and the elaboration of patterns of activity involved both appropriation and invention. For example, structural development of the University of Paris came from the appropriation of guild organization and governance and the invention of faculties and colleges. The norms that regularized the daily round of university life and the content of the university's curriculum also were partly appropriated and partly invented. For example, a good portion of what was taught, but not all, had been taught for some time in the cathedral schools, while the rules that governed the formation of academic policies in the faculties and whole university had only minimal precedents in the practices of other guilds. They also were accretions of the daily life itself (e.g., many of the conventions by which the colleges operated).

Third, the university survived because it was adequately adapted to its environment—fitting the desires of students and their families, nourished by the economic means of the increasingly prosperous commercial classes, and serving the interests of the papacy and later the developing state. In fact, it was the good fit between what was demanded and what the teachers could supply that was the prime basis for their developing power. In this sense, institutions create power, an idea to which I will return when I consider possibilities for new institutional studies of educational organizations.

Let me stress again that, again in accord with Sumner, Durkheim treats institutional formation as primarily a matter of deliberate action rather than emergence. Norms evolve in the course of daily life, but within an institutional frame set in place by design. Designers may borrow structural forms or formally enacted rules from other institutional domains, but they are put in place in the new setting by intentional action. Finally, note that the impact on individuals, the question of regulation and agency, is left in the background

Selznick on the Institutionalization of Organizations

In his influential treatments of institutionalization and bureaucratization, Selznick (1948, 1949, 1957) uses much the same conceptual framework as did Durkheim. However, he introduces in an explicit way the important idea that institutionalization creates values. In institutionalization, the organization itself, or more properly its goals and its rules and conventions about how its work is to be done, become infused with value. When this organizational valorization takes place, an organization's practices become entrenched because of the unwillingness of the staff to alter or depart from what they value so highly. In Selznick's (1949, 256–57) words, "commitments are enforced by institutionalization. . . . Because organizations are social systems, goals or procedures tend to achieve an established, value-impregnated status. We say that they become institutionalized." Moreover, their value extends over and beyond whatever values reside in the organization's technical ability to do its work. Now the organization has a distinctive identity or character, and keeping the organization afloat, with its form and substance intact, is a matter not simply of instrumental survival but also of preserving an entity that is uniquely valuable.

Selznick (1949), like Durkheim on the University of Paris, developed his ideas through a natural history of institutionalization, in this case a study of the accommodation of a new and somewhat fragile organization, the Tennessee Valley Authority, to its local political environment. His students provided other such natural histories—of the Woman's Christian Temperance Union (WCTU) (Gusfield 1955), of a community college (Clark 1960), and of a hospital (Perrow 1961).

In this body of work, the actual mechanisms of value formation are not made entirely clear. Selznick assumes that it is in the nature of social systems to become infused with value, presumably an emergent process. This emergence does not occur everywhere or every time, but Selznick is not entirely clear about the fostering conditions, although his study of the TVA makes it quite clear that powerful external actors can have a strong effect on the institutionalization of both goals and procedures.

Stinchcombe (1968), one of Selznick's students, is clearer in his politics of institutions about both the mechanisms and conditions. He specifies the political mechanisms of institutionalization as control over the selection of successors into organizational leadership and, more generally, over means of persuasion and socialization through which participants are taught the value of the organizational status quo. Moreover, in his essay on the foundation and persistence of kinds of organizations, Stinchcombe (1965) specifies material conditions that affect organizational survival. These conditions include the skill composition of a labor force, the availability of capital, and conditions set by traits of other institutions, such as the stability of political regimes. They have their effects by virtue of the fit of organizational goals and procedures with these constraining environmental properties.

In sum, Durkheim's treatment of the University of Paris and Sumner's ideas in *Folkways* prefigure later developments in the theory of institutionalization. These developments include:

1. the treatment of institutionalization as a process driven by political mechanisms, in particular elites' use of power to realize their interconnected ideal and material interests;
2. the discipline of institutional selection according to environmental fitness; and
3. the use of natural histories to reveal the action of these mechanisms and environmental constraints in institutionalization.

CLASS INTERESTS, THE STATE, AND INSTITUTIONS IN EDUCATION

Sociologists and other social scientists interested in national systems of education continue to debate the reasons for salient differences between these systems. These differences include variation between selective and inclusive access, variation between centralization and decentralization of control, and differences in the place of advanced training and preparation as the chief business of the schools.

The centrality of class interests to the formation of the English and European systems has been firmly established by comparative scholarship. There is less agreement about the American case, and the debate gains particular point in reference to the "exceptionalism" of the American educational system, where it centers on differences between neo-Marxists and their critics. I consider first an example of the work on England and Europe and then turn to the contention about the United States.

Margaret Archer on the Stratification of Educational Systems

Archer's (1979) magisterial treatment of the formation of national educational systems in England, Denmark, France, and Russia is a prime example.[3] This massive work presents extensive natural histories of the development of each of these systems. They are set within a theoretical frame in which structural form, in particular, the intensity of curricular stratification, is explained by political interaction among class-based actors, with elites favoring restricted access, and winning, and nonelites favoring expanded access, and losing.

Archer is careful to stress the importance of rising national states in these situations. In her theory and case histories, as the state gains power, agencies of government become significant actors. She gives primary attention to the state and its agencies as means for expressing the interests of other actors, but her approach is open to the possibility that these agencies and the officials that staff them have interests of their own to pursue.[4]

American Exceptionalism

With respect to the United States, there has been a strenuous debate about the significance of class interests in the formation of the national educational system. This debate centers on the idea of American exceptionalism. It is a debate between neo-Marxists who see the American case, no less than the English and European, as a product of class domination or class conflict and scholars who find the United States truly exceptional. On both sides, the focus is on the process of institutionalization (formation and development), on group interests, and on the politics through which these interests have been realized.

The primary neo-Marxist accounts treat the development of the common school in nineteenth-century New England (Katz 1968, Bowles and Gintis 1976). They rely in large part on natural histories of local events in the mill towns of Massachusetts. These accounts attribute the expansion of common school education, despite working-class and small farmer opposition, to the successful political domination of local business elites whose members wanted a tractable, productive labor force and who sought social order in an increasingly urban and ethnically heterogeneous society.

John Meyer and colleagues (Meyer et al. 1979), Peterson (1985), and Katznelson and Weir (1985) set the stage for a counterargument that was given its most effective statement by Richard Rubinson (1986). Again, the argument is informed by a power- and interest-centered institutional theory. Meyer and his collaborators used data on the correlates of late nineteenth- and early twentieth century common school expansion in the northern tier of American states. They concluded that the religious (ideal) and nation-building (ideal and material) interests of local elites drove the westward expansion of the American common school. Peterson and Katznelson and Weir examined the expanding school systems of American cities during this same period. They employed urban case histories of curriculum change and of the incorporation of racial and ethnic groups into policy making and into the teaching force. They found very little explicit class stratification in the curricula and structure of the cities' schools and that these schools substantially incorporated diverse racial and ethnic groups. They interpret these incorporative characteristics of the schools as consequences of efforts to realize ideal and material group interests in a context of political power and coalition formation.[5]

Rubinson (1986), surveying the argument between the neo-Marxists and their opponents, begins with an inference from allocation theory (Collins 1979). When education becomes consequential for status allocation, educational expansion should be accompanied by pressure from below for access to increasing levels or amounts of schooling because of the devaluation of educational credentials that expansion brings. Because of this continuing pressure, it should be in the interests of powerful elites to restrict access to more than a common base of schooling.

Why, then, did such educational stratification not appear in the United States? Rubinson makes the important observation that an analysis of institutionalization such as Archer's need not be restricted to class and class interests. He argues that group interests in education, whatever their substance and structural basis, are translated into institutional patterns via a political process. From the beginning of state formation in England and Europe, national politics was the predominant politics, and national parties emerged as class parties. For this reason, in the development of national educational systems, elites' efforts to restrict access prevailed. However, in the United States local politics has been more important than national politics in the organization of education, and at the local level parties have expressed in various combinations the interests of diverse economic, ethnic, and, in particular, religious groups. Moreover, in contrast to Europe, universal suffrage came early, giving members of the working and lower classes a political voice at the time the country's educational system was taking shape. As a result, interests favoring open access have more often than not overcome those favoring restriction.

DIRECTIONS FOR RESEARCH

In recent years, there has been very little attention to the mechanisms of educational institutionalization, whatever the level of social aggregation. This inattention is not the result of sparse research opportunities.

The Global Expansion of Education

Most of the work that has been done deals with global expansion, but it has moved in a different theoretical direction, as part of what I would call the "cognitive turn" in institutional research on education. Meyer and his colleagues (e.g., Meyer and Hannan 1979; Meyer, Kamens, and Benavot 1992) have published a provocative series of monographs and articles in which the multiplication of national systems of education across the globe, expansion of enrollment, and curricular content are treated as manifestations of increasingly uniform worldwide beliefs about what nations and their schools should look like.

The mechanisms at work in this process of institutionalization are left tantalizingly vague. These mechanisms, to my mind, would include both the internal politics of nation building and national development and the external politics of national competition and the action of international agencies. To extend the application of a political theory of institutionalization to the global level seems to me a fascinating and potentially productive enterprise. This research, of course, brings the state to center stage, as does Archer's, but the important particulars of how the state and its agencies and agents act and what objectives and interests they pursue still require specification. Bourdieu (1989) has provided an elegant account of the interplay of state and school in the formation and legitimization of professional elites in France, from the Renaissance forward, but it is frustrating empirically. Research on developed countries such as that of Stevenson and Baker (1991) and Muller and Schiller (2000) is promising.

Programs of Educational Reform

These programs in the schools and universities of Europe and Great Britain from the years following World War II onward could provide a fine series of comparative studies of the institutionalization of national systems and an evaluation of the political theory of institutionalization. Burton Clark's (1983) research program made a substantial opening in this direction, but it has not been exploited by others.

The Realization of Class Interests

The thirteen national case studies of educational inequality brought together in *Persisting Inequality* (Shavit and Blossfeld, 1993) raise important questions about the ways in which class interests are furthered or blocked in national educational systems and through national educational policies, but such questions are not addressed consistently in the volume. Current rounds of educational reform in this country provide similar research opportunities. Elisabeth Clemens (Clemens, Fry, and King 2002) is in the midst of an institutionally oriented study of the charter school movement, but again a sustained body of research is lacking.

Behavioral Effects of Institutional Forms

Consider, in concert with Cooley and the Chicago school, that individual identity and conduct may be constituted by participation in social institutions. Then we are led to ask how the national and organizational variety of forms of education affects not only students' educational development but also their interior lives (self-concepts, beliefs, values, and emotions) and patterns of social participation. In effect, we would ask how they negotiate daily life in these settings and to what effect. Again, the literature is sparse (but see, recently, McFarland 2001).

Educational Organizations and Their Control

The cognitive turn in institutional research has had a very strong impact on the analysis of schools as formal organizations. Consider Parsons' (1956) depiction of organizations as creators of power. In his theory of formal organizations, Parsons, like Sumner and Hughes, stresses the instrumental aspect social structure. It is a means for the realization of normatively governed activities—for example, getting a firm's work done, securing money and materials for this work, and gaining legitimacy for the organization. Parsons then considers the political aspects of organizational structure. While Sumner and Stinchcombe view institutions as instruments of the powerful, Parsons treats institutionalized structures as creators of power that actors can use for interest realization.

Parsons posits three generic levels of organizational structure, one concerned with the technical aspects of production, a second with production management (including procurement and distribution), and the third with the management of the organization's legitimacy, finances, and political and cultural support. Parsons argues that each of these domains generates its own power resources because each monopolizes a specific functional domain necessary for the organization to survive and prosper—workers strike, middle managers horde information, and top managers manipulate the flow of funds to one or another part of the enterprise, for example. Here is a potentially significant complement to the treatment of institutions as creators of power—how organizational structure, once institutionalized, provides instruments for the diverse, but socially ordered, interests of an organization's members.

However, work stimulated by Parsons' depiction of organizations went in a different direction, leading to the conceptualization of loose coupling (Weick 1976) and, with respect to education, the presentation of the school as an "institutionalized organization" (Meyer and Rowan 1977). Here we find that the truly productive work is done by top management, namely, the creation and maintenance of an organizational identity that comports well with popular beliefs about what a school should look like (viz., Waller [1932] on the school as a museum of virtue). The technical work is left unexamined and presumably is a local manifestation of the doctrines and procedural rules of the teaching profession (Powell and DiMaggio 1991). In short, compliance is the order of the day: compliance with popular belief (an interesting reading of what Sumner treated as selection according to fitness with the mores) at the level of foreign relations and compliance with professional beliefs and norms in the technical core of instructional work.

This line of analysis has yielded a number of stimulating papers. Nevertheless, it seems to me less interesting to ask about the stability of what in effect is an organizational shell than to ask two questions. I have discussed one already, how schools or systems of schools institutionalize. Brint and Karabel (1991) build on Clark's case study of the community college to move the "new" institutionalism in this direction. The other is how the institutionalized social structures and cultural substance of schools or systems and of their environments affects the daily life of students and teachers. One promising direction for work on the latter question would bring together the institutional analysis of school organization and organizational learning theory—an effort to show how events in the technical core of the school, that is, teachers' work, students' lives, and their interaction take shape within the school's institutionalized moral order and pattern of social organization.

Brian Rowan (1990, 1995) has taken important steps in this direction, drawing on Burns and Stalker's (1961) conceptualization of organizations as organic systems. He shows how institutional properties of the environments of American schools—multiple goals and interests espoused by a complex of local interest groups, coupled with a decentralized polity—bring informal collegial networks of faculty to a central position as loci for diagnosing and solving the never-ending practical problems of teaching.

With Kenneth Frank and Pamela Quiroz, I have presented a theory of school-level organizational control that treats the school as a socially ordered field for the play of group interests (Bidwell, Frank, and Quiroz 1997). This theory was not stated in explicit institutional terms, but it is in fact an argument about the behavioral consequences of institutional forms. In effect, it treats the organization of the faculty workplace as an institutionalized realization of local interests that is constrained by school size. In large schools, these organizational forms are bureaucratic (expressing the aggregated public interest) or marketlike (expressing parental and student interests). In small schools, they are autocratic or oligarchic (expressing the interests of a dominant administrator or faculty elite) or collegial (expressing the interests of a consensual faculty).

The mechanism linking these forms and teachers' instructional behavior is social psychological. Following Simmel (1950) on social types, we treat the forms of faculty workplace organization as distinctive experiential environments for teachers. We argue that these environments foster the formation of distinctive occupational teacher types that are expressed in correspondingly distinctive orientations toward instructional practice. We predict that bureaucracy is associated with rigorous reliance on rules and standards, markets with the manipulation of social distance in relations with students, autocracy and oligarchy with teaching as moral inculcation, and the collegium with teaching that develops higher mental process.

Findings from a sample of high schools provide only partial confirmation of these predictions. The correlation between instructional orientation and workplace form is found for collegia and markets, but not for bureaucracies and either autocracies or oligarchies. The latter organizational forms are not associated with mean faculty scores on any of the four instructional orientations. External domination appears to dampen tendencies toward faculty-level agreement about how to teach.

This negative result and a substantial trend in all of the schools toward department-specific orientations to teaching led Yasumoto and me to think that a more microlevel analysis was called for (Bidwell and Yasumoto 1999). We based this inference also on the low technical interdependence between a school's teachers and the consequent mechanical division of instructional labor. We suspected that the control of teaching has a great deal to do with the particular pedagogical interests of groups of teachers within a faculty and their capacity for the informal control of their members' ways of teaching.

In a complementary vein, I later argued that applying Parsons' three-level model to schools leads to the proposition that the middle level of management (the principalship) is exceptionally weak (Bidwell 2001). Therefore, it is the resources to be found in collegial structures on the shop floor of the school that are of paramount importance as a place for organizational learning. This learning is the learning that is most likely to let schools adapt their technical means to the instructional requisites created by the motives and capabilities of their students, the mission of the school, the demands of parents and other constituents, and professional norms of practice.

However, a body of research on the social organization of teachers' work suggests that the strongly institutionalized school subject matters and their organizational counterparts in local schools (e.g., the academic departments of high schools) may act more often to inhibit than to facilitate a faculty's organizational learning (Johnson 1990; Little 1990; Talbert and McLaughlin 1994; Bidwell and Yasumoto 1999). How teachers acquire, maintain, and adapt local knowledge about teaching and the consequences for what and how much students learn call for investigation (for a modest beginning, see Yasumoto, Uekawa, and Bidwell 2001).

CONCLUSION

Let me return to the questions with which I began, in more general comments about the institutional research agenda in education, pertinent whatever the level of analysis. First, the prime task is to explore the process of institutionalization, rather than the stability that derives from institutionalization. We would do well, I think, to keep in mind Selznick's proposition that institutionalization creates values through which people become committed to the institutional forms in which they participate. This proposition suggests a way to consider the creation and maintenance of social order through a process-centered analysis of institutional dynamics—institutional formation and change.

Second, we need a sustained research program aimed at evaluating and specifying a political theory of institutionalization that embraces both the creation of institutions through the use of power and the creation of power as an aspect of institutionalization. How power is employed in the creation of commitment to institutions, for example, through devices of communication and persuasion, should be explored.

Third, we should pay attention to the notion that institutionalization involves both invention and appropriation. Under what conditions models of form and content become active in spreading institutionalization and the mechanisms that are involved (presumably including political mechanisms) are interesting issues that present work on the global spread of education is just opening up.

Fourth, we must consider not only behavioral mechanisms, such as uses of power, but also, remembering Sumner and Stinchcombe, mechanisms of selection—the constraining and enabling effects of environmental conditions, normative, as well as material and demographic.

Fifth, a matter on which I have touched only tangentially, there is the issue of how institutions in fact regulate conduct—the relative potency and pertinence to educational settings, for both teachers and students, of external constraint or membership, and, as Park and his successors have had it, of membership or marginality in realms of common belief and discourse.

Sixth and finally, with respect to method, in this day, which is still for the most part a day of large sample surveys, we should pay close attention to natural history as uniquely suited to the discovery and demonstration of process.

NOTES

1. Revision of an address prepared for a conference on Advancing the Institutional Research Agenda in Education: From Analysis to Policy, State University of New York at Albany, September 19, 2002. I am grateful for the comments of the con-

ference participants, most notably those of Heinz-Dieter Meyer and Brian Rowan, whose critiques have sharpened and extended the ideas that I present.

2. This way of thinking can be seen for example in the reviews that followed upon the 1991 publication of W. W. Powell and Paul DiMaggio's *The New Institutionalism in Organizational Analysis* (e.g., Abbott 1992) and the 1995 publication of Richard Scott's *Institutions and Organizations* (e.g., Hirsch 1997).

3. Research on national systems of education in non-Western societies are few, with such notable exceptions as Dore's (1984) splendid analysis of how in Japan events in the Tokugawa period prepared the ground for the educational reforms of the Meiji Restoration.

4. In a theoretical vein similar to Archer's, Neil Smelser (1991) has given us a natural history of the development of mass education in nineteenth-century Britain. In his analysis, its emerging form is treated as an outcome of conflict primarily between classes and secondarily between ethnic and religious formations.

5. Historians have written interesting and sociologically useful histories of particular schools (e.g., Labaree [1988] on the Central High School of Philadelphia). Like the account provided by Kaestle and Vinovskis (1980) of nineteenth-century Massachusetts, these histories provide historiographically excellent grist that awaits the mill of theory.

REFERENCES

Abbott, Andrew. 1992. An old institutionalist reads the new institutionalism. *Contemporary Sociology* 21: 754–56.

Archer, Margaret S. 1984 [1979]. *Social origins of educational systems.* Beverly Hills: Sage.

Bidwell, Charles E. 2001. Analyzing schools as organizations: Long-term permanence and short-term change. *Sociology of Education.* Extra issue: 100–14.

Bidwell, Charles E., and Jeffrey Yasumoto. 1999. The collegial focus: Teaching fields, colleague relationships, and instructional practice in American high schools. *Sociology of Education* 72: 234–56.

Bidwell, C. E., K. A. Frank, and P. Quiroz. 1997. Teacher types, workplace controls, and the organization of schools. *Sociology of Education* 70(4): 285–307.

Bourdieu, Pierre. 1996 [1989]. *The state nobility: Elite schools in the field of power.* Trans. Loretta C. Clough. Stanford CA: Stanford University Press.

Bowles, Samuel, and Herbert Gintis. 1976. *Schooling in capitalist America.* New York: Basic Books.

Brint, Steven, and Jerome Karabel. 1991. Institutional origins and transformations: The case of American community colleges. In *The new institutionalism in organizational analysis,* ed. W. W. Powell Jr. and Paul J. DiMaggio, 337–69 Chicago: University of Chicago Press.

Burns, Tom, and George M. Stalker. 1961. *The management of innovation.* London: Tavistock.

Clark, Burton R. 1960. *The open door college.* New York: McGraw-Hill.

———. 1983. *The higher education system: Academic organization in cross-national perspective.* Berkeley: University of California Press.

Clemens, Elisabeth S., Melissa Fry, and Brayden King. 2002. Making a market in education? Charter schools in Arizona. Presented at the annual meeting of the American Sociological Association.

Collins, Randall. 1979. *The credential society.* New York: Academic.

Cooley, Charles H. 1956 [1902]. *Social organization.* Glencoe, IL: Free Press.

Dore, Ronald P. 1984. *Education in Tokugawa Japan.* London: Athlone.

Durkheim, Emile. 1950 [1901]. *The rules of sociological method.* Glencoe, IL: Free Press.

———. 1961 [1912]. *The elementary forms of religious life.* New York: Collier.

———. 1977 [1911]. *The evolution of educational thought: Lectures on the formation and development of secondary education in France.* Trans. Peter Collins. London: Routledge and Kegan Paul.

Gusfield, Joseph. 1955. Social structure and moral reform: A study of the Women's Christian Temperance Union. *American Journal of Sociology* 61: 221–32.

Hirsch, Paul A. 1997. Sociology without social structure: Neoinstitutional theory meets brave new world. *American Journal of Sociology* 102: 1702–23.

Hughes, Everett C. 1936. The ecological aspect of institutions. *American Sociological Review* 1: 180–89.

Johnson, Susan M. 1990. *Teachers at work: Achieving success in our schools.* New York: Basic Books.

Kaestle, Carl F., and Maris Vinovskis. 1980. *Education and change in nineteenth century Massachusetts.* Cambridge: Cambridge University Press.

Katz, Michael. 1968. *The irony of early school reform: Educational innovation in mid-nineteenth century Massachusetts.* Cambridge, MA: Harvard University Press.

Katznelson, Ira, and Margaret Weir. 1985. *Schooling for all: Race, class, and the decline of the democratic ideal.* New York: Basic Books

Labaree, David. 1988. *The making of an American high school: The credentials market and the Central High School of Philadelphia.* New Haven: Yale University Press.

Little, Judith W. 1990. The persistence of privacy: Autonomy and initiative in teachers' professional relations. *Teachers College Record* 91: 509–36.

McFarland, Daniel. 2001. Student resistance: How the formal and informal organization of classrooms facilitate everyday forms of student defiance. *American Journal of Sociology* 107: 612–78.

Meyer, Heinz-Dieter. 2003. Tocqueville's cultural institutionalism. *Journal of Classical Sociology* 3(2): 197–220.

Meyer, John W., and Michael T. Hannan. 1979. *National development and the world system.* Chicago: University of Chicago Press.

Meyer, John W., David H. Kamens, and Aaron Benavot. 1992. *School knowledge for the masses.* Washington DC: Falmer.

Meyer, John W. and Brian Rowan. 1977. Institutional organizations: Formal structure as myth and ceremony. *American Journal of Sociology* 83: 340–63.

Meyer, John W., David Tyack, Joane Nagel, and Audrey Gordon. 1979. Public education as nation-building in America: Enrollments and bureaucratization in the American states, 1870–1930. *American Journal of Sociology* 85: 591–613.

Muller, Chandra, and Kathryn S. Schiller. 2000. Leveling the playing field? Students' educational attainment and states' performance testing. *Sociology of Education* 73: 196–218.

Park, Robert E., and Ernest W. Burgess. 1921. *Introduction to the science of sociology.* Chicago: University of Chicago Press.

Parsons, Talcott. 1951. *The social system.* New York: Free Press.

———. 1956. Suggestions for a sociological approach to a theory of organizations 1. *Administrative Science Quarterly* 1: 63–85.

———. 1990 [1934]. Prolegomena to a theory of social institutions. *American Sociological Review* 55: 319–39.

Perrow, Charles. 1961. The analysis of goals in complex organizations. *American Sociological Review* 26: 854–66.

Peterson, Paul A. 1985, *The politics of school reform, 1870–1940.* Chicago: University of Chicago Press.

Powell, W. W., Jr., and Paul DiMaggio, eds. 1991. *The new institutionalism in organizational analysis.* Chicago: University of Chicago Press.

Rowan, Brian. 1990. Commitment and control: Alternative strategies for the organizational design of schools. *Review of Research in Education* 16: 359–89.

———. 1995. Teachers' instructional work: Conceptual models and directions for future research. Presented at the annual meeting of the American Educational Research Association.

Rubinson, Richard A. 1986. Class formation, politics, and institutions: Schooling in the United States. *American Journal of Sociology* 92: 519–48.

Scott, W. Richard. 1995. *Institutions and organizations.* Thousand Oaks, CA: Sage.

Selznick, Philip. 1948. Foundations of the theory of organizations. *American Sociological Review* 13: 25–35.

———. 1949. *TVA and the grass roots.* Berkeley: University of California Press.

———. 1957. *Leadership in administration.* New York: Harper and Row.

Shavit, Yossi, and Hans-Peter Blossfeld, eds. 1993. *Persistent inequality: Changing educational attainment in thirteen countries.* Boulder, CO: Westview.

Simmel, Georg. 1950. *The sociology of Georg Simmel.* Trans. Kurt H. Wolff. Glencoe, IL: Free Press.

Smelser, Neil J. 1991. *Social paralysis and social change: British working class education in the nineteenth century.* Berkeley: University of California Press.

Stinchcombe, Arthur. 1965. Social structure and organizations. In *Handbook of organizations,* ed. James G. March, 142–93. Chicago: Rand-McNally.

———. 1968. *Constructing social theories.* Chicago: University of Chicago Press.

Sumner, William G. 1906. *Folkways.* New York: Ginn.

Talbert, Joan, and Milbrey W. McLaughlin. 1994. Teacher professionalism in local school contexts. *American Journal of Education* 102: 123–53.

Waller, Willard. 1932. *The sociology of teaching*. New York: Wiley.

Weick, Karl A. 1976. Educational organizations as loosely coupled systems. *Administrative Science Quarterly* 21: 1–19.

Yasumoto, Jeffrey, Kazuaki Uekawa, and Charles E. Bidwell. 2001. The collegial focus and student achievement: Consequences of high school faculty social organization for students' achievement in mathematics and science. *Sociology of Education* 74: 181–209.

FOUR

The Rise and Decline of the Common School as an Institution: Taking "Myth and Ceremony" Seriously

HEINZ-DIETER MEYER

IN THEIR JUSTLY FAMOUS paper "Institutional Structure as Myth and Cere-mony," John Meyer and Brian Rowan (1977) pioneered the idea that organi-zations are built to a large extent on "institutionalized myths." As they put it:

> In modern societies, the elements of rationalized formal structure are deeply
> ingrained in, and reflect, widespread understandings of social reality. Many
> of the positions, policies, programs, and procedures of modern organizations
> are enforced by public opinion, by the views of important constituents, by
> knowledge legitimated through the educational system, by social prestige, by
> the laws, and by the definitions of negligence and prudence used by the
> courts. Such elements of formal structure are manifestations of powerful
> institutional rules which function as highly rationalized myths that are bind-
> ing on particular organizations. (Meyer and Rowan 1977 in Powell and
> DiMaggio 1991, 44)

The idea is that behavior in organizations is determined not by consider-ations of technical efficiency but by the need and desire to comply with widely accepted beliefs, rules, and norms. Despite its prominence in Meyer/Rowan's path-breaking paper, the idea of myths has experienced no empirical or theo-retical development since it was raised to pivotal status in 1977. Researchers have often been content with invoking the importance of myths in the abstract. The new institutionalism calls for more specific analyses of the effect collective beliefs have on the working of institutions (Powell and DiMaggio 1991, Greif 1998). In education, Jerome Bruner (1995) has made an explicit case for the study of institutionalized beliefs and ideas. Education is in his view an embodiment of culture, not just a preparation for it. "Mind" is a prod-uct of culture, a cultural construction, both in the psychological sense, in that there cannot be a single human mind, and in the sociological sense, in that a person's ideas are always developed in interaction with others.

In this chapter I want to extend the Meyer/Rowan account of myths in two directions: (1) I want to direct attention to specific myths and their spe-cific effect on institutions; (2) I want to highlight the role of myths and col-lective beliefs in the change process and the power struggles that always sur-round institutions. In the bulk of the chapter I focus on the myth of the common school. I propose that much of the current problems of the Ameri-can public school are the result of the decline of this founding myth. This account of the problems of American education differs from rational-techno-cratic approaches, which attempt to locate the shortcomings of public educa-tion in flawed policies or insufficient resources.

MYTHS AND EDUCATIONAL INSTITUTIONS: A SOCIAL-CONSTRUCTIVIST ACCOUNT

Why are myths of such importance for the life of institutions? Can we really claim a connection between "myths" and the performance of an institution? To address this question, I will first provide a sketch of a social-constructivist framework of institutions. After that I will detail the special role of the myth mentioned here, followed by a discussion of its decline.

What Is an Educational Institution?

A famous scene in Plato's *Meno* depicts Socrates teaching a young boy Pythagoras' theorem. Standing in a public place, drawing lines in the sand, Socrates leads the boy step by step through Pythagoras' theorem. As the boy realizes that one can find the length of the hypotenuse in a right triangle by taking the square root of the sum of the squares of the other two sides, Socrates tries to prove to the reader that all "learning is remembering."

Whether or not we agree that learning is the unfolding of knowledge that is in some embryonic form "already there," most would agree that Socrates' conversation with the boy qualifies as a simple form of "schooling." Plato's scene consists of a teacher, a student, and a place where they can talk. In some cases the student may actually assume the leading role in the exchange, as in the case of Frederick Douglass, the brilliant leader of the abolitionist movement and runaway slave, who learned to read by "bribing" white school children to explain the alphabet to him. As enticement he used sugar lumps that he took from his slave owner's table. With that minimal outside help, Douglass made himself into one of the most powerful writers and orators in the antislavery movement.

Many other examples attest that schooling goes on wherever people exchange knowledge and ideas. Simple forms of schooling built on this primitive teacher-student dyad have existed for centuries. Most formal education in ancient Greece and Rome took place between a tutor and a student. Practically all of the scientific giants of the eighteenth and nineteenth century were home schooled—a form of education that is on the rise again today. According to Lawrence Cremin, education in the colonial period of the United States was going on everywhere—in local churches, Sunday schools, independent pay schools, charity schools, the subscription school, and private homes (Kaestle 1983, 120). In 1814 Tocqueville (1969) found Americans the best-educated nation, although institutions of formal learning were then few and far between. Ivan Illich's "De-Schooling Society" (1971) is a latter day example of a conception of schooling radically different from today's public school.

The Contingency of Institutions

These few examples may suffice to remind us that schooling of young people has happened on a large scale without recourse to the institutional forms that we take for granted today. In fact, a moment's reflection shows that the modern form of schooling is a highly idiosyncratic institution. There is nothing natural or inevitable about this school as we know it: a dedicated physical space, separated from home or family, where students are graded by age and compelled by law to attend, lest they be counted as "drop-out"; where they are instructed and tested by specialized full-time government employees, whose salary is paid for by taxes. A large number of alternative arrangements exist that could produce the same or similar degrees of literacy and numeracy. Students could learn at home, with peers, with community members, at the parents' workplace, in voluntary organizations, in cyber schools, to mention a few. Instead of full-time educators, teachers could be recruited from the ranks of professionals who take time out from their regular jobs, as Rousseau (1772/1972) recommended. In short: school as we know it is a contingent institution, an institutional form with many feasible alternatives.

Myths and Institutional Legitimacy

The contingency axiom is, in many ways, the starting point of any institutional analysis. It is the idea that a given institutional configuration is only one way of ordering a particular social activity. When we look at education from an institutional point of view, we do not accept what is as inevitable. To be sure: to say that institutions are contingent is not to say that they could assume any imaginable form under the sun. It is also not to say that any established institutional form is necessarily inferior to alternative ones or that it is the result of the political machinations of a particular class. What we say is that the set of feasible alternatives is in most cases larger than zero and that the survival of one institutional option over others is likely to please some social actors more than others. To put it bluntly: to bridge the distance from Socrates' teaching of the young boy to an institution like our system of mass education, many equally possible institutional solutions had to be eliminated, perhaps suppressed. It is quite likely that different social groups or classes had different preferences with respect to the institutional model they preferred. As one model came to dominate the others, it is likely that the political interests of one group gained more than another. That is why students of institutions must beware of the contingency of institutions. As Friedland and Alford (1991, 260) put it: "When social scientists import the dominant institutional logics into their analyses of individuals and organizations in unexamined ways, they unreflectively elaborate the symbolic order and social practices of the institutions they study."

A key step in this quarrel that ends with one institutional design becoming the dominant one is the invention and spread of legitimizing beliefs, the telling of tall tales or myths.

THE "COMMON SCHOOL": A CORE MYTH
OF AMERICAN PUBLIC EDUCATION

In this section I discuss a central myth that has, for over a century, given strength and legitimacy to the American public school: the idea of the *common school*. There are, of course, other important myths legitimizing the public school, for example, the idea of the *efficient school* and the idea of the *locally controlled* school. Either of these two would deserve its own critical discussion. Still, it is not too far fetched to view the common school as the master myth of American public education. In the words of Horace Mann: "Without undervaluing any other human agency, it may be safely affirmed that the common school, improved and energized, as it can easily be, may become the most effective and benignant of all the forces of civilization (Mann in Cremin 1957, 79)."

The common school idea has helped to bridge the gap between different groups' vision of education in the United States. It has assumed mythical status, invoked and reinforced in myriads of daily acts, large and small. Here is one of many examples where the myth is invoked by the nation's highest court:

> It is implicit in the history and character of American public education that the public schools serve a uniquely public function: the training of American citizens in an atmosphere free of parochial, divisive, or separatist influences of any sort of an atmosphere in which children may assimilate a heritage common to all American groups and religions. This is a heritage neither theistic nor atheistic, but simply civic and patriotic. (*Abbington School District v. Schempp*, 372 U.S. at 241–42 [1963])

The view of the 1963 Supreme Court that the common school is inclusive, equitable, assimilative, preparing the students for participation in civic life, is repeated in a multitude of statements such as the following: "The public schools of this country serve the admirable function of bringing together on common ground students from a diversity of cultural and religious backgrounds. The introduction of public prayer into such a setting jeopardizes the sense of community and unnecessarily introduces an emotional and divisive faction" (Rabbi Daniel Polish, Testimony to US House of Representatives, on behalf of the Synagogue Council of America, September 8, 1980). The ideals of the common school continue to be invoked. Education analyst Joseph Viteritti only recently noted that the concept of the common school is a basic dogma of the "American civic religion," which many researchers accept "as an act of faith" (2003, 235).

By building the American public school on the idea of the common school, American public education has received a highly particular rationale: to assimilate the children from otherwise diverse and heterogeneous groups (socioeconomically as well as religiously), making the school the engine of the construction of a civic community. Yet there is nothing inherently necessary about a narrative that legitimizes the public school by referring to its alleged social and societal effects. In the narratives of other countries, such considerations did not play much of a role. To understand the distinctiveness of the common school myth, a brief review of an alternative narrative will be instructive.

The Distinctiveness of the Common School Idea: A Comparison with Bildung

To sharpen our understanding of the distinctiveness of the common school, a brief comparison with an alternative concept is instructive. Where Americans converged on the common school idea, mass schooling in Germany was institutionalized in the name of Bildung. *Bildung* (from the German verb *bilden*, to "build," to "construct") is a secular ethic of conduct promulgating a person's cultural self-education. In the Bildungs ethic a person must strive lifelong to shape and perfect himself into a harmonious, fully developed individual. He does so in a sustained encounter with the best that human arts and sciences have produced. The process of Bildung may be initiated by a school but reaches far beyond its limits. In essence, it is an ongoing struggle in which man's higher faculties strive to refine and cultivate the lower ones. While a teacher can help, Bildung is essentially autodidactic.

This is one important difference from the common school idea. While the common school strives to make better citizens for a better republic, Bildung is focused on the self-perfecting individual—conceived as a philosopher or artist, not the bourgeois. In "On the Limits of the Effectiveness of the State" Humboldt offered Bildung as an alternative to Western rival conceptions: "The ancients devoted their attention more exclusively to the harmonious development of the individual man, as man; the moderns are chiefly solicitous about his comfort, his prosperity, his productiveness. The former looked to virtue; the latter seek for happiness" (Humboldt, 1791/1993, 69).

There are at least two differences that distinguish Bildung from the common school ideal. First, the goal of the common school is not the broadening of a person's intellectual capacities per se but the creation of social inclusion and moral consensus. The target is the individual as citizen, and the tools are tax-supported schools, teaching the three Rs and the Protestant bible. In Bildung, the target is man's inner self, and its tools are the arts and sciences. Second, while the common school was promoted by a class of egalitarian, urban, middle-class intellectuals (who also played a role in the antislavery movement), the pivot for the German movement were artists and philosophers. The first purposes of the common school promoters were more equality and social justice. As Horace Mann (1848) put it:

> According to the European theory, men are divided into classes—some to toil and earn, others to seize and enjoy. According to the Massachusetts theory, all are to have an equal chance for earning, and equal security in the enjoyment of what they earn. [. . .] The operative or laborer of the present day has no employment, and therefore no bread, unless the capitalist will accept his services. The vassal had no shelter but such as his master provided for him. Not one in five thousand of English operatives, or farm laborers, is able to build or own even a hovel; and therefore they must accept such shelter as Capital offers them. (in Cremin, 1957, 85)

In sum: the common school is an institution to create and strengthen democratic community as inclusive, equitable, and assimilative. It replaces a loose, inchoate system of local and private education. Bildung, by contrast, is indifferent to the social condition of the people. It aims at the individual's inner self. While the common school is a sharp weapon against social exclusivity in education, it is a rather blunt instrument when it comes to improve the quality of learning. Bildung, by contrast, lends itself more readily to underscore the importance of educational quality, comprehensiveness, and performance. These are some of the practical implications of the two institutionalized ideas.

THE ORIGIN OF THE COMMON SCHOOL MYTH

Inspired by the Prussian education system, Horace Mann began a campaign to replace the loose, unregulated, decentralized, yet reasonably effective New England school system by a uniform, centralized, wall-to-wall system. The common school became shorthand for this uniquely American view of schooling to uplift, cultivate, assimilate, and morally transform. Yet this change meant centralization, secularization, and taxation—three big departures from a tradition of decentralized, locally controlled schooling. Inevitably, such a project would run into strong resistance by anyone who opposed centralization, secularization of the school's religious mission, and higher taxes.

To appreciate the significance of the common school idea, it is important to recall what problem it was designed to solve. I mentioned above that for decades schooling in New England was more like a quilt than an evenly woven cloth. Yet the results were quite impressive. Many Americans had no reason to be particularly unhappy with their messy and disorganized system of schooling, which satisfied the needs of a largely rural society. The call to centralize and systematize this loose arrangement of educational venues did not come from the agrarian middle classes of New England. It was made by the emerging class of urban intellectuals and reformers who believed that the uneven and disjointed nature of the system conflicted with the imperatives of equality and democracy. Some reformers pointed to the fact that the United States had a system of higher education that served the upper classes well, while general education was relegated to second-class status. As Noah Webster put it in 1790: "The constitutions are republican and the laws of education are monarchical" (in Kaestle 1983, 6).

Widespread Resistance against School Centralization

To many Americans of the early nineteenth century the common school idea was an open invitation to secularize education and place it under the control of "big" government. Since its implementation implied higher taxes, expanded government, and weaker religious impact, the number of groups who resisted the common school was impressively large:

- poor rural towns had no money to support a more comprehensive and more expensive system of schools; for many the idea to raise taxes to educate "other people's children" was akin to "reaching into neighbor's pockets to finance one's own children's education";
- many defenders of local autonomy saw a centralized school system, governed from Boston rather than their local town, as a threat to their local self-government;
- the members of the various Protestant groups and sects saw a religiously uniform school system as a vehicle of secularization. Unlike local schools that could follow the beliefs of the preponderance of the local community, common schools would have to teach a watered-down version of Protestantism, something that would satisfy no one;
- whereas Protestants were concerned that the common school would no longer teach the specific sectarian version of their beliefs, non-Protestant groups, especially Catholics, saw Horace Mann's project as a way to establish Protestant dominance over all other religions;
- non-Anglo Saxon ethnic minorities who used schooling as a means to pass their cultural and language heritage to their children likewise were suspicious of the idea to centralize and standardize the system;
- last, but not least, upper-class families were not keen to have their children mix with, as John Locke and Thomas Jefferson had called it, "the rubble." One upper-class student quoted his father as saying that he would "rather send me to jail than to public school in Boston" (Kaestle 1983, 59). The children of the well-to-do did not need improved schools for their upbringing. The private education they enjoyed was far superior to anything the public system could provide.

Thus, in the early nineteenth century few social groups saw the need for a reform of the magnitude Horace Mann envisioned, and the resistance against a system of public schools was formidable. To forge a coalition strong enough to overcome the resistance against the creation of a public system of general education, a rationale was needed that a large number of the stakeholders found compelling. This rationale was found in the common school. But even then it took a social crisis and the resulting widespread concern of the upper and middle classes to make the common school stick.

Mass Immigration: A Window of Opportunity for Change

A key event in the acceptance of a centralized and secularized tax-supported public school was the midnineteenth-century mass immigration, which made a continuation of gradual assimilation of the newcomers through the established institutions of church and township impossible. Not only were the immigrants too numerous to be readily absorbed into American culture. Their cultural and ethnic origin also put them directly at odds with the dominant Anglo Saxon Protestants, who saw the mass immigration as a threat that would cause civic disorder, urban riots, and religious segregation. Coincidentally, the new factories in the nascent New England textile industry needed laborers that could not readily be found among the ranks of rural Americans. To be useful for factory work, they needed English-language skills and youngsters socialized to American standards of discipline and authority. Seen against that background, the erstwhile resisters saw the common school in a new light. Perhaps such an institution could provide the necessary assimilation and socialization that would turn these newcomers into more reliable members of American society—both civically and economically (Bowles and Gintis 1985; Katznelson and Weir 1976). The coincidence of institutional change and mass immigration was not limited to Massachussetts. Diane Ravitch pointed out that in New York, "each major reorganization of the school system was the result of intense political struggle, and that each of these battles coincided with a huge wave of new immigration" (Ravitch 1988, xxix).

The rhetoric of social reformers such as Horace Mann, who described the common school as "protection of society against the giant vices which now invade and torment it"; as well as a "great equalizer of the condition of men; source of civilization, of economic prosperity" suddenly fell on fertile ground.

The End of the Myth of the Common School

> If the tempest of political strife were to be let loose upon our common schools, they would be overwhelmed with sudden ruin, struck down by the hand of political patricide.
> —Horace Mann, 1848

Protestant hegemony, combined with social egalitarianism, defines school as engine of social progress, the instrument to transform nominal democracy into real democracy. The only way this works, however, is by stretching the compass of moral consensus, by building an ever wider roof under which a growing disparity of beliefs would fit. Inevitably, the larger the roof, the shallower the convictions that were supposed to unite all Americans under the common school's roof. Yet, this increasingly thin blanket of shared convictions would inevitably invite the resurgence of religious sectarianism—one of the greatest dangers to the common school, as Horace Mann well knew.

The American public school's defining feature was to be a school with a mission. That mission originated with the first Protestant settlers' need to induct the young and new immigrants to the Protestant faith (Bailyn 1972). It later metamorphosed into a mission to Americanize those who began to arrive en mass with a professedly different faith. In its final version, the mission became one of preparing the young for full participation in the American dream. Ironically, as that mission nears completion, the American public school seems to become increasingly "despirited." The unifying force of the common school is increasingly neutralized and overwhelmed by the divisive forces of socioeconomic differentiation, litigation, and cultural heterogeneity. Yet in the past three decades this school for all, designed to instill the same American ideals in everyone and to offer everyone a chance to improve him/ or herself, had to make silent, but all the more important concessions to reality: an aggressive secularism has replaced religious denominationalism; a "life preparation" curriculum has replaced "the people's college"; deep socioeconomic cleavages have replaced the inclusive community.

For more than a century the common school has provided the rationale for the American project of public education. One of its main functions was to provide a narrative that was acceptable to a large number of diverse interest groups who seemed ill equipped to unite in support of the institution of the public school. Some of the major change movements of the twentieth century took the theme of the common school and urged greater efforts at closing the gap between its claims and the reality on the ground.

Today, however, the common school, forced to make deep and irreversible concessions to reality, is losing traction (Cibulka 1995). In Mann's view, the common school rested on the key pillars of socioeconomic inclusion, moral-religious inclusion, and cultural-civic assimilation. All of these pillars show signs of erosion.

• The all-important idea of (socioeconomic) inclusiveness comes up hard against a reality of growing socioeconomic segregation (Kozol 1992). The lines of segregation run not only between schools with widely differing resources but also within schools where tracking creates classes of learners that echo socioeconomic and racial lines (Ogletree 2004). The robustness of this segregation suggests that the public school is no longer "common," serving no longer as an engine of socioeconomic integration.

• The idea of religious-moral inclusiveness has given way to an aggressive secularism that recognizes only each individual's freedom of belief. The United States has moved from a self-conception as a Protestant country to one in which Protestantism is only one among a large and increasing number of faiths, none of which the school endorses. Instead of Mann's "denominational" Protestantism the only belief that students and parents have in common today is the belief in the freedom to believe anything they want. The public school today espouses a variant of moral-religious relativism, for which Protestantism and voodoo worship are equivalent forms of personal belief.

• Finally, the 1990s have replaced the idea of cultural assimilation by the notion of multiculturalism. The key change here is the recognition of the fact that a large number of religious and ethnic communities in the United

States, while sharing certain civic and cultural tenets, have incommensu-rably different commitments to culturally shared beliefs, values, and priori-ties. No longer do we maintain that these differences interfere with being American. Rather, diversity and difference are celebrated as constitutive of the American cultural fabric (Berlin 1998; Walzer 1995; Taylor 1996). We even accept that differences of race or ethnicity will affect students' reading of curricular content (e.g., the history of slavery in the United States). The common school as the great machine of cultural assimilation has been replaced by the public school as an arena for the celebration of cultural diversity (Schlesinger 1998, Glazer 1997). Horace Mann knew that the common school would be severely tested if ever the country were to allow a plurality of cultural and religious options. As long as "the controverted points, compared with those about which there is no dispute, do not bear the proportion of one to a hundred" the common school was unproblem-atic. "It is obvious, on the other hand, that if the tempest of political strife were to be let loose upon our common schools, they would be overwhelmed with sudden ruin," "struck down by the hand of political patricide." (Mann in Cremin 1957, 96).

Through most of its history—until the 1960s—the American high school was energized by its "not yet." It had "not yet" reached 100 percent of the boys and girls of an age group; it had not yet managed to disabuse all parts of the population of their foreign, traditional, obsolete ideas and values; it had not yet realized equality of opportunity for all. As long as there was still a gap between the mission and the reality of full inclusion, the American high school could retain its missionary faith. Then, in the late 1960s two things happened: (1) the high school became universal, racial segregation was torn down, at least on paper, and the melting pot burst; (2) henceforth, statistics would no longer report the number of young people who managed to attend high school, but rather the number of people who did not or who left early.

Thus, the American public school lost its institutional mission. No longer could it claim to bring greater parts of the population under the umbrella of Americanism because that American unity had, indeed, become problematic. No longer could it claim that it was the great engine of opportunity, because under conditions of tracking and suburban quasiprivate schools opportunity was clearly dished out inequitably. Besides, the knowledge demands of most occupations and professions have risen so dramatically that a high school degree alone no longer opens many doors.

Like other institutions that decline because they succeeded, the Ameri-can school has lost its energizing mission. Having brought practically the entire age cohort of the young under its roof, it no longer knows what to strive for. In the face of great cultural, ethnic, and religious plurality, it does not know what kind of community it is supposed to engender. In the face of a reality of segregation (by "academic achievement," class, and belief), it does not know how to create inclusiveness. In the face of a high school diploma that opens no doors, it does not know the meaning of opportunity. Having lost the belief in an overarching American mission, and having witnessed the breakup of a homogeneous population into so many fragments of multiculturalism, the institution of the American school is for some time now merely "going through the motions." This lack of mission and of a homogeneous basis makes itself felt the older and more independent the students become. By the time they reach high school, the American school turns, for many, into a custodial institution.

A NOTE ON INSTITUTIONAL CHANGE

In this chapter I describe the creation of the common school, which initially was strongly resisted by a majority of groups who feared a change from a decentralized, small-scale, predominantly rural school system to a centralized, large-scale, urban system. To gain analytical leverage, I want to use the case of the common school to develop a stylized model of institutional change. The model highlights the role of collective beliefs and of the punctuated equilibrium (Krasner 1984). In this model, change occurs as the result of an equilibrium-altering window of opportunity of which a dominant coalition manages to take advantage. In a schematic sketch, the constellation of forces might have looked like this (table 4.1):

In the status quo ante, five out of seven major social constituents—including the farming families and rural towns where the majority of people then lived and the small but powerful group of aristocrats and patricians—opposed the idea of the common school with its concomitant new taxes, loss of local control, and shift to secularism. It is hard to imagine a weakening or major change in that strong anticommon school coalition but for an event that shook up the confidence of the leading Boston Brahmins and patricians. The unprecedented influx of masses of non-Anglo immigrants in the ports of Boston and New York turned out to be a uniquely challenging test of the social fabric of midnineteenth-century New England. Irish, Polish, Italian, Jewish, German, and French immigrants were not Protestants, nor was English their mother tongue (with the exception of the Irish). Especially their young sons misperceived the democratic, unauthoritarian nature of the public order as a free-for-all, flooding urban centers such as Boston and New York with unassimilated people and ethnicities, who seemed bent on upholding their peculiar ideas and customs. Conjuring up the specter of social disruption and disturbances, the aristocrats now saw a use for the common school that had escaped them before. By making the new immigrants attend public school, they might in time become sufficiently accustomed to WASP American values and cus-

TABLE 4.1
Institutional Change as Punctuated Equilibrium

Pro/Con	Socioeconomic Group	Position/Interest	Degree of Organization
Con	Farmers; rural towns;	reject imposition of central, tax-costly school system; children receive enough schooling in pre-Horace Mann system	Low
Con	Puritan-Protestant groups, ministers	reject watered down ("denominational") curriculum prefer loose patchwork of assuredly religious education over centralized and secularized system	Low
Con	Catholic church/ families	reject imposition of a Protestant curriculum; control fairly widespread system of parochial schooling	High
Con	Ethnic minorities	reject centralized system that imposes English as mandatory language	Low
Ambivalent	Workers	weary of new taxes; but public and free system of education may improve social status of children	Intermediate
Before: Con	Aristocrats/ Patricians/ Boston Brahmins	do not want to see their children go to the same schools as the urban "rubble"; children are well served by privately organized education	High
After: Pro	Aristocrats/ Patricians/ Boston Brahmins	embrace public education to assimilate non-Anglo immigrants and quell danger of urban crisis/riots	High
Pro	Urban reformers/ intellectuals	disjointed, uneven system of local schooling is undemocratic and unjust; intellectuals stand to benefit from jobs created by centralization of schooling	High

toms to make them useful and employable members of the community. As table 4.1 shows, only one of the seven groups had to switch sides for the old stable state to become sufficiently punctuated to make room for a new dominant coalition becoming the building block for a new equilibrium.

By joining the urban reformers and intellectuals who had been the lone group calling for the common school, the wealthy Brahmins (in conjunction with the workers who were ambivalent vis-à-vis the new institution) caused the scales to tip. The old legitimizing rationale for general education that saw education anchored in family, community, and religion changed to a socially progressive, egalitarian rationale. The table includes rough estimates of the degree to which the various groups were organized and thus able to speak with one voice. Again, the advantage goes to the reformers and the patricians who were highly organized and articulate and able to influence public opinion.

Three things are important about the idea of a punctuated equilibrium:

1. Endogenous and exogenous changes qualify as triggers for "punctuation," i.e., the switch from the traditional to a new equilibrium. While exogenous changes are typically easier to recognize, endogenous changes (i.e., changes that are driven by a specific dynamic of the institution itself) may often prepare the ground and make the institution "ripe" for effective attack from external forces or events.
2. The illustration shows how institutional changes are accompanied and prompted by changes in the distribution of power—in the above case the switching sides of the wealthy Brahmins that enables reformers, patricians, and workers to join a new dominant coalition.
3. It also shows how long periods of stability and inertia can be brought to an end by entirely accidental circumstances that nobody could have foreseen. Most early nineteenth-century New Englanders would have been fairly proud about the degree of literacy and education that was to be found in the new nation, created by immigrants. That they might be forced by new waves of immigrants to change their ways in education, few people could have anticipated.

In sum: institutional change is made by identifiable individuals or groups who pursue identifiable goals and objectives (in this analysis: the prevention of an urban crisis). While change typically will have self-interested driving forces and motives, it would be wrong to reduce every change to the selfish motives of this or that group. In certain historic moments institutional innovations, even if pushed by only a part of the social forces available, may yet happen to advance the greater good of all.

CONCLUSION

The American public school is one of the core institutions of American society. It is embedded in a grand narrative of social inclusion and opportunity for all. Its creation was testimony to the American faith in social progress, the power of reason, and the promise of human perfectibility. Very few of the great American narratives do not turn, at one point or another, on the public school as a master mechanism for opportunity and advancement. In many ways the public school has been the American dream machine. Hence, the ideological, political, and symbolic importance of that institution is hard to overstate as well as the beliefs on which it is founded. As those beliefs weaken, as people, one by one, stop seeing the school as common and inclusive, a launching path of opportunity, as they demand choice and a higher degree of control over the education of their children, in short, as the founding myths crumble, so does the institution. If, for the time being, parents and students keep coming, it may be more due to tradition and habit than conviction or faith.

By reviving the study of the role of myths and beliefs in the rise and decline of institutions, institutional theory can produce analytical leverage that other perspectives on education lack. It can produce more plausible and more comprehensive explanations for some of the persistent problems of educational practice, such as the institution's persistent failure to innovate. Based on this view, a key problem of the American public school is not that it is rooted in nonrational beliefs and myths, but that the grip of these myths on the American collective conscience is waning, while suitable alternatives are not yet in sight.

REFERENCES

Abbington School District v. Schempp, 1963. 372 U.S. at 241–42.

Bailyn, Bernard. 1972. *Education in the forming of American society*. New York: Norton.

Berlin, I. 1998. *The crooked timber of humanity*. Princeton, NJ: Princeton University Press.

Bowles, Samuel, and Herbert Gintis. 1976. *Schooling in capitalist America: Education reform and the contradictions of economic life*. New York: Basic Books.

Bruner, Jerome. 1995. *The Culture of Education*. Cambridge, MA: Harvard University Press.

Cibulka, James G. 1995. The institutionalization of public schools: The decline of legitimizing myths and the politics of organizational instability. In *Advances in research and theories of school management and educational policy*, ed. Rodney T. Ogawa, 3: 123–58. Greenwich, CN: JAI.

Cremin, Lawrence A., ed. 1957. *The republic and the school: Horace Mann on the education of free men*. New York: Teachers College Press.

DiMaggio, Paul J., and W alter W. Powell. 1983. The iron cage revisited: Institutional isomorphism and collective rationality in organizational fields. *American Sociological Review* 48: 147–60.

Friedland, Roger, and Robert R. Alford. 1991. Bringing society back. In *The new institutionalism in organizational analysis*, ed. Walter Powell and Paul J. DiMaggio, 232–66. Chicago: University of Chicago Press.

Glazer, Nathan. 1997. *We are all multiculturalists now.* Cambridge, MA: Harvard University Press.

Greif, Avner. 1998. Historical and comparative institutional analysis. *American Economic Review* 88(2).

Humboldt, Wilhelm. 1791/1993. *The Limits of State Action.* Ed. J. W. Burrow. Indianapolis: Liberty Fund.

Illich, Ivan. 1971. *Deschooling society.* New York: Harper and Row.

Kaestle, Carl F. 1983. *Pillars of the republic: Common schools and American society, 1780–1860.* New York: Hill and Wang.

Katznelson, Ira, and Margret Weir. 1985. *Schooling for all: Class, race, and the decline of the democratic ideal.* New York: Basic Books.

Kozol, Jonathan. 1992. *Savage inequalities: Children in America's schools.* New York: Sagebrush.

Krasner, Stephen D. 1984. Approaches to the state: Alternative conceptions and historical dynamics. *Comparative Politics* 16(2): 223–46.

Mann, Horace. 1957. Report No. 12 of the Massachusetts School Board (1848). In *The republic and the school: Horace Mann on the education of free men.* New York: Teachers College Press.

Meyer, John, and Brian Rowan. 1977. Institutionalized organizations: Formal structure as myth and ceremony. *American Journal of Sociology* 83: 340–63; reprinted in *The New Institutionalism in Organizational Analysis,* ed. Walter Powell and Paul J. DiMaggio. Chicago: Chicago University Press.

Ogletree, Charles J. 2004. *All deliberate speed: Reflections on the first half-century of Brown v. Board of Education.* New York: Norton.

Plato. 2002. The Meno. In *Five Dialogues.* New York: Hackett.

Powell, Walter, and Paul J. DiMaggio, eds. 1991. *The New Institutionalism in Organizational Analysis.* Chicago: University of Chicago Press.

Ravitch, Diane. 1988. *The great school wars.* New York: Basic Books.

Rousseau, Jean Jacques. 1972. *The government of Poland.* Bobbs-Merrill.

Schlesinger, Arthur. 1998. *The Disuniting of America.* New York: Norton.

Taylor, Charles. 1996. Two theories of modernity. *The Responsive Community,* Summer, 16–25.

Tocqueville, Alexis. 1969. *Democracy in America.* New York: Doubleday.

Viteritti, Joseph P. 2003. Schoolyard revolutions: How research on urban school reform undermines reform. *Political Science Quarterly* 118(2), Summer, 233–57.

Walzer, Michael. 1995. The concept of civil society. In *Towards a Global Civil Society,* ed. Michael Walzer, 7–28. Providence, RI: Berghahn.

FIVE

The School Improvement Industry in the United States: Why Educational Change Is Both Pervasive and Ineffectual

BRIAN ROWAN

A GREAT DEAL OF RESEARCH suggests that educational change in the United States is faddish and has little real or lasting impact on the core function of schools—instruction.[1] Two lines of argument have been used to explain this pattern. One focuses on issues of school organization, culture, and leadership, arguing that schools are inherently conservative institutions and that deep and lasting change can come about only through transformational leadership and a fundamental restructuring of schools as organizations.[2] Another blames this pattern of educational change on the decentralized and pluralistic nature of educational governance in the United States. Here, patterns of educational governance in the United States are seen as promoting multiple and incoherent reform efforts that lead to loose coupling within schools, and the key to lasting change is seen as the development of "systemic" policy arrangements that produce coherent and focused education reforms.[3]

Neither of these arguments fully explains patterns of educational change in the United States. A few case studies of American schools, for example, have shown that changes in school organization, culture, and leadership can produce dramatic instances of school improvement. But many more such studies find that transformational leaders and/or school restructuring efforts typically lead to weak and inconsistent results from school to school.[4] Similarly, after a decade of systemic reform in the United States, there is some evidence of positive changes in student outcomes, but only in some of the states pursuing systemic reforms. Overall, research suggests that instruction and instructional outcomes in U.S. schools are not dramatically different than they were a decade ago, even in states vigorously pursuing systemic approaches to educational reform.[5]

All of this suggests that something is missing from our usual theories of educational change. In this chapter, I argue that the missing element is attention to the large set of organizations in U.S. education that exist alongside of, and interact regularly with, schools and governing agencies. The purpose of this chapter is to develop an argument about the ways in which these organizations (rather than schools and governing agencies) affect the scope and pace of change in American education. In doing so, I focus on a set of organizations that make up what I call the school improvement "industry" in the United States. Understanding how these organizations are structured and function, and how they interact with schools and governing agencies, will round out our knowledge about change in American schools.

The argument I build in this regard is based on two premises. First, I argue that the instructional core of schools—not only in the United States, but everywhere—is built around the extensive use of texts and tests obtained *outside* of schools. In the United States, however, I will argue that economic conditions in the publishing industry force schools searching for textbook and testing resources to engage in market transactions with publishing firms that exist in a highly concentrated industry, where firms succeed by achieving economies of scale through pursuit of a national marketing strategy. In this environment, textbook and testing firms tend to invest a great deal in new product launches, to be quite slow to innovate, and to be quite unresponsive to the unique, local demands arising in schools. As a result, local efforts at instructional change often bump up against inertial forces in the publishing industry, producing the pattern of stability so often observed in the instructional core of American schools.

A second premise is that schools—everywhere—look outside their boundaries for information, training, and program development resources germane to instructional improvement. In the United States, however, the organizations that provide these resources almost always exist in an extremely pluralistic and heterogeneous environment in which new organizational forms, while easy to found, are also quick to fail. In this situation, local schools looking to gain new information, devise new training schemes, or adopt new programs confront a social environment in which critical information, training, and program development resources are extremely heterogeneous and short lived because the organizations providing such resources either come and go quite rapidly or change directions on a dime. This situation, I argue, produces the renowned "faddishness" in American education—the constant swirl of innovation and reform. But even though innovation is ever present and much sought after locally, it cannot much affect the instructional core of schools, since activities in the core are substantially stabilized by transactions with large, stable firms adapted to economic conditions in the publishing industry.

The critical issue for this chapter is why these conditions obtain in the United States. Why, for example, is the textbook industry in the United States so concentrated? Why do firms in the textbook publishing industry pursue a national marketing strategy? And why are the firms in this industry so slow to adapt to local demands? Moreover, why are the organizations providing schools with information, training, and new programs so quick to be founded, so quick to fail, and so enamored with adapting quickly to changes in the marketplace for ideas? To answer these questions, I argue that researchers need to move beyond an analysis of schools and governing agencies in order to look more closely at the school improvement industry.

THE SCHOOL IMPROVEMENT
INDUSTRY IN K–12 EDUCATION

Many discussions of educational improvement focus on relations between schools and their governing agencies. But there is much more to the K–12 education that warrants the attention of any serious effort to understand educational change. For one, education is a huge institutional enterprise, and its very scale gives rise to a great deal of organizing outside of schools and their governing agencies. The vast number of employees hired by educational organizations, for example, has given rise to several hundred occupational and professional associations in the field.[6] Moreover, this vast employee base created a huge and recurrent demand for "professional development" and other forms of employee training. To meet this demand, institutions of higher education each year graduate roughly two hundred thousand individuals with degrees in education.[7] Alongside this enormous enterprise, there is also a lively and constant market for other continuing education opportunities, which are provided not only by schools, governing agencies, and universities but also by hundreds of private firms and membership associations in the field.[8]

The education sector also consists of many different businesses providing a host of support services to schools and school systems. These include a large number of firms providing "back office" services (such as accounting, insurance, and so on), others providing more visible food, transportation, architectural services, and even a small set of firms that contract with local school systems to provide instructional services directly to students. Overall, more than 80 percent of all local education agencies in the United States contract with

outside sources for professional and technical services in a given year, services
that are provided by over thirty-seven hundred business establishments earning over $3.7 billion per year. Quite apart from all of this activity, there is also
a continuing demand for research services in K–12 education, with over four
hundred establishments (apart from universities) providing roughly $550 mil-
lion in education research and development in the sector. Finally, the sector is
served by a large number of manufacturing firms catering to the needs of
schools and school systems for manufactured goods, including office supplies,
textbooks, furniture, heating and cooling systems, and so on. Here, textbook
publishers alone ship over $1.85 billion worth of goods to schools each year,
with other manufacturing organizations adding to this total.[9]

THE SCHOOL IMPROVEMENT INDUSTRY

This chapter focuses on a particular subset of these organizations, namely,
those that form the K–12 school improvement *industry*. In coining this term,
I mean to denote a group of organizations whose main aim is to provide goods
and services directly relevant to school—and especially instructional—
improvement. In looking at this industry, I will focus especially on three kinds
of organizations: (a) for-profit firms, including both publicly and privately
held firms that operate primarily as suppliers and contractors to schools and
school systems; (b) membership organizations, which I define as organizations that rely primarily on dues or subscription fees and that exist largely to
serve the interests of their members, including various occupational and/or
professional associations, trade associations, and/or networks of organizations;
and (c) not-for-profit (often quasipublic) organizations that secure a large
portion of their funding from fee-for-service arrangements and/or government or foundation grants.

To argue that a set of organizations comprises a school improvement
"industry" is to argue that these organizations seek to produce something of
value for consumption by local school systems and/or governing agencies
interested in school (and especially instructional) improvement. Throughout
this chapter, I call attention to four classes of such commodities: information,
training, materials, and programs. With respect to information, I focus on the
provision of research, advocacy, and other forms of analysis, especially as
these bear on problems of instructional improvement. The boundary between
information and a second commodity of interest—training—is loose, but in
the sense implied here, training involves the direct use of information to
socialize or instruct others, as in programs of professional development
and/or training. Materials can be defined as the usual array of textbooks,
software, tests, manipulatives, maps, and so on, as well as the supplementary
guides and users manuals associated with these. Programs, for my purposes,

are defined as deliberate and conscious efforts to combine information, training, and materials into a package of instructional activities designed to be enacted by a school.

ORGANIZATIONAL NICHES AND POPULATIONS IN THE SCHOOL IMPROVEMENT INDUSTRY

In a previously published paper on this topic (Rowan 2002), I used ideas from organizational ecology (and closely related work on strategic groups within industries) to analyze the school improvement industry.[10] The key ideas in this analysis were first, that the school improvement industry could be analyzed as populations or "strategic groups" of organizations, and second, that all of the organizations in a particular population would have a similar structure and pursue a similar business strategy, in large part because all of them were operating in a similar social environment, where each tried to exploit similar resources and was subject to similar economic and competitive forces.

Niches in the School Improvement Industry

In that same analysis (Rowan 2002), I argued that organizations in the school improvement industry existed in three fundamental "niches" defined by the kinds of resources the organizations depended upon for survival. Two kinds of resources served as the basis for classifying these niches. The first were *primary resources*, that is, resources used to establish an enterprise and/or to extend or expand the enterprise at later points. I further defined three primary resource types: capital, membership subscriptions, and endowments. The second dimension of resources defining niches in the school improvement industry were *transactional resources*. These are resources that accrue to organizations as a result of the economic exchange relationships they have with other organizations or constituencies in the education sector. Here, I defined three transactional resources in American education: exchanges with local school systems, exchanges with education employees, and exchanges with granting agencies.

Some Fundamental Premises about Niches in the School Improvement Industry

Table 5.1 shows how the two resource dimensions just described define nine potential niches in the school improvement industry. In the table, the rows list types of primary resources, the columns list types of transaction-based resources, and the cells define joint occurrences of resources, that is, the various niches in the school improvement industry. In this chapter, I focus only

TABLE 5.1
Fundamental Niches in the School Improvement Industry

	Transactions with School Systems	Transactions with Education Employees	Transactions with Granting Agencies
Capital-Based	1	2	3
Membership-Based	4	5	6
Endowment-Based	7	8	9

on the three shaded cells in the table, which I define as the "primary" niches in the school improvement industry. The rest of the chapter discusses key organizational forms located in each of these cells and the role these organizations play in promoting school improvement in the United States. The central argument of the chapter is that organizations in each of these cells (or niches) face unique competitive and selective pressures and that it is these pressures and the ways organizations respond to them that accounts for much of what we observe in the area of educational change in the United States.

Capitalized Firms and Local Schools (Cell 1)

Let us begin by looking at the competitive dynamics and selective forces operating inside cell 1 of table 5.1. We have already seen that this niche includes all kinds of for-profit firms engaged in economic transactions with local school systems. This is not surprising. Capital-based organizations are in the business of generating profits and increasing shareholders' returns, and school systems are very desirable customers for these firms because, for most of the twentieth century, school-system budgets have been not only reasonably stable but also growing. As a result, capital-based firms have been *especially* interested in exploiting resources emerging from transactions with local schools.

Within this niche, the most significant actors in terms of instructional improvement are textbook publishers.[11] A central feature of textbook publishing in the United States, however, is that profits are achieved mainly through economies of scale. As a result, firms in the textbook industry compete relentlessly to gain market share, and the industry as a whole tends to move toward concentration. Today, for example, there are only six major publishing firms in the K–12 textbook market, each firm having been created through the merger of several formerly independent firms. Moreover, these major firms make a good deal of their profits from a limited number of products—mostly textbook *series* designed for use in the major academic subjects taught in schools.

While small in number, the dominant textbook firms are large in scale, economically dominant in their markets, and politically powerful.[12]

As a direct result of economic concentration in the textbook market, local schools and school systems lack power and control in the market place. This results, in part, from patterns of educational governance in the United States, which allow the concentrated power of textbook suppliers to be exercised against the dispersed demand of local school systems. In this situation, any single school system is far more dependent on textbook suppliers than are textbook suppliers dependent on a given school system.[13] As a result, textbook publishers do not need to be particularly sensitive to the unique demands of local school systems. In theory, of course, the power of textbook companies could be counteracted through concentrating consumer demand. In fact, statewide textbook adoption laws were designed early in the twentieth century at least in part to achieve this aim, and thirty-two states now adopt textbooks on a state-wide basis. But most analysts agree that statewide adoption laws do little to defuse the power of textbook publishers.[14]

Still, textbook publishers are not completely insulated from local demand, largely because they are in fierce competition with other dominant publishers for market share. To fend off competitors and maintain economies of scale, however, the few firms producing textbook series adopt a national marketing strategy in which unique, local demands are accommodated simply by expanding existing texts. In this way, American textbooks end up being a "mile wide and an inch deep." K–12 textbooks in the United States are larger in size than textbooks from most other nations, containing both more topics and more diverse topical coverage.[15] But this is a logical outcome of market dynamics and should not be seen solely as the conscious preference of school systems. Moreover, because of their dominant market position, major textbook producers avoid radical changes in their products, not so much in response to the inherent conservatism of local school systems—although that is a factor publishers keep in mind—but more importantly because radical, new products present publishers and their shareholders with higher levels of risk. As a result, textbook publishers are a classic case of what organizational ecologists call "K-strategists"—organizations that launch new products slowly and only after careful investigation and copious investment of resources.[16]

This is not to say that innovating organizations are completely driven out of the niche defined by cell 1 of table 5.1. In fact, the large and powerful publishing firms just described exist alongside a number of other, much smaller and more innovative publishers of instructional materials, firms that actually outnumber the dominant firms. But these smaller publishers of educational materials survive in the niche defined by cell 1 as a result of what organizational ecologists call "resource partitioning." Since dominant firms make profits largely from economies of scale, they avoid many of the smaller and more specialized markets in education. Their avoidance of these markets, however,

provides business opportunities for other firms and is one source of real innovation in the instructional core of schools. However, in American education,
publishing firms exploiting marginal markets in education have not been a
source of *lasting* innovation for two reasons. First, marginal firms that manage to develop a profitable market niche are often purchased by dominant
firms and thus adopt the K-strategy preferred by these firms. Moreover, firms
operating in marginal markets often fail (precisely because their markets are
marginal). As a result, their innovations cannot have much lasting impact on
schooling.

Membership-Based Organizations and Private Transactions

I move now to a description of a second important niche in the school
improvement industry, one in which membership organizations seek to capitalize on resources derived from transactions with employees in the field.
Many organizations in American education use membership fees as their primary resource base. For example, the American Society of Association Executives (ASAE) lists 567 such organizations in the field of education alone, an
estimate that probably underrepresents the actual number of such organizations operating in the field.

As an organizational form, dues- or subscription-based organizations are
among the very oldest of organizational forms in American education.[17] Originally, membership-based organizations in education pooled practitioners in
the field, offering them a forum for political advocacy and professional development. Usually, these purposes were accomplished through the convening of
annual (or more frequent) meetings—which provided opportunities for both
political action and continuing education—and additionally through publication of a journal or newsletter. Today, these basic attributes continue to define
the main form of membership-based organizations, demonstrating the enormous stability and legitimacy of this form, not only in American education
but also in society at large.

What is interesting about membership-based organizations in American
education is their central role as information providers in the school improvement industry. For example, with few exceptions, the market for education
periodicals in the United States is dominated by the publications of these
organizations—*not* by publications produced by capital- or endowment-based
organizations. This is easily explained, however. In the competition among
organizational forms to secure a private subscription base for periodicals,
membership organizations have an inherent competitive edge over all other
organizational forms—ready access to built-in membership lists and the ability to fold the costs of publication into membership fees.

Another major function of membership organizations is the provision of
training. Here, too, membership-based organizations have an advantage in a

particular market—the private market for school improvement training, that is, school improvement-related training paid for through the private budgets of education employees. In this market, however, membership organizations face stiff competition, mainly from universities. As a result, a kind of resource partitioning has emerged. Teachers and administrators interested in markedly improving their salaries often purchase degrees or credit-hour instruction from universities, taking advantage of the financial incentives provided in most of the salary schedules of local school systems. But this leaves membership organizations free to provide yet a third form of information and training—the provision of short-term, low-cost training programs that can earn continuing certification or meet local contractual obligations for continuing education.

The information and training provided by membership-based organizations has some peculiar features that are important to school improvement patterns in the United States. Both the periodicals and the training programs these organizations offer tends to cater to the extreme specialization of their membership bases. In American education, the specialization of membership-based organizations is common and results from several sources. One is the progressive differentiation of occupational specialties within education, and the consequent founding of new, and ever more specialized, membership organizations. A second is the lack of large, integrating organizations capable of projecting a unified voice in the field of education. The result is a kind of hyper-pluralism in the field of education in the United States, with hundreds of membership organizations catering to the interests and needs of specialized groups.

All of this, of course, has very important implications for U.S. education. The hyper-pluralism of membership-based organizations contributes to the sheer cacophony of the education reform environment, as hundreds of narrow problems are surfaced by specialized interests and placed on the reform agenda through the publications of periodicals and the provision of brief training sessions at annual meetings. More important, the very niche in which membership-based organizations exist contributes to the faddishness of reform efforts. Most membership-based organizations lack an ample source of working capital. As a result, they have little to invest in sustained program development and thus thrive by catering to the temporally emergent needs of their members. In this sense, most membership-based organizations resemble r-strategists. They move quickly—in their publications and in their training programs—to capitalize on fresh ideas and new trends, in large part because their position in the competitive periodicals and training markets depends on such actions. This is not to say that membership-based organizations are unimportant to educational reform. Indeed, their actions sometimes gain very high visibility (as with the National Council of Teachers of Mathematic's [NCTM's] efforts to push reforms in mathematics education). But, as a whole, the niche that membership-based organizations try to exploit in American education seems to "select against" organizations pursuing a stable, long-term strategy of school improvement and instead to favor organizations that cater to temporal variations in the specialized interests and needs of diverse groups of employees.[18]

Endowment-Based Organizations and the Grants-Based Economy of School Improvement

The final niche discussed in this chapter is cell 9 of table 5.1, where endowment-based organizations seek to exploit transactions with granting agencies. The most visible organizations in this niche include universities engaged in sponsored research and technical assistance projects, the numerous "think tanks" providing educational analysis and advocacy, hundreds of nonprofit research and development organizations, and a host of quasigovernmental technical assistance agencies.

The number of endowment-based organizations operating in American education is easily several hundred—not including universities. More than two hundred nonprofit establishments (excluding universities) provide about $300 million in educational research and development in education,[19] and hundreds of nonprofit and quasigovernmental organizations provide information, advocacy, and technical assistance in the K–12 sector. Added to this are universities, which provide over $500 million in educational research, as well as the many technical assistance and information clearinghouses supported through federal funding, and the hundreds of nonprofit organizations providing well-packaged, instructional improvement programs.[20]

Despite the success of endowment-based organizations in the school improvement industry, the high dependence of such organizations on a grants-based economy leads most to be marked by a peculiar organizational form that is "project-based." In this respect, endowment-based organizations are classic r-strategists—that is, organizations that move quickly into newly opening markets by making only minimal investment in new start-ups. But, while these organizations can move quickly into opening markets, they also suffer very high failure rates. This is because within endowment-based organizations, grant-funded projects come and go with great frequency. Thus, while many endowment-based organizations are themselves quite stable, the products they market in the school improvement arena turn over at a rapid pace.

All of this occurs because grants-based funding in American education has two important features. First, it is marked by much temporal variation in which grants-making agencies frequently change priorities, abandoning some areas of interest to move into other areas. In this environment, organizational ecologists predict that r-strategists (organizations that can move quickly to exploit emerging opportunities) have a competitive advantage over K-strategists (that are better adapted to more stable and fine-grained environments). The long-run consequence of this selection process, however, is that research, technical assistance, and program development "projects" in the United States come and go in great numbers as a result of heavy reliance on transactions with granting agencies.

There is a second sense in which the grants-based environment affects school improvement. While the overall amount of grant funding available to endowment-based organizations has been growing over time, funding has been increasingly spread over an ever-larger number of priorities, keeping the amount of resources devoted to any single priority small in comparison to the total amount of grants funding available. As a result, endowment-based projects operating in the grants-based environment face a kind of double jeopardy. Not only do they run the risk of having their project funding terminated, but as a result of multiple funding priorities among granting agencies, the amount of funding available to the typical project is often small. In this environment, projects often are forced to pursue a local marketing strategy and to forego investment in activities that stimulate long-term development in favor of achieving more visible, short-term successes.

We have thus arrived at a second explanation for the "faddishness" of educational change in American education. The grants-based economy promotes the development of large populations of r-strategists. Many small, short-term, local, and resource poor projects are founded, and most fail (i.e., go out of existence). But this is a natural outcome of the grants-based environment, for funding for national, long-term projects, with heavy development costs, is difficult to come by, promoting a preponderance of project-based organizations whose very survival is enhanced by use of an r-strategy.

THE ECOLOGY OF SCHOOL IMPROVEMENT AND EDUCATIONAL CHANGE

Having discussed the organizational ecology of the school improvement industry, we are now in a position to return to the central problem of this chapter—developing an explanation for the peculiar pattern of educational change in the U.S. school system. Earlier I argued that educational change in the United States is marked by two seemingly contradictory tendencies—a tremendous amount of innovation (even faddishness)—coupled with a great stability in core instructional processes. What explains this pattern of change?

I have argued that the organizational ecology of the school improvement industry—the processes of natural selection occurring within various niches in the K–12 education sector—seems to be a central dynamic in explaining patterns of change in American education. Faddishness results from the extreme specialization of membership associations in American education, and the resulting issue-driven, hyperpluralism and temporal "faddishness" of their activities. Faddishness also results from selection processes operating within the grants-based economy that produces a high rate of innovation but also a high rate of failure in research and development, technical assistance, and the production and dissemination of innovative instructional programs.

Still, the school improvement industry in the United States does produce a lot of truly innovative and potentially effective technical assistance and instructional innovation, a lot of which is adopted by local school systems. But all of this innovation confronts (and ends up being inconsistent with) the stable features of instruction in these school systems—especially the textbooks and tests manufactured by the K–12 publishing industry in the United States. In fact, the importance of standardized texts and tests in American schools cannot be overemphasized. They are a basic feature of the core technology of schooling and figure in upwards of 80 percent of all instructional activities. They influence both the content of lessons in classrooms and the methods teachers use to teach lessons. Thus, the stability of textbooks is an important part of our story.

All of this suggests that our usual theories of educational change—both the ones that proclaim the power of local school system autonomy and the ones that call for unified, state-directed reform—are lacking in major respects. As a result, a new image of educational change in the United States might be needed, one that sees educational change as arising out of what Chester Finn (1997, 248) calls "a decentralized universe of diverse models, multiple providers, and consumer choices." But in this revamped imagery, the consumers making choices are not simply parents choosing among public and private schools but also a wide variety of schools choosing among many different school improvement products; and the providers in this system are not simply public and private schools but also the very large number of for-profit organizations, membership-based organizations, and endowment-based organizations providing information, materials, technical assistance, and new programs to these schools.

Attention to the ways in which market and government forces can be used to encourage organizations operating in the school improvement industry to produce goods and services that promote innovative and lasting change in instruction therefore seems essential to understanding school improvement. New policies directed at the school improvement industry—for example, policies directed at how investments are made in the organizations operating within the industry, how market failure in the provision of goods and services can be counteracted, or how political provision of services can be made more effective—might produce patterns of educational change that differ from the ones just described.

However, there is a problem in developing new policies in this area. We simply do not know enough about the school improvement *industry* at this point in time to formulate wise policy about it. Therefore, I would argue that more—and different—kinds of research on educational change and improvement are needed. Such research, I argue, could proceed in two directions. The first would be intensive case studies of the school improvement industry in the United States that would shed more light on the nature and functioning of the school improvement industry and/or how developments within this industry shape patterns of educational change. Another important direction would be cross-national studies. If societies other than the United States have differently configured textbook industries, different grants-based economies, and different patterns in the formation of membership organizations, then patterns of educational change in these countries should differ from those observed in the United States. Research comparing the school improvement industries in different nations is badly needed if we are to confirm the hypotheses I have advanced in this chapter and thereby develop a more complete understanding of the dynamics of educational change.

NOTES

This is a revised version of a paper prepared for a Spencer Foundation funded conference on the Social Geographies of Educational Change: Contexts, Networks, and Generalizability, University of Barcelona, Barcelona, Spain.

1. The work of Larry Cuban and David Tyack is especially helpful in illustrating these points. For a discussion of change efforts in American education over the past century, for example, see Tyack and Cuban (1995). For evidence on the stability of instructional practices in American schools, see Cuban (1993).

2. The classic argument on the inherent conservatism of school cultures is Sarason (1996). Schein (1985) describes the conservative influence of organizational culture on change efforts in organizations more generally. Arguments about organizational and leadership factors involved in promoting organizational change in education can be found in Fullan (1991) and Murphy and Louis (1994). The 1990s also saw the emergence of a large literature on school restructuring as a source of educational change. Good discussions here are Elmore and associates (1990) and Murphy (1991).

3. An important early statement about how patterns of educational governance in the United States affect school change can be found in Meyer and Rowan (1978) and in Meyer and Scott (1983, especially part 3). A more recent argument, paying special attention to the problem of *instructional* change can be found in Cohen and Spillane (1992). The classic argument in favor of systemic reform is Smith and O'Day (1991).

4. Some recent case studies of positive change in instruction and student achievement resulting from leadership and restructuring are discussed in Meier (1995) and Elmore and Burley (n.d.). For a broader set of cases, however, see the program of research on school restructuring conducted by researchers at the University of Wisconsin during the 1990s. These researchers studied a national sample of schools nom-

inated for their exemplary efforts at school restructuring. The overall findings of this research are discussed in Newmann and Wehlage (1995), but especially noteworthy is the finding reported by Berends and King (1995). Only 25 percent of the schools in this nationally nominated sample had broken away from traditional patterns of instruction and school organization as a result of their exemplary efforts at school restructuring.

5. Temporal trends in student achievement in the United States have been analyzed by David Grissmer and colleagues (see Grissmer et al. 1994; Grissmer and Flanagan 1998; and Grissmer et al. 2000). In general, Grissmer's work shows that achievement in the United States is increasing, in large part because of changes in family composition, but that increases in achievement above and beyond what would be predicted by changes in family composition are also evident. Grissmer's work shows that additional improvement due to moves toward "systemic" reforms in some states occurs, but only in *some* states pursuing this approach. In fact, state-level variables other than systemic reform seem be more important in explaining the patterns of educational improvement observed by Grissmer and colleagues.

6. Estimates on the number of membership associations in education were taken from the web site of the American Society of Association Executives (www.asae.org).

7. See the U.S. Department of Education (1999), *Digest of Education Statistics.*

8. See the U.S. Census Bureau (1999), *1997 Economic Census*, Professional, Technical, and Scientific Services Series.

9. The figures cited here are from the U.S. Census Bureau (1999), *1997 Economic Census*, Manufacturing Series and U.S. Census Bureau (1999), *1997 Economic Census*, Professional, Technical, and Scientific Services Series. The estimate that 80 percent of all districts contract for one or more services is from DeSchryver (2000).

10. The most well known statement on organizational ecology can be found in Hannan and Freeman (1989). For a good review of empirical research in this tradition, see Baum (1996). For a critique of organizational ecology as a theoretical perspective, see Young (1988), as well as the rebuttal by Hannan and Freeman (1989). For work on "strategic groups" undertaken from a different perspective, see Porter (1980).

11. For discussion of other for-profit firms operating in the school improvement industry and their role in school improvement, see Rowan (2002).

12. It is impossible to get the most current data on concentration in the textbook industry, as it has not yet been published from the *1997 Economic Census*. However, the *1997 Economic Census* report on the "information" industry (found in the manufacturing series) does show that there were just thirty establishments shipping $1.85 billion of textbooks to schools in 1997, with about half the revenue coming from shipments to elementary schools and the other half coming from shipments to secondary schools. While these data suggest that a few firms are doing a very large business in this industry, they do not provide unambiguous evidence of concentration. For that, information provided by Sewall and Cannon (1991) is more useful. These authors used a variety of sources to estimate that the top three textbook publishers in the United States (MacMillan, Harcourt Brace Janovich, and Simon and Schuster) controlled about 45

percent of the textbook market in the 1990s, a fairly high degree of concentration. We should be careful, however, not to overstate the case here. Most analysts agree that there is still competition among firms in the textbook industry, although the amount of such competition probably varies by market niche. For example, Sewall and Cannon (1991) observe that about 45 percent of all sales in the elementary school market are basal reading series, and another 25 percent are mathematics series. Moreover, they observe that for the past two decades, the number of firms competing in this market has been dwindling. There is probably more competition in the markets for textbooks in more specialized niches, allowing textbook publishers who do not compete in the mass market for textbook series to profit by operating in more marginal markets. It is worth noting also that high levels of concentration in the U.S. textbook industry are not new. Sewall and Cannon (1991) note that in 1890, a trust composed of five large firms controlled roughly 75 to 80 percent of the textbook market. However, widespread exposure of the corrupt business practices of these firms, plus market pressure from the roughly 170 other firms in the industry at the time, apparently turned the tide toward more competition in the textbook market over the next several decades. By the 1960s, however, the industry was moving back toward concentration. A major point, then, is that the textbook industry in the United States apparently naturally evolves toward concentration. Today, a very small number of firms operate in the K–12 textbook industry, and only a few firms dominate the *mass* markets for textbooks in K–12 education.

13. For the logic of this argument, see Thompson's (1967) analysis of power and dependence in interorganizational exchange relations.

14. Brief histories of state-level textbook adoption rules can be found in Sewall and Cannon (1991) and Apple (1991). State adoption laws were passed in some states, at least in part, to combat the textbook trust. However, such laws were widely seen as ineffective—even corrupt—as Apple (1991) discusses. More recent discussions of state adoption laws and procedures can be found in Tyson-Bernstein (1988) and Tulley and Farr (1985).

15. These features of American textbooks have been discussed in Schmidt, McKnight, and Raizen (1997).

16. Although my discussion to this point has dealt exclusively with textbook publishing, it should be noted that the major textbook publishers in American education also have, for the most part, acquired the major achievement test publishers. Thus, all of the market dynamics discussed with respect to texts apply equally as well in an analysis of test publishing.

17. For a historical overview of these organizations, see Mattingly (1975) and Haber (1991).

18. An exception to this rule is the National Education Association, which appears to have pursued a stable reform agenda since the 1960s. However, the NEA is unique among membership associations in education in that it has gained the ability to deduct membership dues directly from members' paychecks. This no doubt has contributed to the NEA's substantial financial capital, as Lieberman (1997) observes.

19. The relevant data on profit and nonprofit research organizations in the United States (excluding universities) can be found in U.S. Census Bureau (2000), *1997 Economic Census*, Professional, Scientific, and Technical Services Series, where data on organizations providing educational research and development are listed separately within the data.

20. A list of federally funded assistance centers can be found on the U.S. Department of Education web site under "education resource organization directory." Lists of organizations providing full-blown instructional programs to school systems are a bit more difficult to find. However, for the 1980s, a partial list of such organizations—and the programs they operate—can be found in U.S. Department of Education's publication, *Programs That Work*. The number of programs in this bulletin was always in the hundreds, and these lists included only programs that were receiving funding from the National Diffusion Network (NDN). Because the NDN was terminated as a federal program in the 1990s, I have taken a more recent estimate of the number of program providers operating nationally from a list of programs receiving funding under the Comprehensive School Reform Demonstration (CSRD) Act, as published on a web site maintained by the Southwest Educational Development Laboratory (www.sedl.org). Here too, over 100 programs are listed, but the reader is cautioned that, once again, this is simply a list of programs receiving federal support under CSRD. The interesting point is that both lists suggest that at any point in time, there are probably 150 to 200 federally supported school improvement programs being vended by endowment-based organizations on a national basis.

REFERENCES

Altbach, P. G., G. P. Kelly, H. G. Petrie, and L. Weis, eds. 1991. *Textbooks in American society: Politics, policy, and purpose.* Albany: State University of New York Press.

American Educational Research Association. 1999. Gorrillas in our midst: Emerging themes on how to improve educational research. On capital hill, August/September, http://www.aera.net/gov/archive.

Apple, M. W. 1991. Regulating the text: The socio-historical roots of state control. In *Textbooks in American society: Politics, policy, and purpose*, ed. P. G. Altbach, G. P. Kelly, H. G. Petri, and L. Weis, 7–26. Albany: State University of New York Press.

Baum, J. A. C. 1996. Organizational ecology. In *Handbook of organizational studies*, ed. S. R. Clegg, C. Hardy, and W. R. Nord, 77–114. Newbury Park, CA: Sage.

Berends, M. and M. B. King. 1995. *A description of restructuring in nationally nominated schools: Legacy of the iron cage?* Santa Monica: Rand.

Chubb, J. E. 1997. Lessons in school reform from the Edison Project. In *New schools for a new century: The redesign of urban schools*, ed. D. Ravitch and J. P. Viteritti, 86–122. New Haven: Yale University Press.

Chubb, J. E., and T. M. Moe. 1990. *Politics, markets, and America's schools.* Washington, DC: Brookings Institution.

Church, R. L., and M. W. Sedlack. 1976. *Education in the United States: An interpretive history.* New York: Free Press.

Cohen, D. K. 1982. Policy and organization: The impact of state and federal educational policy on school governance. *Harvard Education Review* 52: 474–99.

Cohen, D. K., and J. P. Spillane. 1992. Policy and practice: The relations between governance and instruction. In *Review of Research in Education,* ed. G. Grant, 18: 1–49. Washington, DC: American Educational Research Association.

Cuban, L. 1993. *How teachers taught: Constancy and change in American classrooms, 1880–1990.* New York: Teachers College Press.

DeSchryver, D. A. 2000. *Creating a revolution from the boardroom to the classroom: New partners in education.* Washington, DC: Center for Education Reform.

Elliot, D. L., and A. Woodward, eds. 1990. *Textbooks and schooling in the United States: Eighty-ninth yearbook of the National Society for the Study of Education, part 1.* Chicago: University of Chicago Press.

Elmore, R. F., and Associates, eds. 1990. *Restructuring schools: The next generation of educational reform.* San Francisco: Jossey-Bass.

Elmore, R. F., and D. Burney, ed. Improving instruction through professional development in New York City's Community District no. 2. *CPRE Policy Bulletin.* Philadelphia: University of Pennsylvania, Consortium for Policy Research in Education.

Finn, C. E., Jr. 1997. The politics of change. In *New schools for a new century: The redesign of urban schools,* ed. D. Ravitch and J. P. Viteritti, 226–50. New Haven: Yale University Press.

Fullan, M. 1991. *The new meaning of educational change.* New York: Teachers College Press.

Grissmer, D. W., A. Flanagan, J. Kawata, and S. Williamson. 2000. *Improving student achievement: What state NAEP scores tell us.* Santa Monica: Rand.

Grissmer, D. W., S. N. Kirby, S. Williamson, and M. Berends. 1994. *Student achievement and the changing American family.* Santa Monica: Rand.

Haber, S. 1991. *The quest for authority and honor in the American professions, 1750–1900.* Chicago: University of Chicago Press.

Hannan, M. T., and Freeman, J. H. 1989a. *Organizational ecology.* Cambridge, MA: Harvard University Press.

———. 1989b. Setting the record straight on organizational ecology: A rebuttal to Young. *American Journal of Sociology* 95 (2): 425–37.

Hill, P. C. 1997. Contracting in education. In *New schools for a new century: The redesign of urban schools,* ed. D. Ravitch and J. P. Viteritti, 61–85. New Haven: Yale University Press.

Jepperson, R. L., and J. W. Meyer. 1991. The public order and the construction of formal organizations. In *The new institutionalism in organizational analysis,* ed. P. J. DiMaggio and W. W. Powell, 204–31. Chicago: University of Chicago Press.

Kerchner, C. T., and J. E. Koppich. 1997. *United mind workers: Unions and teaching in the knowledge society.* San Francisco: Jossey-Bass.

Lieberman, M. 1997. *The teacher unions: How the NEA and AFT sabotage reform and hold students, teachers, and taxpayers hostage to bureaucracy.* New York: Free Press.

Lips, C. November, 2000. "Eduprenuers": A survey of for-profit education. *Policy Analysis* no. 386. Washington DC: Cato Institute.

Mattingly, P. H. 1975. *The classless profession: American schoolmen in the nineteenth century.* New York: New York University Press.

Meier, D. 1995. *The power of their ideas: Lessons for America from a small school in Harlem.* Boston: Beacon.

Meyer, J. W., and B. Rowan. 1978. The structure of educational organizations. In *Organizations and environments,* ed. M. W. Meyer et al., 78–108. San Francisco: Jossey-Bass.

Meyer, J. W., and W. R. Scott. 1983. *Organizational environments: Ritual and rationality.* Beverly Hills: Sage.

Moe, M. T., K. Baily, and R. Lau. 1999. *The book of knowledge: Investing in the growing education and training industry.* Merrill Lynch, Global Securities Research and Economics Group, Global Fundamental Equity Research Group, Report 1400, April.

Murphy, J. 1991. *Restructuring schools: Capturing and assessing the phenomenon.* New York: Teachers College Press.

Murphy, J., and K. S. Louis, eds. 1994. *Reshaping the principalship: Insights from transformational reform efforts.* Newbury Park, CA: Corwin.

Newmann, F. M., and G. Wehlage. 1995. *Successful school restructuring: Highlights of findings.* Madison: University of Wisconsin, Wisconsin Center for Educational Research.

Porter, M. 1980. *Competitive strategy.* New York: Free Press.

Sarason, S. 1996. *Revisiting the culture of the school and the problem of change.* New York: Teachers College Press.

Schein, E. H. 1985. *Organizational culture and leadership: A dynamic view.* San Francisco: Jossey-Bass.

Schmidt, W. H., C. C. McKnight, and S. A. Raizen. 1997. *A splintered vision: An investigation of U.S. science and mathematics education.* Dordrecht/Boston/London: Kluwer.

Scott, W. R., and J. W. Meyer. 1983. The organization of societal sectors. In *Organizational environments: Ritual and rationality,* ed. J. W. Meyer and W. R. Scott, 129–54. Beverly Hills: Sage.

Sewall, G. T., and P. Cannon. 1991. The new world of textbooks: Industry consolidation and its consequences. In *Textbooks in American society: Politics, policy, and purpose,* ed. P. G. Altbach, G. P. Kelly, H. G. Petrie, and L. Weis, 61–69. Albany: State University of New York Press.

Smith, M. S., and J. O'Day. 1991. Systemic school reform. In *The politics of curriculum and testing,* ed. S. F. Fuhrman and B. Malen, 233–67. London: Falmer.

Thompson, J. T. 1967. *Organizations in action.* New York: McGraw Hill.

Travers, R. M. W. 1983. *How research has changed American schools: A history from 1840 to the present.* Kalamazoo: Mythos.

Tulley, M. A., and R. Farr. 1985. The purpose of state-level textbook adoption: What does the legislation reveal? *Journal of Research and Development in Education* 18(2): 1–6.

Tyack, D., and L. Cuban. 1995. *Tinkering toward utopia: A century of public school reform.* Cambridge, MA: Harvard University Press.

Tyson-Bernstein, H. 1988. *A conspiracy of good intentions: America's textbook fiasco.* Washington: Council for Basic Education.

U. S. Census Bureau. 1999. *1997 economic census.* Washington DC: Government Printing Office.

U. S. Department of Education, National Center for Education Statistics. 1999. *Digest of education statistics.* Washington, DC: Government Printing Office.

Vinovskis, M. A. 1999. *History and educational policymaking.* New Haven, CT: Yale University Press.

Young, R. C. 1988. Is population ecology useful paradigm for the study of organizations? *American Journal of Sociology* 94(1): 1–24.

SIX

The Institutional Environment and Instructional Practice: Changing Patterns of Guidance and Control in Public Education

JAMES SPILLANE
PATRICIA BURCH

THE NOTION OF "loose coupling" has held considerable sway in education research, frequently invoked to account for the rather weak ties between policy and administration, on the one hand, and classroom work, on the other hand. We argue that coupling—a potent construct—has been misused. Treating instruction as a monolithic or unitary practice, scholars too easily and readily conclude that instruction is loosely coupled from policy and administration. We argue that analyses of relations between institutional environments and instruction be predicated on at least two ways of thinking about instruction. First, we argue that instruction is about subject matter. Institutional environments shape instruction in and around particular subjects. Second, even within a given subject area, instruction is not a single dimensional activity. It involves numerous elements including the content, the academic tasks students work on, teaching strategies, ways of representing ideas to students, student grouping practices, and student work assignments. Institutional environments can be tightly coupled with some dimensions of instructional practice, whereas loosely coupled with others.

In the late 1970s and 1980s, institutional analyses of organizations tended to be built around Parson's (1960) ideas about the inevitability of loose coupling between the technical and institutional levels of management in organizations. Parson's idea was that actions taken to align organizations with societal norms and values frequently came into conflict with technical activities designed to foster organizational goal attainment, leading to what he saw as a "qualitative break" across the technical and institutional levels of management in organizations. Schools in the United States were pointed to as a prime example of loose coupling (Meyer and Rowan 1978; Weick 1976). Operating in a societal sector characterized by fragmented, multi-layered, and pluralistic governance, schools in the United States were seen as striving to conform to many different, and potentially inconsistent, rules and regulations in order to gain societal support. But faithful implementation of these diverse rules was thought to be impossible, since it would produce conflict and uncertainty in classrooms or would be impossible to implement given the great variability of local instructional activities.

However, the argument that institutionalized rules and regulations could *never* be tightly coupled to the technical core of organizations struck many organization theorists as overdrawn (see, for example, Perrow 1986; DiMaggio and Powell 1991), and as a result, many analysts began to question the postulate that schools are necessarily loosely coupled (see, for example, Meyer 1983; Rowan and Miskel 1999; Rowan 2002). A decade of educational reforms designed to bring systemic reform to educational governance in the United States, the development of standards-based curricula and intensified instructional guidance for local schools, and the ever increasing use of testing and systems designed to hold teachers and administrators directly accountable for student learning all raise doubts about the assumption that schools in the United States are loosely coupled systems.

THE PROBLEM

This chapter revisits arguments about loose coupling in American schools from the perspective of implementation research conducted in educational organizations over the past decade. The purpose is not to rehash previous discussions of loose and tight coupling in schools but to contribute to the further development of institutional theory. To achieve this purpose, we attempt to spell some of the various mechanisms that bring about couplings in institutional sectors. Following Weick (1976), we analyze this coupling process along three fronts.

First, we focus on processes that couple institutionalized rules to classroom instruction. But rather than treating "instruction" as an undifferentiated construct, we see it as situated in particular curricular domains (e.g., mathematics, reading/language arts). Thus, when we talk about instruction in this chapter, we are talking about instruction in a particular curricular area, not instruction generally.

Second, we treat instruction as a multidimensional activity. Instruction involves the teaching of specific academic content, using particular materials and teaching strategies, possibly either under different instructional grouping conditions or through the deployment of different discourse activities.

Third, we avoid making vague statements about elements being coupled. We do not, for example, talk broadly about coupling between policies and practices or about couplings of administration and the technical core. These statements do not tell us much about who or what is being coupled in a given institutional sector. Instead, we talk about specific agents and agencies—including state agencies, professional associations, role incumbents, and so on.

(RE)CONCEPTUALIZING THE TECHNICAL CORE

In our view, a more nuanced analysis of the technical core in schools involves moving away from views of "instruction" as a monolithic or unitary practice. Drawing selectively on studies of teaching and leadership in elementary and high schools, for example, we will identify two salient dimensions of teaching and learning in schools—the subject matter being taught and the practices being used. When the specific curricular area being taught is identified, and when particular dimensions of instruction in these subject areas are taken into account, it will become obvious that complex patterns of both loose *and* tight coupling exist within the American educational system.

Coupling and Subject Matter

As we demonstrate, educational activities in American society are organized quite differently—both in the broader social environment and in local school settings—across different curricular domains. In fact, following Rowan (this volume), we assert that within the broad K–12 education sector, there are distinctive institutional environments built up around different academic disciplines or subject areas.

Consider how the institutional environments of schools differ by subject area. To begin with, government agencies regulate the different school subjects differently. In particular, mathematics and language arts have received far more attention from state policy makers than other subjects. Indeed, most states developed curricular standards and student assessments for mathematics and language arts well before they did so for science and social studies. Similarly, state and local accountability systems have tended to focus more frequently on mathematics and language arts, often to the exclusion of science and social studies. But there are other ways in which local and state education agencies treat school subjects differently as well. For example, the federal government's attempts to influence instruction have differed by subject area, with some federal programs (e.g., Title 1, Eisenhower Mathematics and Science Program, No Child Left Behind) requiring local responses in particular subject areas and ignoring others.

Differences across subject areas are also reflected in the organization and activities of nongovernmental agencies operating in education, including textbook and test publishers, professional associations, and postsecondary institutions that prepare teachers and school administrators. Thus, standardized achievement tests are available and widely used for school subjects such as reading and mathematics, but much less available for other school subjects. Textbook markets are more likely to be concentrated for the sale of textbook series in the core subjects of reading/language arts and mathematics, and less concentrated for more peripheral subjects such as foreign languages, music, or art. Each subject also has a unique disciplinary or professional society. Some of these associations are well organized at the national and/or state level with teachers and other education professionals. A growing body of work shows that such associations can influence teachers' work but that such influence can vary across subject areas (Talbert and McLaughlin 1994; Spillane and Thompson 1997). For example, a study of teachers in nine diverse Michigan school districts conducted by Spillane (2004) found that almost 50 percent of the teachers reported being either fairly or very familiar with National Council of Teachers of Mathematics (NCTM) Curriculum and Evaluation Standards, but that only 16 percent of teachers were fairly or very familiar with Science for All Americans, produced by the American Association for the Advancement of Science (AAAS).

Subject matter differences are also evident in the postsecondary institutions where teachers and other education professionals receive preservice and in-service training. Many studies, for example, have documented the existence of distinctive disciplinary cultures in higher education (Clark 1987; Becher 1987). Each subject area in American education, for example, seems to be built around its own unique set of epistemological assumptions and practices, and each is constituted by very different patterns of large, macrosocial organization. As we shall see, such differences have real importance in the "technical core" of schools, in large part because the epistemological assumptions and practices of the various subject areas and the various artifacts (such as textbooks, tests, curricular guides, etc.) organize and lend meaning to instruction inside classrooms.

A number of studies conducted over the past decade have shown how subject matter serves as an important context for teachers' practice. In high schools, for example, it has been found that cognitive and normative assumptions embedded in disciplinary cultures are reflected in departmental subcultures and exercise a pervasive influence on teachers' practice (Ball 1981; Little 1993; Siskin 1994). Subject matter complexes, for example, influence how teachers enact their roles, with high school teachers differing in their conceptions of their subjects on dimensions that include the degree of definition or agreement about subject content, scope or homogeneity of the subject, degree of sequencing of the material, whether the subject is static or dynamic, and the degree to which a subject is viewed as core or basic (Rowan 2002; Stodolsky and Grossman 1995).

What is important about this literature is that differences in teachers' conceptions of subject matter influence the degree of curricular control, standardization of curriculum, and agreement around instructional practice and coverage in schools. As one might expect, given the importance of definition and sequence in the field, mathematics teachers in high schools have been found to report significantly less control and autonomy over content than social studies and English teachers (Grossman and Stodolsky 1994). Thus, it appears that the greater the sequencing of a subject's content, the tighter the coupling among classrooms and across classroom and administrative components in schools. Other work points to the importance of subject matter in understanding relations between instruction and the institutional environment. For example, in a study of high school departments in the United Kingdom, Ball (1981) found that teachers' responses to a multiability classroom initiative varied by subject departments; the English department embraced the initiative, while foreign language teachers argued against the reform.

While most elementary teachers are not subject matter specialists and do not work in departmentalized contexts, subject matter is nevertheless also an important context of elementary teachers' work (Stodolsky 1988, 1989). A study of fifth-grade classrooms, for example, found that topics, sequence of instruction, and intellectual goals were more uniform across classrooms in mathematics than social studies (Stodolsky 1988). Some recent implementation research also suggests that elementary teachers' response to the policy environment varies depending on the subject; teachers' conceptions of themselves as teachers and as learners about teaching differ from language arts to mathematics, influencing how they respond to policy (Spillane 2000; Drake, Spillane, and Hufferd-Ackles 2001).

Administrators' work practices also vary across subjects, as a recent study of distributed leadership in fifteen Chicago elementary schools demonstrates. To begin with, school administrators in this study (especially principals) tended to manage instruction differently depending on the subject. At the time of the study, the Chicago Public Schools, like other urban districts in the United States, had created high-stakes accountability systems that targeted language arts and mathematics in particular. As one might predict based on institutional theory (Meyer 1983), these shifts in the policy environment contributed to shifts in the internal administration of schools.

School administrators took district policies in these areas seriously, and improving classroom instruction in the two core subjects of language arts and mathematics was central to their work. In these schools, then, the so-called technical core did not appear to be decoupled or even loosely coupled from administration and the policy environment. For example, over 80 percent of the teachers in the study identified the school principal as an influence on their instruction (Spillane, Hallett, and Diamond 2003). Furthermore, principals actively participated in meetings about instruction. Moreover, district policies, including policies about district curricular standards and student test data, were prominently featured in both school leaders' and teachers' day-to-day work on improving instruction.

However, the coupling of administration and teaching varied by subject area in the fifteen elementary schools. Most striking, and partly reflecting the policy environment, was that in most schools science teaching remained mostly decoupled from administration and the policy environment, while language arts and mathematics were more tightly coupled. An urban elementary teacher captured the situation when she remarked, "So I go to my grade chairperson and she'll give me a list of the ten objectives in reading and math that I must teach. Science and social studies are more flexible because the students are not tested on the IOWA's [Iowa Test of Basic Skills] in science and social studies so that's more . . . on the teacher's personal decision." A school administrator noted, "You know science isn't one of your guides for whether a child is promoted or graduates. So reading and math are what are stressed because those are what everybody looks at . . . that's what the teachers look at too."

Differences between subjects, however, were not simply a matter of tight or loose coupling—the mechanisms through which instruction was coupled with school administration, district policy, and other aspects of the institutional environment differ by subject. While language arts and mathematics instruction were more tightly coupled with school and district administration than earlier work would suggest, the coupling mechanisms were different. These differences were reflected in the school routines designed to connect administration and instruction, the involvement of school administrators in these routines, and the formally designated positions, among other things (Hayton and Spillane, under review; Spillane, Coldren, and Sherer, under review). In all schools, there were numerous routines and structures designed to connect administration and the technical core, including leadership team meetings, grade level meetings, curricular committee meetings, and so on. Language arts consumed a majority of these routines, and, moreover, these routines happened much more frequently in language arts than compared to mathematics. School principals and assistant principals played more prominent roles in these routines and structures related to language arts as compared to mathematics. Further, six of the eight schools had language arts coordinators who had reduced teaching loads or in some cases no classroom teaching responsibilities. Lead teachers, often with official designations as "mathematics teacher leader" and sometimes with some release time from teaching, typically took the helm in organizational routines related to mathematics instruction. In most schools, the typical involvement of the school principal with mathematics instruction involved recruiting and supporting the work of the school's external partners, programs, and lead teachers.

At Adams School—a K–8 school on Chicago's Southside, for example, organizational routines designed to connect the technical core to administration and the broader institutional environment happened more than twice as often as similar routines for mathematics (Spillane and Sherer 2004). Three or four formally designated leaders (e.g., principal, assistant principal, language arts coordinator, special needs coordinator) were always in attendance playing an active role in leading the discussion. In contrast, school administrators were not always in attendance, when they were it was typically only one, and they never led the discussion or played an active role in it. Taken together, these patterns suggest that the ways in which administration and the technical core are coupled differs by curricular domain.

These differences were reflected in school leaders' beliefs about the work of leadership. School leaders' schemata for leadership work differed depending on the subject (Burch and Spillane 2003). While school leaders identified reading and mathematics as priorities—core subjects—their beliefs about leading change in these subjects were different. For example, 80 percent of school leaders in the study saw expertise for reforming literacy as existing internally within the school and as essentially "home grown." In contrast, these same leaders saw expertise for reforming mathematics instruction as beyond the schoolhouse, associated with external programs. Further, school leaders emphasized the integration of literacy instruction across the curriculum, while in mathematics they emphasized sequencing content across grades. These findings suggest that while language arts and mathematics instruction may be more tightly coupled with the institutional environment than earlier work would suggest, the mechanisms by which they are coupled differ.

The studies discussed earlier illuminate how the institutional environment lends organization and meaning to the technical core of schooling differently depending on the subject. Taken together, these studies suggest that the subject is a key variable in understanding the extent to which instruction is loosely or tightly coupled with the wider institutional environment. The activity formats teachers use, their conceptions of knowledge and instruction, the extent to which teachers cooperate with one another, and the ways leaders operate to manage instruction all depend on the subject area. Academic subjects organize instruction, shaping how the technical core operates and connects with the institutional environment even in elementary schools. Not only do norms of subject matter pervade schools, but they also work in and through policy making and governance at other levels. Patterns of loose and tight coupling look different for different subjects. Instruction is not uniformly decoupled or loosely coupled from the institutional environment. These findings suggest the need for greater sensitivity to issues of subject matter in studying relations between instruction and policy and administration.

Instruction as a Multidimensional Practice

Another way to sharpen discussions about couplings between the institutional environment and the technical core is to treat instruction as a multidimensional practice. This is consistent with trends in government policy making over several decades, where state and local policy making have attempted to regulate some dimensions of instruction more than others. For example, in the seventies and eighties, many states specified basic competencies that students should master in particular subjects. Hence, the focus here was chiefly on academic content. Indeed, state policy has focused mostly, though not exclusively, on what content should be taught, in what sequence, to what level of mastery, and (in some states) on the classroom materials associated with this work. Even the standards movement is premised on the notion that state government should specify content standards and acceptable levels of mastery, while individual schools should determine the best teaching strategies for achieving these standards.

It is not only the states that treat dimensions of instruction differently. For example, textbook publishers focus on content coverage and sequencing and increasingly provide guidance about teaching strategies, suggesting activities that teachers might use to introduce particular content. Test publishers, by contrast, focus mostly on student mastery of particular content. Differences are also evident in the postsecondary sector, especially when it comes to teacher education. In many teacher education programs, prospective teachers learn the intellectual content they will teach in disciplinary departments—chemistry, English, history, and so on. However, these same teachers learn about teaching strategies, curricular materials, and student grouping practices in general education schools. In the preservice preparation of teachers, universities treat different dimensions of the technical core differently.

These circumstances in the institutional environment suggest that treating the technical core as a unitary practice is problematic. The empirical evidence concurs. Some implementation research suggests that the policy environment connects unevenly with instructional practice; some dimensions of instructional practice are more tightly coupled with the policy environment than others (Cohen and Ball 1990). To understand this relevancy of dimensions of instruction to the problem of coupling, consider a study of a suburban school district's efforts to align instructional policies in support of more intellectually rigorous learning goals for language arts (see Spillane and Jennings 1997). The Parkwood School District (pseudonym) developed curriculum guidelines outlining ambitious learning goals for each grade level, describing materials and strategies that teachers could use to achieve these goals. The curriculum guides encouraged the use of "real" literature, the integration of reading and writing, attention to students' stages of literacy development, and detailed descriptions of teaching strategies. District policy makers aligned curriculum materials, student assessments, and staff development for teachers with these guides.

Studying the implementation of these policies in nine classrooms in three different schools, researchers found that the district's messages made their way into classroom practice. For example, consistent with the district policy, all nine teachers used literature exclusively to teach reading, used a variety of literary genres, emphasized students' ability to comprehend text, and integrated reading and writing instruction. While these teachers did not rely exclusively on district policy for guidance about the language arts, the evidence suggests a relatively tight coupling between instruction and district policy.

However, moving beyond dimensions of instruction such as the materials used, the activities teachers used, and the aspects of literacy focused on, significant differences were evident among classrooms. For example, the discourse norms that teachers established in their classrooms around reading differed. While some teachers asked students for their opinions about the materials they read and simply thanked them for their ideas, other teachers pressed them to justify their ideas with a convincing argument based on evidence from the text.

This evidence suggests that some dimensions of teaching were tightly coupled with the policy environment, while others were loosely coupled. One reason for this was the clarity of the district policies. District policies were quite explicit about the materials teachers were to use. Classroom policies also pressed teachers to have students react critically to text, but here the policies offered only very general goal statements as guidance. In this case, the less elaborated accounts of reformed practice produced less consistency among classrooms.

Because teachers use their prior knowledge and experience to make sense of the ideas pressed by policy, policy to practice connections are mediated by teacher sense making. Thus, understanding policy implementation requires more than the assumption that teachers understand what policy is asking them to do and that they should simply adopt, ignore, or modify policy guidance. Instead, the role of sense making in policy implementation suggests that when policies are less elaborated, teachers' sense making produces qualitatively different understanding among teachers. Thus, the institutional tradition needs to pay more attention to human agency in its efforts to understand relations between policy and the technical core.

Other implementation studies similarly document patterns of tight and loose coupling between policy and instruction and generated ample evidence of policy getting beyond the classroom door (Firestone, Fitz, and Broadfoot 1999; Hill 2001; Spillane and Zeuli 1999). A recent observational study of a national sample of K–12 mathematics and science lessons involving 364 teachers in thirty-one schools suggests some interesting patterns of tight and loose coupling between the technical core and the institutional environment, depending on the dimension of instruction under consideration (Weiss et al. 2003). With respect to content coverage, state and district curriculum standards were especially influential in three out of four of the mathematics and science lessons observed nationally. With respect to teaching strategies, however, these policy documents were much less influential with only 5 percent of the teachers in the study reporting that these documents were influential. Teachers reported having a great deal of autonomy in choosing teaching strategies with 90 percent of teachers identifying their own knowledge, beliefs, experiences, as the most salient influence. Seventy-one percent of the teachers, however, reported relying on textbooks and/or curricular programs to some extent in selecting teaching strategies: only 5 percent cited state and district curriculum standards, and only 7 percent referenced state and district tests and accountability systems (Weiss et al. 2003).

While there appears to be more "loose" coupling of policy and practice around issues of teaching strategies, there appears to be "tighter" coupling around issues of academic content. Further, while the teaching strategies dimension of the technical core can be loosely coupled with one part of the institutional environment (e.g., state and federal agencies) it can be tightly coupled with another part of the institutional environment (e.g., textbook publishers).

Finally, whether a particular dimension of instruction is tightly or loosely coupled with the institutional environment will depend on the subject area, although here the available evidence is less clear, since implementation studies typically focus only on a single subject area or fail to disaggregate data by subject area. The study of distributed leadership in Chicago elementary schools, mentioned earlier, offers some evidence on these matters. Specifically, teachers' conversations in organizational routines (e.g., grade-level meetings, curricular committee meetings) and informal meetings (e.g., lunch conversations) focused on issues such as the textbook and materials, lesson plans, and time shortages in both mathematics and language arts. While discussions about mathematics were typically limited to these issues, discussions about language arts also focused on teaching strategies, student thinking and learning, and even teacher learning. In sum, discussions among school staff in organizational routines and structures covered more dimensions of the technical core when language arts was the topic of conversations rather than mathematics. So there is much here for scholars working in the institutional tradition to investigate.

DISCUSSION

We argue that investigating relations between the technical core and the institutional environments of schooling in ways that are sensitive to both subject matter and dimensions of instruction is an important area for institutional scholars working in the education sector. Of course this work poses conceptual and methodological challenges, but it also suggests some potentially fruitful lines of inquiry.

One challenge involves analyzing instructional practice in actual schools and classrooms while still treating the broader institutional system as the relevant unit of analysis (Rowan and Miskel 1999). The challenge, then, is to develop an understanding of *what* people do, *how* they do it, and *why* they do it, while simultaneously attending to the institutional structures at various levels of the system that enable and constrain that activity. The challenge here is that scholars working in education often confined their work to one level of the system. For example, research on teaching practice often treats teachers' development of their instructional practices as occurring in an institutional vacuum, ignoring or treating lightly the broader school and school system contexts. Studies of student learning also often pay scant attention to the broader institutional context. Many scholars who study the institutional context have tended to ignore, or treat as a black box, leadership and teaching practice instead of focusing on student outcomes and on understanding those institutional structures, roles, functions, and norms that enable and constrain change in these outcomes.

A second challenge involves thinking more systematically about the different dimensions of instruction. We think about instruction as involving academic content, academic tasks, teaching strategies, student grouping arrangements, classroom discourse or interaction norms, and instructional materials. *Content* refers to topic coverage and sequencing and the amount of time spent on particular topics. *Academic tasks* are the "basic treatment unit" in classrooms, defining the intellectual products students are to produce and the approaches they are to take in producing these products (Doyle 1983, 162; 1980). Academic tasks draw students' attention to particular aspects of content as well as to particular ways of thinking about and using that content. In other words, students can encounter the same content (e.g., multiplication of decimals) very differently depending on the academic task on which they work. *Classroom discourse* norms refer to the ways the teacher and students talk with each other and what they discuss. Classroom discourse norms can substantially transform academic tasks as presented by the teacher (Doyle and Carter 1984). *Teaching strategies* refer to the strategies that teachers use to engage students, including the types of questions they ask and the types of representations they use. *Student grouping* concerns how students are grouped for instruction including whole class, individual, and small-group arrangements. *Instructional materials* include among other things textbooks, curricular materials, and manipulatives. These different dimensions of instruction are not mutually exclusive, but by treating instruction as a unitary practice, scholars easily gloss over subtle patterns of tight and loose coupling. The future of implementation research lies not in assertions about loose and tight coupling generally, but about how different dimensions of instruction are loosely or tightly coupled with particular elements of the institutional sector (e.g., state agencies, district offices, school administration) and why this occurs.

Thinking about research in this area leads us to several propositions that might focus future studies, including some theory-testing studies.

Proposition One

The extent to which the technical core is loosely or tightly coupled with *particular* elements of the institutional environment will vary by curricular domain, even in elementary schools. There is empirical evidence to support this proposition for high schools, where subject specific departmental structures and teacher specialization in subject areas are the norm. The evidence to support this proposition for elementary schools is still scarce suggesting that scholars might investigate patterns of tight and loose coupling between the technical core and elements of the institutional environment in elementary schools. By emphasizing particular in this first proposition, we mean to underscore that the institutional environment should not be treated as a monolith, but rather that attention must be given to different agents and agencies in the institutional environment.

Proposition Two

Within curricular domains, different dimensions of the technical core (e.g., content, materials, teaching strategies) can be both tightly and loosely coupled with different elements of the institutional environment. Some dimensions of technical core (e.g., academic content) appear to be more tightly coupled with the state and district policy environment compared with other dimensions (e.g., teaching strategies). Systematic investigations of the extent to which different dimensions of instruction are coupled with different elements of the institutional environment across two or more curricular domains would shed considerable light on relations between the technical core and its institutional environments.

Proposition Three

The *mechanisms* or *means* through which the technical core is coupled with elements of the institutional environment will differ by curricular domain.

Even in cases where the technical core in two subject areas is relatively tightly coupled with the policy environment (e.g., language arts and mathematics), this coupling may be enabled by different in-school mechanisms (e.g., organizational routines, structures, and tools) depending on the subject area. Hence, attention to the day-to-day means in schools through which the technical core is coupled with different elements of the institutional environment merits attention from scholars.

Proposition Four

Shifts in the institutional environment will contribute to changes in the internal working of schools, but these in-school changes will differ depending on the curricular domain. While changes in the federal and state policy environment (e.g., standards, high stakes accountability) have contributed to a tighter coupling between the technical core and the policy environment in both mathematics and language arts, this tighter coupling has been achieved in different ways within schools depending on the subject. School leaders and teachers' cognitive scripts for instruction and how to improve it differ for language arts compared to mathematics. Reflecting these differences, schools apprehend similar policy pressures in different ways depending on the curricular domain. Hence, tighter coupling can be achieved through different means to and to different degrees *in* schools depending on the curricular domain.

CONCLUSION

The specter of loose coupling has had something of a stranglehold on implementation scholarship. Treating instruction as a monolithic or unitary practice, it was relatively easy to conclude that instruction was decoupled or loosely coupled from administration and policy. We showed, however, drawing on recent implementation research that treating teaching as a unitary practice is problematic in that it glosses over patterns of tight and loose coupling between the institutional environment and instruction. Looking carefully *within* instructional practice and acknowledging its multiple dimensions is critical to understanding tight and loose coupling in education.

As we discussed here, institutional environments do in fact shape the technical core in schools. Institutionalized norms linked to distinctive subject area subcultures contribute to distinct patterns of tight and loose coupling across disciplines, even in elementary schools, where subject specialization is unusual. Administration and the technical core tend to be more tightly coupled in some subjects than in others. At the same time, subjects that tend to be tightly coupled also can vary in the extent of that coupling. We posited that patterns of coupling in the education sector can also vary by dimension of instruction.

While policy and administration may be loosely coupled with one dimension of practice (such as the representations teachers use to teach students) it may be tightly coupled with another dimension (such as the topics taught by a teacher). Hence, not only do institutional theorists need to consider types of organizations within an institutional sector (Whittington 1992), but they also need to disaggregate the technical core in particular sectors.

Attention to day-to-day work practices—organizational routines, structures, and tools—used in particular schools is critical if institutional theorists want to understand the mechanisms through which coupling is achieved. Policy makers, administrators, and teachers do not simply conform to institutionalized norms, values, and technical; they are instead active agents in the development of the common meaning systems and symbolic processes that build up within and around particular aspects of the technical core. Particularly important in this process are the routines, structures, positions, and tools that link different levels of the educational system—government agencies, nongovernment agencies, administration, and teaching. We argue that understanding how ideas, practices, tools, policies, and so on move from one level of the system to another and come be constitutive of, and constituted in, work at different levels is critical to understanding patterns of tight and loose coupling.

NOTE

Work on this chapter was supported by the Distributed Leadership Study (www.distributedleadership.com) and funded by grants from the National Science Foundation (REC-9873583) and the Spencer Foundation.

REFERENCES

Ball, S. J. 1981. *Beachside comprehensive*. Cambridge: Cambridge University Press.

Becher, T. 1987. The disciplinary shaping of the profession. In *The Academic Profession*, ed. B. Clark, 271–303. Berkeley: University of California Press,.

Burch, P., and J. P. Spillane. 2003. Elementary and subject matter: Reforming mathematics literacy instruction. *The Elementary School Journal* 103(5).

Clark, B. 1987. *The academic profession*. Berkeley: University of California Press.

Cohen, D. K., and D. L. Ball. 1990. Relations between policy and practice. *Educational Evaluation and Policy Analysis* 12.

DiMaggio, P. D., and W. Powell. 1991. The iron cage revisited: Institutional isomorphism and collective rationality in organizational fields. In *The new institutionalism in organizational analysis*, ed. W. W. Powell and P. J. DiMaggio. Chicago: University of Chicago Press.

Doyle, W. 1983. Academic work. *Review of Educational Research* 53: 159–99.

Doyle W., and K. Carter. 1984. Academic tasks in classrooms. *Curriculum Inquiry* 14: 129–49.

Drake, C., J. Spillane, and K. Hufferd. 2001. Storied identities: Teacher learning and subject matter context. *Journal of Curriculum Studies* 33(1).

Firestone, W. A., J. Fitz, and P. Broadfoot. 1999. Power, learning, and legitimation: Assessment implementation across levels in the United States and the United Kingdom. *American Educational Research Journal* 36(4): 759–93.

Grossman, P., and S. Stodolsky. 1994. Considerations of content and the circumstances of secondary school teaching. *Review of Research in Education*.

Hayton, P., and J. Spillane. under review. *Professional communities in elementary schools: How the subject matters.*

Hill, H. C. 2001. Policy is not enough: Language and the interpretation of state standards. *American Educational Research Journal* 38(2).

Little, J. W. 1993. Professional community in comprehensive high schools: The two worlds of academic and vocational teachers. In *Teachers' work: Individuals, colleagues, and contexts*, ed. J. W Little and M. W. McLaughlin, 137–63. New York: Teachers College Press.

Meyer, J., and B. Rowan. 1978. The structure of educational organizations. In *Environments and Organizations*, ed. M. W. Meyer. San Francisco: Jossey-Bass.

Meyer, J. W. 1983. Innovation and knowledge use in American public education. In *Organizational environments: Ritual and rationality*, ed. J. W. Meyer and W. R. Scott, 233–60. Beverly Hills: Sage.

Parson, T. 1960. *Structure and process in modern societies*. Glencoe, IL: Free Press.

Perrow, C. 1986. *Complex organizations: A critical essay*. Glenview, IL: Scott, Foresman.

Rowan, B. 2002. Teachers' work and instructional management, part 1: Alternative views of the task of teaching. Ann Arbor, MI: Unpublished manuscript.

Rowan, B., and C. G. Miskel. 1999. Institutional theory and the study of educational organizations. In *Handbook of research in educational administration*, J. Murphy and K. S. Louis, 359–84. San Francisco: Jossey-Bass.

Siskin, L. S. 1994. *Realms of knowledge: Academic departments in secondary schools*. Washington, DC: Falmer.

Spillane, J. 2000. A fifth-grade teacher's reconstruction of mathematics and literacy teaching: Exploring interactions among identity, learning, and subject matter. *The Elementary School Journal* 100(4).

Spillane, J. P. 2004. *Standards deviation: How local schools misunderstand policy*. Cambridge, MA: Harvard University Press.

Spillane, J. P., A. Coldren, and J. Sherer. under review. *Distributed leadership: Leadership practice and the situation.*

Spillane, J. P., T. Hallett, and J. B. Diamond. 2003. Forms of capital and the construction of leadership: Instructional leadership in urban elementary schools. *Sociology of Education* 76(1): 1–17.

Spillane, J. P., and N. E. Jennings. 1997. Aligned instructional policy and ambitious pedagogy: Exploring instructional reform from the classroom perspective. *Teachers College Record* 98: 449–81.

Spillane, J. P., and J. Sherer. 2004. A distributed perspective on school lLeadership: Leadership practice as stretched over people and place. Paper presented at the Annual Meeting of the American Educational Research Association, San Diego, CA, April 2004.

Spillane, J. P., and C. L. Thompson. 1997. Reconstructing conceptions of local capacity: the local education agency's capacity for ambitious instructional reform. *Educational Evaluation & Policy* 19: 185–203.

Spillane, J. P., and J. S. Zeuli. 1999. Reform and teaching: Exploring patterns of practice in the context of national and state mathematics reforms. *Educational Evaluation and Policy Analysis* 21(1): 1–27.

Stodolsky, S. S. 1988. *The subject matters: Classroom activity in math and social studies.* Chicago: University of Chicago Press.

———. 1989. Is teaching really by the books? *Yearbook (National Society for the Study of Education)* 88: 159–84.

Stodolsky, S. S., and P. L. Grossman. 1995. The impact of subject matter on curricular activity: An analysis of five academic subjects. *American Educational Research Journal* 32(2).

Talbert, J. E., and M. W. McLaughlin. 1994. Teacher professionalism in local school contexts. *American Journal of Education* 102.

Weick, K. E. 1976. Educational organizations as loosely coupled systems. *Administrative Science Quarterly* 21, 1–19.

Weiss, I., J. Pasley, S. Smith, E. Banilower, and D. Heck. 2003. *A study of K–12 mathematics and science education in the United States.* Chapel Hill, NC: Horizon Research.

Whittington, R. 1992. Putting Giddens into action: Social systems and managerial agency. *Journal of Management Studies* 29(6).

SEVEN

The New Institutionalism Goes to the Market: The Challenge of Rapid Growth in Private K–12 Education

SCOTT DAVIES
LINDA QUIRKE
JANICE AURINI

INTRODUCTION: GROWING MARKET FORCES IN EDUCATION

PRIVATE EDUCATION IS GROWING in a variety of forms throughout North America. At least 14 million American children are now in private schools, charter schools, magnet schools, or home schooling (Fuller 2000, 42; see also NCES 2004). The proportion of Canadian students enrolled in private schools grew by 20 percent over the past decade; the corresponding percentage in Ontario, Canada's largest province, was 40 percent. About 6 percent of all Canadian youth are enrolled in private schools, but in Toronto's growing market, that figure is 9.7 percent. About 13 percent of all nonreligious schools are now private. Likewise, tutoring has been transformed from a small cottage industry into a corporate enterprise, supported by a surging demand. Recent surveys suggest that 24 percent of Ontario parents with school-aged children have recently hired tutors (Livingstone, Hart, and Davie 2003; see also Davies and Hammack 2004).

Alongside this expansion of choice, a "standards" movement has gained strength. For twenty years, North American politicians have accused schools of being substandard and sought ways to improve their quality. The choice and standards movements converge in the form of "consumer report" initiatives that advertise school-by-school rankings on standardized test scores, with the rationale of giving parents the needed information to choose wisely from a menu of local schools. Such initiatives are often justified under the banner of market reforms in education.

This chapter discusses the implications of the growing and increasingly varied private education market for new institutional theory and evaluates the utility of that theory for comprehending these changes. Institutional theory is the preeminent theory of educational organizations, famous since the late 1970s for depicting public schools as loosely coupled and isomorphic organizations. When new institutional theory was first developed, there were few charter schools or voucher programs in the United States, and schools were rarely judged by standardized test scores, as is common today. In Canada, there were far fewer private schools and almost no tutoring businesses of which to speak, but today both of these private forms have a strong presence. According to their advocates, such marketlike arrangements in education have the potential to create school organizations that are neither uniformly isomorphic nor loosely coupled, and as such they may pose a stark challenge to institutional theory.

To investigate these issues, we draw on our research in Toronto, Canada, where for several years we have studied developments among private schools and tutoring businesses. These entities represent educational organizations that are subject to more marketlike pressures than are public schools. They evade many hierarchical regulations, collect funds directly from fee-paying parents, and survive only by attracting clients. Indeed, these Toronto-based organizations operate in a "purer" market environment than do American charter schools or voucher-receiving schools, which are usually seen as the prototype of the new "market-driven" school among researchers. Facing minimal guidelines from the province and lacking government subsidies, they are directly exposed to the discipline of the market and charge what the market will bear.[1]

By examining private schools and tutoring businesses, this chapter takes institutional theory beyond regular K–12 schools and heeds Rowan's call (1999/2002) to recognize the larger assembly of organizations that service schools and students. Parallel to his "school improvement" industry, we see tutoring businesses as part of a broader "student improvement" industry that includes tutors, consultants, and various educational advisors (also see McDonough 1994). More importantly, tutoring businesses are ideal test cases of market-driven educational organizations. Their tasks are clearly educational, and their content is shaped by public schools, yet they are not regulated by any board, state, professional body, or accrediting organization. Since they cannot offer credentials, in theory they should be insulated from pressures to conform to public norms, and since they are not chartered to socialize students into societal values, they ought to be freer to maximize their academic productivity than are public schools. Such issues as the freedom to pursue pedagogical goals are key themes in discussions of educational markets, and we describe them in further detail later.

THEORY: THE CHALLENGE OF MARKETS

In now-classic articles (Meyer 1977; Meyer and Rowan 1977, 1978; Meyer, Scott, and Deal 1981), the new institutionalists portrayed schools in the 1970s and 1980s as "loosely coupled" and "isomorphic." They argued that this organizational form has been institutionalized over the past century, not only across North America but throughout the world (Meyer, Kamens, and Benavot 1992; Meyer and Ramirez 2000). But while institutional theory is famous for linking school structures to their environment, in many crucial respects that environment has changed. The famed image of the loosely coupled and isomorphic school, we argue, should be placed in context of the 1970s and 1980s heyday of the "shopping mall" public school (Powell, Farrar, and Cohen 1985), with its indifferent standards and bland conformity. Over the past twenty years, privatization, along with the standards and testing movements, has rocked education. Moreover, a body of theory has emerged that identifies markets as a dramatic transforming force on schools. Extrapolating from a large literature (e.g., Chubb and Moe 1990; Hoxby 2003; Ouchi 2003; Peterson 1990) that we dub "market theory," we next describe a series of mechanisms that are said to fundamentally alter school organization.

Markets are hailed by their advocates as injecting an entrepreneurial dynamism into education via a fundamental principle: to shift funding power from central bodies to parents. According to Chubb and Moe (1990), the most renowned market theorists, public funding arrangements encourage schools to conform to legal conventions rather than provide effective service. Unions demand the hiring of certified teachers, boards force compliance to curricular guidelines, and governments leverage school practices by various funding formulae. These bureaucratic shackles, they argue, make public schools unresponsive to their clients, like any inefficient monopoly. Market reforms are seen to pry schools from the grip of central administration and create competitive pressures similar to those faced by for-profit firms (Hoxby 2003, 6). Many choice arrangements thus weaken hierarchical regulations and force schools to survive by collecting funds directly from fee-paying clients.

This imperative to attract clients, according to the theory, spawns variety and can dismantle the "one best system" imposed by public bureaucracies (c.f.,

Tyack 1974). Mass generic schools, critics argue, are antiquated among today's students and teachers, whose preferences for pedagogy are now more varied and specialized. While public bureaucracies remain aloof and slow to change, markets are touted as the optimal medium to match the tastes of parents and educators. Deregulated choice is seen to encourage the entry of new educational providers, who bring innovative "breakthrough thinking" (Murphy 2003) in schooling, and devise more customized programs for their clients.

This links to another claim: greater student achievement is a necessary byproduct of markets (Chubb and Moe 1990; Hoxby 2003; Ouchi 2003). The advertising of school-by-school test scores, common practice in many American jurisdictions, has a strong affinity with market reasoning. Customers, needing to judge differences in school quality, are presumed to search for a simplified benchmark or "gold standard," such as superior records of achievement. Since schools collect revenue directly from recruited students, then markets are said to make schools accountable for minimal outcomes and create a "feedback mechanism" for continual quality improvement (Bidwell 2001; Ouchi 2003). Hence, according to this theory, by imposing clear standards and real sanctions, markets should reconnect school performance to its resource exigencies.

In sum, as market conditions become increasingly pervasive in education, institutional theorists can no longer simply assume that schools are loosely coupled and governed by ceremonial conformity (Rowan 2002, 15–16). If market theory is accurate, the fusion of markets and test scores makes school environments more "technical" and less "institutional" and should have at least three fundamental impacts on schools' organization:

1. *Isomorphic versus Divergent Change:* New institutional theory emphasizes how a strong normative environment in education causes unconventional schools to risk legitimacy. In contrast, market logic suggests that schools seek niches if their survival depends on accommodating unmet client preferences, and thus markets can reverse pressures for isomorphism and spawn a variety of instructional themes.
2. *Recoupling through Competitive Accountability:* Institutional logic holds that schools will retain a loosely coupled structure by evading direct monitoring of their instructional effectiveness, whether by evolving nonmeasurable goals, creating new mandates, or embracing norms of teachers' professional discretion. Theories of markets, in contrast, suggest that market-based schools must signal their quality to parents and hence should systematically report their outcomes, whether in the form of test score rankings, ratings, or widely recognized curricula.
3. *Formal Structure:* While new institutionalists suggest that the deeply diffused image of "school" tends to limit educational innovations, market theory highlights how lesser regulation in the private sector may weaken formal structures. Since relatively unregulated private schools need not adhere

to those conventions adopted by public schools only to procure legitimacy, private schools may dilute standard forms of physical plants, extracurricula, or teacher qualifications, for instance.

OUR RESEARCH ON TORONTO'S PRIVATE EDUCATION MARKET

Since 2001 we have collected data on various forms of private education in the greater Toronto area, documenting their growth, interviewing key actors, conducting site visits, and attending events. To date we have conducted seventy-five interviews with a variety of actors, including parents, principals, tutors, business people, preschool educators, home schoolers, and representatives from regulatory agencies, franchise associations, and instructor training programs. The largest portion of our project deals with private schools. We have compiled data on all nonreligious private schools and all public schools in the city. These data have four components. One consists of information on all 551 public schools in Toronto, using official sources. Another component consists of data on 82 private schools, the full population of nonreligious private schools in the city, based on phone interviews, official sources, promotional material, in-person interviews, and site visits. This component compares Toronto's 18 "elite" private schools, defined by membership in Canada's well-known Conference of Independent Schools, with the city's 64 "third-sector" schools, defined as all other private schools that the provincial ministry of education does not list as religious, language, or reform schools (for further details see Davies and Quirke 2005). The third component consists of rich qualitative data on private schools based on forty-five site visits and interviews with principals at third-sector private schools. The final component examines private tutoring businesses, using thirty interviews and site visits with representatives of these enterprises. Among this sample of interviewees were representatives of all major corporate franchises that operate in Canada, as well as several owners of small, independent tutoring businesses. Additional information came from a one-year participant observation study conducted by Janice Aurini, who tutored at a large franchise (Aurini 2004).

CHARACTERISTICS OF PRIVATE EDUCATION ORGANIZATIONS IN TORONTO

Isomorphism

Do private education organizations strive to be isomorphic with mainstream public schools, or do they seek their own paths and occupy various niches? To judge this, we use the Toronto public school board as a benchmark. Specialized public schools in the city are relatively few and far between, representing fewer than 10 percent (55 of 588) of all schools. These include alternative schools, French immersion, arts-centered schools, and a few academic-intensive schools. Otherwise, 9 in 10 public schools assume a standard, generalist form.

The elite sector in some ways represents an isomorphic yet upscale version of the public system. Almost all elite schools are generalists (with the exception of a French-language school and a special education school) that offer very similar types of broad, liberal education. In comparison to the third sector, the elites are far more similar to the public system and largely represent an "up-market" version of the standard school form, with only more expensive staffs and physical plants.

In contrast, third-sector schools differ greatly from both public and Elites in terms of their diversity. More than 90 percent of these schools offer some sort of specialty, creating an astonishing array of programs, mandates, and philosophies of teaching. These schools defy any common blueprint. Among the sixty-four third-sector schools, there were various niches based on unique curricula and pedagogical themes. We found specialty schools that range from intensive academics, woman-centered, liberal arts, social justice and environment issues, museum-based studies, multiple languages, "core knowledge," accelerated learning, and even a few "alternative" schools. Some schools also founded niches distinguished by special services, offering alternate hours, part-time, or per-credit courses. A few schools catered to diverse student populations, such as gifted students, athletes, dancers, those with Caribbean origins, or those with learning disabilities or special needs. By offering such specialized diversity, third-sector providers reverse trends toward isomorphism.

These schools serve a niche by being specialized alternatives for the urban upper-middle class. Many have intimate classes of about ten students. Tuition is generally probative, ranging from ten thousand to twenty thousand dollars. To reduce costs, most trim their physical plant, doing without playing fields, vocational programs, and various extracurricula. To provide an illustrative example, one school was founded by a PhD without a teaching background who believed that local public schools ought to use more inquiry-style pedagogy. She designed a "museum-centered" curriculum to exploit her school's location in a genteel urban neighborhood near the Royal Ontario Museum. Attracting a middle-class clientele who seek a more arts-based education, this school is staffed largely by individuals who lack teacher training but have impressive credentials in the world of the arts. Just down the street is a competing school that is similarly housed in a former mansion. Founded by a group of teachers who left a private school, the school specializes in classical education. Students wear uniforms, take instruction in several languages, and are generally prepped for liberal arts programs in universities. One distinguishing characteristic of these schools is their informality. All teachers know all students personally, and most preach "education for education's sake," readying their students for university while not reducing the experience to a competition for grades or test scores.

Tutoring businesses occupy a middle ground, in that they face an intriguing mix of isomorphic and divergent pressures. On the one hand, they operate in a setting defined by the dominant institutional form of education. Their demand is shaped by the contours of the main school system. Its pressures of competition fuel the need for improved grades and test prep. Its curricular content is shaped by schools, as is its timing, since most clients come after school hours from September to June. Many personnel come from the education sector—retired teachers and university students make up the bulk of the tutoring force. Thus, the tutoring market is embedded in a wider institutional environment and is shaped by its dynamics. Public schools cast a long shadow on it, hence it is called *shadow education* (Stevenson and Baker 1992).

However, small independents and the large franchises have both assumed interesting hybrid forms. As small businesses, independent tutors often operate rather informally. Most do not hire certified teachers; they operate out of small buildings or houses. As for-profit enterprises, they face market pressures for efficiency that push them toward niches, such as specializing in math, language, or science. Thus, while small independent tutors operate in the shadow of schools' institutional environment, their market conditions lead them to specialize and to create idiosyncratic forms of organization.

The large franchises also operate in the shadow of public schools, and in many ways they set up operations that parallel school content. Like schools, they do diagnostic testing, have sequential programs, and employ "educational directors" who play a role analogous to a vice principal. They often borrow labels and prestigious namesakes from the world of public education. Further, like a school board, the franchiser imposes a standardized model on the franchisees, closely dictating product lines, service delivery, educational materials, and physical plant. Thus, in many ways, they parallel local schools, offering a true supplementary form of education.

But franchises differ from schools by offering a wider array of services and product lines that span age groups, credential levels, and formal educational forms. Unlike any school, a typical tutoring franchise will offer services ranging from preschool, K–12, adult literacy, and university test prep. No single public school would offer such a diverse range of services across age groups. The cause of this diversity is that tutoring franchises have additional pressures for isomorphism: as corporate businesses, they are expected to conform to prevailing business forms. They have other organizational models to mimic, and these models hail from other industries. In some respects, tutoring businesses copy franchises from outside of the realm of education.

For instance, most of the large franchises are members of a business association—the Canadian Franchise Association (CFA), an organization that represents enterprises in hundreds of industries, ranging from restaurants, coffee shops, and car rentals to parcel services. These associations spread norms and strategies for business practice that lending banks come to expect. This is important, because franchises need to generate larger revenues than do small independents because of the existence of franchise fees. Successful franchises often require sizable investments, far beyond those needed in small independent businesses. One common franchise strategy to extend revenues is to develop services that can secure customers for extended periods and allow a business to expand into new taste markets. This has led to the advent of "centers" in several industries. For instance, many gyms have transformed themselves into "fitness centers" and now stretch beyond athletic and weight training to offer on-staff physiotherapists, massage therapists, nutritionists, and personal trainers, as well as having counters that sell juices, fitness gear, and nutritional supplements. Rather than simply providing an exercise space, fitness centers now give customers an "assessment" and place them in a "program." This expansion and diversification of product lines is designed to maximize revenue sources.

We are finding that tutoring franchises have similarly expanded beyond their traditional base of K–12 supplementary education. New franchises have greatly expanded their range of product lines, now offering preschool programs, standardized test prep, on-line tutoring, adult literacy, vocational training, and courses for high school credit. In some cases, they have developed into full-fledged private schools. Thus, the imperatives of the franchise business form has led tutoring enterprises to mimic schools in some ways but to also expand beyond into a wider array of services that span several age groups and credential levels. These pressures push direct franchisers toward new organizational templates that differ from schools. Many use business models for physical plants and services, and in interviews, many considered teachers to be undesirable franchise owners, portraying them as lacking the entrepreneurial spirit necessary to run a profitable business.

Coupling

Do markets compel private education organization to tighten their structures? That is, do they advertise their quality using performance indicators? Again, we can use Toronto public schools as a point of comparison. All public schools have their average standardized test scores advertised on the board's web site, though these tests remain relatively "toothless," with no sanctions as yet following results. Further, a well-known conservative think-tank (the Fraser Institute) takes those data and compiles a rating for each school. Thus, Toronto public schools are required to report these presumed indicators of quality. A few (3 percent) go further to focus their academics and adopt the International Baccalaureate curriculum. None advertise the placement of graduates into prestigious universities.

Following market theory, we hypothesized that Toronto private schools should welcome opportunities to engage in competitive comparisons. A major finding, however, is that only one type of private education organization, the elite schools, does so. The majority of elite schools indeed engage in some competitive comparison, with most partaking in the Fraser ratings, several reporting some quantitative score, and most advertising the successful placement of their graduates in prestigious American and European universities (i.e., Ivy League, Oxbridge). Almost all sought and received accreditation from a private assessment body, and almost all of the secondary schools used the International Baccalaureate (IB) or Advanced Placement (AP) curricula. Judging by this diverse set of indicators, elite schools readily engage in competitive rating schemes and signal their presence in a broad, international field.

In sharp contrast, the other private education organizations retain a loosely coupled form. Very few third-sector schools, for example, use any quantitative indicator. Almost none report test scores, university placement rates, or league table rankings. Fewer than 9 percent participate in the province's testing initiatives, and only 13 percent volunteer to be rated by the Fraser Institute. Only one of thirty schools with web sites advertise any quantitative indicators. Only 10 percent of secondary schools used either the IB or AP. Thus, the vast majority of third-sector schools opt out of any competitive ranking scheme. Similarly, tutoring businesses do not engage in competitive accountability. Though the logic of market theory suggests that they should be compelled to demonstrate their effectiveness, we found a very different situation. These businesses typically do not guarantee raised school grades nor use external standardized tests to measure their clients' progress. In fact, we did not find a single example of a large franchise attempting to measure its effectiveness.

When inquired about such guarantees, most tutoring interviewees explain that the multifaceted, uncertain nature of tutoring makes any guarantee a profound risk. Many instead develop alternate strategies in the name of accountability. One is to create their own internal evaluations of their students' progress, rather than using external standards such as school grades or standardized tests. A more pervasive practice has been to evolve new, nonmeasurable goals. For instance, many businesses now boast expansive mandates, such as stimulating their clients' emotional development, including "leadership skills," "self-development," "self-esteem," "self-confidence," and so on. Further, franchises are increasingly pursuing a broad "skill-building" model of tutoring, downplaying traditional tutoring as a mere band-aid solution to a much larger problem. They avoid short-term promises of improved school grades in favor of more diffuse goals such as developing cognitive abilities and closing skill gaps. One even claims to nurture metacognitive awareness—a vague trait that is certainly difficult to measure.

The impetus for these practices comes back to classic institutional arguments about the benefits of loose coupling: direct inspections of effectiveness could expose inconsistencies or inefficiencies. Being free of any formal governing body, professional association, or government regulator to impose coupling mechanisms, tutoring businesses have the luxury of constructing their own yardsticks of success. But a crucial difference is that pressures for loose coupling in tutoring businesses stem from market conditions. One consequence of being a market-driven enterprise without any credentialing authority is that tutors have little leverage over students. Tutoring is optional; clients are free to withdraw at any time, and tutors' evaluations pose no direct consequences to student grades or accreditation. Tutors lack the authority to penalize students for incomplete work and dissident behavior. Lacking direct links to formal school outcomes, tutors are acutely aware of the difficulty of retaining willing students and parents.

As a consequence, tutors have developed a series of strategies to keep customers happy, even at the cost of superseding instructional goals. Some will periodically relax instruction when problems arise, allowing difficult students to work on less challenging material or sit quietly until the session is over. One major franchise has students reflect during the last five minutes of every session, relaying to the tutor what they have accomplished that day, and then repeat these phrases to their parents. While this ritual does not actually measure instructional effectiveness, it provides parents an account of how their money has been spent, thus serving a legitimizing function. Such decoupling permits tutors to maintain the positive client relations that are critical for continual enrollments in market conditions.

Formal Structures

Our final concern is whether private education organizations weaken their formal structures and seek new sources of legitimacy. As a baseline comparison, we again turn to Toronto public schools. All are in traditional academic space, marked by large buildings with standard classrooms and large yards. All are legally obliged to hire accredited teachers, and all principals are former teachers. Given this benchmark, do private education bodies adopt standardized forms?

We found that only elite private schools are concerned with conforming to the dominant image of a "school." Almost all of the Elite schools had traditional physical plants; indeed, many were "up-market" versions of the traditional school. More than 72 percent were the epitome of the venerable prep school, with sprawling playing fields, great halls, and other symbols of prestige. These expensive formal structures command legitimacy within an idiom of tradition. From their vaulted market position, Elite schools act as bearers of standards, not as educational mavericks. They are run in a bureaucratic, rule-bound manner, with most principals and teachers having formal credentials, often paid in excess of the public system rate.

In contrast, the third-sector schools have distinct physical plants. Because of their sensitivity to the cost of rent, only one-quarter of these enterprises rented floor space from public schools; none owned a school. The remainder were typically located in humble locales, such as office buildings, store space in shopping plazas, old houses, or former churches, fire stations, and banks. These unorthodox locales forced many third-sector schools to either improvise their extracurricular activities or to forego them altogether. Most lack playing fields, gyms, pools, or music rooms. To provide such services, several use community facilities, such as nearby YMCAs, private health clubs, public parks, or tennis courts. Thus, they broke from the isomorphic model of a school through their physical plant.

Another way that markets affect formal structure is through the hiring of teachers with formal credentials. Mostly running small enterprises with tight budgets, third-sector principals spoke of their restricted spending relative to public schools. Teacher salaries are their largest expense, and third-sector schools often adapted to their market position by relaxing hiring requirements. Fewer than half of third-sector principals were accredited Ontario teachers (members of the Ontario College of Teachers [OCT]) themselves, and several had no teaching background at all. Only 14 percent of these schools were staffed entirely with OCT teachers. While all principals talked of wanting to pay teachers well, most claimed it difficult to match the wages expected by credentialed teachers. Given these pressures, they staffed their schools in creative ways, hiring noncertified teachers among the ranks of unemployed graduate students or utilizing talented yet noncertified people in their social networks. Principals rationalized this practice by proclaiming formal teaching qualifications to be irrelevant to most parents and to the success of students.

Similarly, tutoring businesses did mimic the formal structure of a "school" in some ways, but pragmatically adjusted to financial pressures. For instance, like schools, they create workbooks, lessons, diagnostic testing, and report cards and hold parent-teacher meetings. Franchises employ "education directors," a position separate from the administration of the business, who serve a vice principal role, liaising between parents and tutors and ensuring the integrity of their program. Yet, while mimicking some characteristics of public schools, learning centers are free to shed costly features, such as hiring credentialed teachers. Out of thirty owner-interviewees, only eight were certified teachers, and only two of the six major franchises require their tutors to hold a teaching certificate. Their isomorphism is thus only partial and is highly selective.

What promotes this strategy? To survive, third-sector schools constantly look to trim costs and often dilute organizational components they deem to be less essential, such as fully credentialed teachers or traditional physical plants. But such tactics can be risky. According to institutional theory, any dilution of these formal structures would risk legitimacy, and indeed third-sector principals spoke frankly of having a "selling job" to do on parents who feared their enterprise "didn't look like a school." To assuage this problem, most third-sector schools traded standard formal structures in favor of small classes and personal service. Almost all had class sizes that were not only sub-stantially smaller than those in public schools but also much smaller than the elite average. By creating intimate surroundings, these schools could offer an environment tailored to students and cultivate personal relations with parents. Principals saw customized attention as their major selling point. Operating with precarious profit margins, the owners of third-sector schools and tutor-ing businesses alike told us that market competition forced them to be accountable to their clients not via performance indicators but by providing one-on-one contact, personal service, and an "open-door" policy by which their clients could directly inspect their practices. Though many of the older establishments admitted that once they grew more financially stable, they then adopted a more closed-door policy, in general, the third sector has a strong customer service ethos.

In summary, market forces had a variety of effects on private education orga-nizations in Toronto. Elite private schools were isomorphic, embodying a gener-alist form and embracing standard emblems of school but were also oriented toward competitive accountability. Third-sector schools, in contrast, sought niches and diluted formal structures, as would be predicted by market advocates, yet they avoided performance indicators. Similarly, small independent tutoring businesses also occupied niches and diluted their formal structures, yet they too avoided performance indicators. Franchises also avoided competitive account-ability yet took on hybrid forms, drawing influences from schools but also from franchises in other industries. Importantly, none of these bodies was fully iso-morphic with public schools *and* loosely coupled, as might be predicted by insti-tutional theory, neither were any niche-driven *and* recoupled, as might be pre-dicted by market theory (for a summary of these findings, see table 7.1).

DISCUSSION: THE INTERPLAY OF MARKETS AND INSTITUTIONS

The pace of educational change over the past decade, particularly initiatives for market competition and higher standards, poses a challenge to institu-tional theory. The renowned image of the isomorphic, loosely coupled school needs to be contextualized as a product of particular social conditions, namely, an era of relatively stable public funding, less credential competition, and weaker testing technology. It was also a time when the "choice" movements of

TABLE 7.1
Organizational Characteristics by Type of Private Education

	Elite Schools	Third-Sector Schools	Tutoring Franchises	Independent Tutoring Business
Isomorphism: Do they emulate standard public school models?	Yes, adopt generalist forms	No, diverge into many niches	Adopt hybrid forms	No, diverge into many niches
Tighter Coupling: Do they advertise performance indicators?	Yes, strongly oriented to testing	No, avoid performance indicators	No, use only internal tests	No, avoid performance indicators
Formal Structures: Do they use dominant symbols of schooling?	Yes, bolstered formal structures	No, make pragmatic adjustments	No	No, make pragmatic adjustments

the day—for free and alternative schools—sputtered within a few short years, serving only to bolster isomorphism in the main system. However, choice movements, political discord in education, greater credential competition, and standardized testing have in some ways disrupted these tendencies. Today, not all educational organizations drift toward isomorphic and loosely coupled forms, and market conditions appear to be a source of change. What specific impacts do markets have on schools?

The Impact of Markets on Schools

Our study suggests several broad ways in which markets can affect school organizations. One is to expose educational organizations to a broad array of structural templates beyond the mass public school. For instance, we found that corporate franchising pressures tutoring businesses to adopt organizational forms that are legitimate in the world of business, but not necessarily in the world of schooling. In our study of tutoring franchises, and as Janice Aurini is currently finding among other corporations that offer educational services, pressures to expand revenues lead them to embrace innovations from other industries, such as diversifying their product lines and quickly embracing new technologies in ways that transgress the regular boundaries of schools.

Markets also affect school organizations by encouraging the use of customized attention as a niche-building strategy. For instance, third-sector schools face an already crowded K–12 market, populated by a generally well-funded public system and a host of established elite private schools. In such an environment, divergent change, not mimicry, allows new schools to enter the playing field. A crowded marketplace encourages educators to offer what their competitors do not: specialized curricula and small-scale, personalized attention. The ability to tap this otherwise untapped source of consumer demand permits their growth. Indeed, the lone common denominator among various growing forms of private education—new private schools, tutoring businesses, and home schooling—appears to be a capacity to offer a tailored and individualized educational experience.

A third way that markets can affect educational organizations is to promote coupling, though here the story is more mixed. Markets that have norms of test score comparisons appear to generate tighter coupling, as we saw among Toronto elite schools and as is becoming a norm in American education. But in some conditions, markets generate other forms of accountability. In Toronto, private organizations face less state regulation than do public schools, so they can evade testing initiatives. In such a setting, the impact of markets can be to foist upon schools a kind of accountability based on customer service, as we saw among third-sector schools and tutoring businesses. Time can only tell if sustained market environments encourage educational organizations to tighten their structures by reporting performance indicators. While such standards remain unformed in relatively new sectors such as third-sector schools or tutoring businesses, as these industries mature they may be compelled to adopt more coupled forms.

These market-generated variations among school organizations pose a challenge to new institutional theory. We next speculate how the theory can be retooled by incorporating notions of how these market effects are embedded in surrounding institutional environments.

Markets Embedded in Institutions:
Resources, Regulation, Competition, Controls

Many of the original ideas in institutional theory have perhaps become implicit in recent discussions of education. For instance, tenets of isomorphism assume the existence of governing bodies that accredit schools, regulate their competition, and offer stable funding in exchange for conformity to various rules. They are premised on captive client bases and assurances of stable resources. Likewise, the tenet of loose coupling reflected the arrangements of the 1970s and 1980s when technology to monitor school effectiveness was used less and when educational competition was less intense. But today, market arrangements can loosen regulation, intensify competition, make clients less captive, make resources less stable, and generate stiffer pressures to perform. These changes highlight four key variables:

resource stability, credential competition, amount of regulation, and strength of technology.

School organizations are affected by their resources, and one impact of markets is to make resource allocations increasingly variable. Some educational markets are highly stable, and others are very competitive. For instance, though Toronto's elite private schools are nominally in a market environment, drawing no government subsidy and needing to charge high tuition fees, they are very comfortable, blessed with large endowments, waiting lists, and legacies of high-powered alumni. In stark contrast, third-sector schools epitomize the "lean and mean" market-driven organization, being financially precarious and constantly needing to attract clients. These differences affect how each responds to pressures of isomorphism and coupling. Elite private schools are well resourced, serve an upper-class clientele, and are driven to signal legitimacy by adopting generalist formal structures. In contrast, relative newcomers such as third-sector schools lack such resources, so they avoid competition by developing some sort of distinctiveness.

The larger theoretical point is that market competition can create vast differences in resource stability among educational organizations, which in turn shape organizational forms. Institutional theory's tenet of isomorphism was premised upon a public school system that provided a well-regulated, stable environment, but the emergence of market competition can generate greater variation. Stability encourages education organizations to be isomorphic, and conversely, instability can pressure them toward niches.

This issue of stability raises larger issues of regulation and control. Compared to most American jurisdictions, Toronto's private market is less regulated, and its standardized testing regimen is weaker (see table 7.2). Ontario's provincial government enforces few regulations on private schools and does not compel them to participate in standardized testing. In contrast, most American schools of choice must comply with testing initiatives, and indeed, standardized tests have been hailed as a new coupling mechanism for American

TABLE 7.2
Institutionalized Differences Between Canada and the United States

	Canada	United States
Postsecondary Competition	Less intense, regional	Intense, national
Technology	Weat testing culture	Strong testing culture
Regulation of Schools of Choice	Very weak	Relatively strong for charter schools, voucher programs

schools. The key point, however, is that the use of these tests varies internationally (Rowan 2002). Canada's testing culture is weaker than its American counterpart, with no equivalent of the SAT at the postsecondary level, and almost no high-stakes tests at the K–12 level. Ontario's new testing regime, devised in the late 1990s, remains "toothless," with no consequences attached to a school's performance.

These national differences create an intriguing interplay between market forces and institutional settings. The lack of a surrounding test score culture dissipates pressures for recoupling in some sectors of Toronto's private-school market. For instance, third-sector schools' precarious financial situations made them doubly sensitive to inspections, and the same competitive pressures that created niches among these schools have the effect of undercutting recoupling. This is important for theory: loose coupling was actually encouraged by competitive market pressures because there was no strongly institutionalized technology. Needing to attract clients, markets instead push these organizations toward more consumer-friendly practices. This is in contrast to American charter schools and to Toronto elite schools, both of which tend to embrace the test-score culture.

The anomaly posed by Toronto's elite schools engagement in a test-score culture highlights one further variable: credential competition. American high schools operate in a national-level competition to enter a postsecondary system marked by a steep status hierarchy. More than in most countries, American colleges are arrayed on an elaborate rank order, ranging from humble state colleges to the world-renown Ivy League, and this hierarchy has created a growing national market for undergraduate admissions (Geiger 2002). In contrast, the Canadian undergraduate system is less hierarchical, has a smaller national market, and thus generates fewer nonlocal ambitions among high school students (see Davies and Hammack 2004).

These varying shapes of credential competition explain patterns in the Toronto private-school market. The elite schools have more tightly coupled forms because they strive to place their graduates in international universities. Though residing north of the border, their frame of reference is largely the peak of the American hierarchy. Aspiring to place graduates in the Ivy League, they are brought into the orbit of American institutional practices. In contrast, the third sector's frame of reference is local. These schools advertise the placing of their graduates only in local universities and bill themselves as only offering advantages over public schools in gaining admission to southern Ontario institutions. In fact, a few interviewed principals emphasized that they must tell parents to scale down unrealistic dreams of sending their child to Harvard or Yale.

A key theoretical implication is that broad institutional settings can set the parameters for educational markets. Elite schools, though nominally unregulated, are isomorphic and tightly coupled because their frame of reference is the U.S. postsecondary system. Otherwise, Ontario's weak testing apparatus allows other private schools to opt out of rating schemes without sanction because consequential parties such as universities, media, assessors, and tuition-paying parents are not yet using them to appraise schools. Along with a local frame of competitive reference, these institutional forces combine to channel market forces toward a "niche logic."

CONCLUSION

Revising Institutional Theory for a New Era

By incorporating variations in resources, regulations, credential competition, and control technology, a revised institutional theory can readily comprehend the impact of markets on education. It can illuminate how markets interact with institutional formations to trigger what appears to be a widening variety of educational organizations.

It can reveal how new American schools of choice are products not only of market forces but also of an institutional formation with a strong testing culture and intense credential competition. Conversely, it can show how other institutional formations can direct market forces in different directions. Unregulated markets in weak testing environments can create a diversity of niche-occupying schools that are loosely coupled, as we saw among third-sector schools and tutoring businesses. Market forces do not always compel schools to improve their academic quality if they lack a surrounding infrastructure of control.[2]

Our major conclusion, then, is that while educational markets necessitate some revision to institutional theory, they also illustrate its continuing utility. Reforms for choice have altered the educational landscape, but the theory can reveal how such markets are embedded in institutional settings and how those settings can then channel those forces in different directions.

NOTES

1. The ecology of school choice differs somewhat in Ontario vis à vis American jurisdictions. Ontario has no charter, magnet, or voucher schemes. Catholic schools are fully funded. Unlike some Canadian jurisdictions such as the city of Edmonton, Ontario public school boards are not mandated to provide a full menu of choice. As a result, a sizable nonreligious private education market has emerged. These private schools face few regulations. The provincial government will accredit a private school as long as it enrolls at least five students, complies with health and safety guidelines, and broadly follows the provincial curriculum.

2. Future research can investigate whether there is an inherent tension between two market-oriented reforms: choice schemes that aim to stimulate pedagogical diversity and testing initiatives that aim to create high-standard and more tightly coupled schools. The paradox is that test-based standards can encourage schools of choice to narrow their goals and avoid experimentation for fear of risking weak test scores. This provisional conclusion is suggested not only by Toronto elite schools but also by recent American studies of charter and voucher-receiving schools. Despite their billing as exemplars of innovation, some researchers see little pedagogical novelty among these schools, believing that minimal test score requirements serve to constrain their practices (Lubienski 2003; Murphy 2003). It is interesting that while it is also unclear whether charter schools or vouchers actually boost test scores, they do raise levels of parent satisfaction (Goldhaber 1999). Such a finding bolsters our conjecture that educational markets may push schools to be more concerned with satisfying customers than with raising academic quality.

REFERENCES

Aurini, Janice. 2004. Educational entrepreneurialism in the private tutoring industry: Balancing profitability with the humanistic face of schooling. *Canadian Review of Sociology and Anthropology* 41(4): 475–91.

Aurini, Janice, and Scott Davies. 2004. The transformation of private tutoring: Education in a franchise form. *Canadian Journal of Sociology* 29(3): 419–38.

Bidwell, Charles E. 2001. Analyzing schools as organizations: Long-term permanence and short-term change. *Sociology of Education* (extra issue 2001): 100–14.

Chubb, John, and Terry Moe. 1990. *Politics, markets and American schools.* Washington, DC: Brookings Institute.

Davies, Scott, and Floyd Hammack. 2005. The channeling of student competition in higher education: Comparing Canada and the U.S." *Journal of Higher Education* 76(1): 89–106.

Davies, Scott, and Linda Quirke. 2005. Providing for the priceless student: Ideologies of choice in an emerging private school market. *American Journal of Education* 111(4): 523–47.

———. 2006. Innovation in educational markets: An organizational analysis of third sector private schools in Toronto. In *School sector and student outcomes*, ed. Maureen Hallinan. Notre Dame, IN: Notre Dame University Press.

DiMaggio, P., and W. Powell. 1991. The iron cage revisited: Institutional isomorphism and collective rationality in organizational fields. In *The new institutionalism in organizational analysis*, ed. W. Powell and P. DiMaggio. Chicago: University of Chicago Press.

Fuller, Bruce. 2000. Introduction. In *Inside charter schools*, ed. Bruce Fuller, 1–11. Cambridge: Harvard University Press.

Geiger, R. L. 2002. The competition for high-ability students: Universities in a key marketplace. In *The future of the city of intellect: The changing American university*, ed. Steven Brint, 82–106. Stanford, CA: Stanford University Press.

Goldhaber, Dan D. 1999. School choice: An examination of the empirical evidence on achievement, parental decision-making, and equity. *Educational Researcher* 28(9): 16–25.

Hoxby, Caroline. M. 2003. *The economics of school choice*. Chicago: University of Chicago Press.

Livingstone, David W., Doug Hart, and L. E. Davie. 2003. *Public attitudes towards education in Ontario 2002: The 14th OISE/UT survey*. Toronto: Orbit.

Lubienski, Christopher. 2003. Innovation in education markets: Theory and evidence on the impact of competition and choice in charter schools. *American Education Research Journal* 40(2): 395–443.

McDonough, Patricia A. 1994. Buying and selling higher education: The social construction of the college applicant. *Journal of Higher Education* 65: 427–46.

Meyer, John W. 1977. The effects of education as an institution. *American Journal of Sociology* 83: 55–77.

Meyer, John W., David H. Kamens, and Aaron Benavot. 1992. *School knowledge for the masses*. Washington, DC: Falmer.

Meyer, John W., and Francisco Ramirez 2000. The world institutionalization of education. In *Discourse formation in comparative education*, ed. Jurgen Schriewer. Frankfurt: Peter Lang.

Meyer, John W., and Brian Rowan. 1977. Institutionalized organizations: Formal structures as myth and ceremony. *American Journal of Sociology* 83(2): 340–63.

———. 1978. The structure of educational organizations. In *Environments and organizations*. San Francisco: Jossey-Bass.

Meyer, John W., W. Richard Scott, and Terrance E. Deal. 1981. Institutional and technical sources of organizational structure: Explaining the structure of educational orgnanizations. In *Organization and the human services: Cross-disciplinary reflections*, ed. Herman D. Stein, ch. 6. Philadephia: Temple University Press.

Moe, Terry M. 2001a. *Schools, vouchers, and the American public*. Washington, DC: Brookings Institute.

———. 2001b. Teachers unions and the public schools. In *A primer on America's schools*, ed. Terry M. Moe, 151–84. Stanford: Hoover Institute.

Murphy, Joseph. 2003 Has marketization improved the quality of education? The case of charter schools. *Journal of Educational Change* 4(1): 72–80.

National Center for Education Statistics (NCES). 2004. 1.1 million homeschooled students in the United States in 2003. Accessed August 5, 2004, at http://nces.ed.gov/pubs2004/2004115.pdf.

Ouchi, William G. 2003. *Making schools work: A revolutionary plan to get your children the education they need*. New York: Simon and Schuster.

Peterson, Paul E. 1990. Monopoly and competition in American education. In *Choice and Control in American Education*, ed. W. Clune and J. Witte, 47–79. New York: Falmer.

———. 2001. Choice in American education. In *A primer on America's schools*, ed. Terry M. Moe, 249–84. Stanford: Hoover Institute Press.

Powell, Arthur G., Eleanor Farrar, and David K. Cohen 1985. *The shopping mall high school*. Boston: Houghton Mifflin.

Rowan, Brian. 2002. The new institutionalism and the study of education: Changing ideas for changing times. Paper presented at the conference Advancing the Institutional Research Agenda in Education, State University of New York, Albany.

Schneider, Mark, Paul Teske, and Melissa Marschall. 2000. *Choosing schools: Consumer choice and the quality of American schools*. Princeton: Princeton University Press.

Stevenson, David Lee, and David P. Baker. 1992. Shadow education and allocation in formal schooling: Transition to university in Japan. *American Journal of Sociology* 97(6): 1639–57.

Tyack, David, and Larry Cuban. 1997. *Tinkering toward utopia: A century of public school reform*. Cambridge, MA: Harvard University Press.

EIGHT

Growing Commonalities and Persistent Differences in Higher Education: Universities between Global Models and National Legacies

FRANCISCO O. RAMIREZ

INTRODUCTION

Mᴜᴄʜ ᴏꜰ ᴛʜᴇ ʟɪᴛᴇʀᴀᴛᴜʀᴇ on universities emphasizes the importance of the national context in shaping its institutional goals and organizational forms. Within this literature differences in how universities react to a wide range of educational innovations reflect differences in historical legacies. In formal organizational terms these historical legacies constitute the organizational decisions and structures, which add up to the path dependencies, which in turn explain persistent differences in higher education across national contexts. Within this scholarly tradition the weight of historical legacies is paramount in explaining university trajectories across national contexts. An alternative perspective focuses on the world context and emphasizes the degree to which world models of progress and justice have influenced nation-states and national educational institutions. From a world society perspective one expects to find growing educational commonalities across nation-states. In organizational parlance one expects growing institutional isomorphism, as different universities increasingly experience common rationalizing influences from a common organizational field.

Throughout this chapter I reflect on both growing commonalities and persistent differences. The first part of the chapter focuses on the worldwide expansion of higher education between 1965 and 1995. My goal is to highlight a worldwide trend, to indicate how a world society perspective accounts for this trend, and to contend that expanded higher education involves a shift from a socially buffered to a socially embedded model of the university. The latter calls for a socially responsive, organizationally flexible, and broadly inclusive university. Next, I consider in what ways Oxford and Stanford embody different models of the university and to what extent these differences persist or get eroded in the latter part of the twentieth century. I shall argue that symbolic differences persist even as organizational transformations lead Oxford closer to a socially embedded university model. The modernization of Oxford is contrasted with the situation at Stanford, a university that from its origins illustrated the socially embedded model. I conclude by directly considering the tensions between the influence of historical legacies and common frames on universities and on their sensibilities toward educational innovations.

World Society and Educational Expansion

After World War II the phenomenal growth of first primary and then secondary education in country after country raised a serious challenge to theories of schooling that emphasized societal or national contextual explanations. If schooling was a response to industrialization or urbanization, then one should expect to observe its growth in the more but not in the less industrialized or urbanized countries. If a democratic regime or culture were the main trigger of educational growth, the nondemocratic countries would exhibit very different patterns of educational development. But in fact the world educational revolution truly swept the entire world (Meyer et al. 1977). Moreover, the countries of the world also enacted compulsory education laws and established national educational ministries (Ramirez and Ventresca 1992). Furthermore, national curricula began to look more and more alike with respect to what subjects were taught and how much time was allocated to different subjects (Meyer, Kamens, and Benavot 1992). Common justifications informed these common educational trends, from an earlier emphasis on education for development to a more recent one on education as human right (Chabbott 2003). An earlier and often contentious vision of schooling for the masses had become an established and nationally legitimating model of mass schooling. Nation-states and nation-state candidates would commit themselves to this model, though the expected societal benefits from expanded schooling were often not realized (see Chabbot and Ramirez 2000 for a review of empirical studies of education and development).

To make sense of growing common trends with respect to mass schooling, trends that cannot be adequately accounted for via utilitarian explanations, world society theory postulates a logic of appropriateness and a dynamic of nation-state enactment of appropriate nation-state identity. The underlying argument can be briefly summarized:

1. Becoming a nation-state in the latter part of the twentieth century increasingly involved adhering to rationalizing models of nation-statehood that had emerged and triumphed throughout the nineteenth and twentieth centuries.
2. These models emphasized education for nation building and for individual development. The authority and influence of these models increased over time, producing educational expansion and standardization at an increasing rate.
3. The influence of endogenous national economic, political, and social factors on national educational policies and practices declined over time.
4. These models were earlier transmitted from core nations to peripheral ones, but more recently the models increasingly diffuse from international organizations and from scientists, professionals, and other educational experts.
5. The more a nation-state is linked to these models and to their organizational carriers the greater the likelihood that its educational system will be attuned to the world models and will change in directions in line with changes in world emphases.

This argument would lead one to expect changes in the direction of educational expansion or massification of schooling, of standardization of educational goals, organization, curricula, and pedagogy, of a rise of educational expertise "without borders," and of international educational organizations and conferences within which educational expertise could be displayed. Many of these changes have in fact taken place in the realm of education (Meyer and Ramirez 2000), and more broadly, with respect to science and scientific activity (Drori et al. 2003). As nation-states seek to enact a world-validated "imagined community" pursuing standardized progress and justice goals much national and educational isomorphism ensues. Educational distinctiveness is difficult to manage when the influential educational blueprints tend to be universalistic in tone, be their sources the Chicago Boys selling education as human capital formation or the Disciples of Paolo Freire preaching education as human right and empowerment (Ramirez 2003). Despite their obvious differences these educational blueprints are advanced to be applicable worldwide. The strong underlying assumption is that given the correct educational conditions all can learn or be empowered; the educability of peasants, the working class, people of color, or women is no longer an issue.

This argument and the empirical evidence consistent with its key premises are more fully developed elsewhere (Meyer et al. 1997). But the immediate question is whether the argument applies more so with respect to mass schooling and less so with respect to higher education? While mass schooling was linked to the nation-state from its emergence in the age of nationalism, in some countries some universities, Oxford, for example, predate the nation-state by centuries. To the extent that universities like other organizations are influenced by the ideas and forms that were dominant when they were born (Stinchcombe 1965), some universities should be less subject to the influence of subsequent rationalizing models. However, it is important to keep in mind that most of the universities of the world today were founded after 1945 (Riddle 1989). This was a period of accelerated higher educational growth in the United States, leading one critic to wryly observe that Americans seemed to be acting as if there was "no salvation outside higher education" (Shills 1971). But was this pattern of expansion also true elsewhere?

Figure 8.1 traces the growth of tertiary enrollments as a percent of the appropriate age cohort between 1965 and 1995, for Western (N=21) and non-Western countries (N=64). The West here is a geocultural concept and includes Western European countries as well as the United States, Canada, Australia, and New Zealand. For both sets of countries the pattern is one of growth. In the West the national average tertiary enrollment ratio jumps from 10 to nearly 45 percent in three decades. The similar trend for non-Western countries involves an increase from a national average tertiary enrollment ratio of fewer than 5 to nearly 15 percent. The gap between the Western and non-Western countries increases during these three decades. But note that by 1995 the non-Western world has surpassed the Western world of 1965 with respect to the average level of tertiary enrollments. Debates about what constitutes a university and what is the appropriate university response to proposed or ongoing innovations in their curricula, organization, and funding take place within the broader world context of accelerated entry into higher education institutions, including universities.

As observed earlier this is an era of increased university foundings; in the West the growth is from a national average of twenty to thirty-one universities. (The United States is not included in this comparison because it is an outlier, and its inclusion would inflate the Western national average.) For the rest of the world universities grow from a national average of six to eleven during the same period. The certification society has become a reality in much of the world (Collins 1979), and it is a highly legitimated reality as well as a source of legitimacy itself. All sorts of life chances are contingent on obtaining a higher education degree, and there is little contentiousness over occupational allocation based on educational certification (Brint 1998).

FIGURE 8.1

Growth of Tertiary Enrollment as a Proportion of the Twenty to Twenty-four Age Group:
Comparison of the Western and Non-West Countries (N=21 and 64)

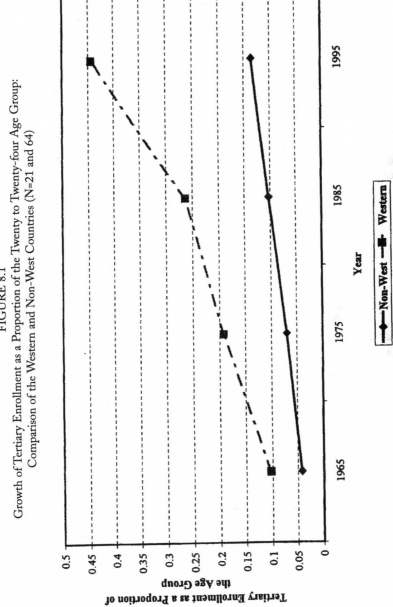

The broader context also reveals differences in the trajectories of different academic majors or fields of concentrations in higher education. Figure 8.2 reveals a pattern that shows growth in social science enrollments and decline in humanities enrollments as percentages of total tertiary enrollments. This pattern is strikingly similar for both the Western (N= 21) and non-Western countries (N= 64). The world context thus involves overall growth in enrollments, a general decline in what was once an elite humanities enclave, and the ascendancy of the social sciences. The latter includes business studies but also economics, sociology, political science, and a range of newer ventures such as women's studies (Drori and Moon 2006; see also Frank and Gabler 2006 for similar trends regarding the faculty compositions of universities; their study shows the relative ascendance of the social sciences and the relative demise of the humanities faculty).

The ascendancy of the social sciences and of new university subjects in general constitutes curricular innovation that more readily takes place in universities and academic systems that are more open or more vulnerable to external social influences. Focusing on university industry ties some writers (from Veblen to Slaughter) have critically noted the expanded role and influence of business in higher education in the United States. American universities, I contend, are and always have been more open to all sorts of social influences, including business but also ethnic and religious groups, local associations, foundations, and more recently, new advocacy groups such as racial minorities, women, environmentalists, and so on. This greater openness leads to earlier curricula innovations as regards not only business subjects but also engineering, the social sciences, computer science, ethnic studies, women's studies, and ecological studies, for example. The recent rise of enrollments in interdisciplinary studies illustrates the permeable character of university curricula in the United States (Brint 2002).

The crucial dimension is university openness to all nonstate influences, not just the degree of business influence over the universities. The important question is whether universities are primarily embedded in society or buffered from it. Both Ben-David and Zloczower (1962) and Flexner (1930) recognize the socially embedded character of American universities relative to their more socially buffered European (and especially German) counterparts. Both of their comparative assessments of universities go beyond the issue of who funds the university to also consider what constitutes valid university research, teaching, and other activities. European and American universities have historically differed not only with respect to who underwrote the research but also, even more fundamentally, on what constitutes a university and university-based knowledge (Stichweh 1999). Curricular and funding issues are thus both relevant in ascertaining which model of the university is in play. So too is the question of whether the public goals of universities are compatible with private funds and nonstate influences. Issues of organizational autonomy, disinterested scholarship, and public service also

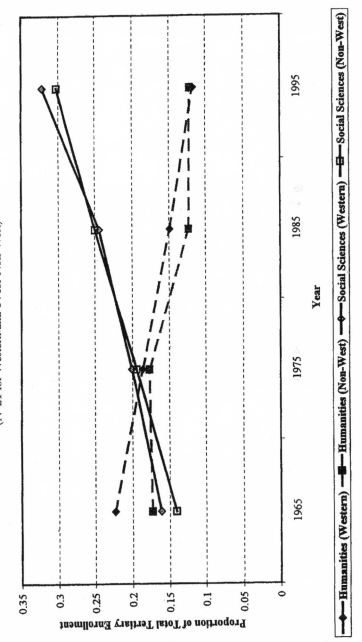

FIGURE 8.2
Disciplines' Share of Higher Education:
Humanities and Social Sciences as a Proportion of Total Tertiary Enrollment
(N=21 for Western and 64 for Non-West)

surface in debates on the character of the university and on educational innovations therein.

Many American universities, from public land grant universities to the private Stanford University, have a historical legacy of being heavily engaged in the business of society and its upgrading. On the contrary, with few exceptions, the older European universities were expected to be more distant from society and more linked to high centers of canonical knowledge and value, to the institutions of church and state, for instance.

Today, however, European universities increasingly hear and heed the transnational drummer that favors the socially embedded university and move in this direction as well. The declarations of twenty-nine European secretaries of education constitute the most recent embodiment of the transnational drummer. The Bologna Declaration called for more socially useful and inclusive universities, rather directly undercutting the socially buffered university model (Lenhardt 2002). But an enormous amount of prior discourse favoring the socially embedded and more open university has piled up in international organizations and conferences, the carriers of world models of progress and justice. Not surprisingly though, the defense of the socially buffered university often takes the form of protests against the Americanization associated with university changes (Weiler 2003). Even within the United States, though, critics of university/industry ties, a specific manifestation of the socially embedded university, have depicted these ties as a degenerative condition called "academic capitalism" (see Slaughter and Leslie 1997; Press and Washburn 2000).

From a world society perspective the rationalization of the university is the broader dynamic, which leads to both higher educational expansion as a desired goal and the socially embedded university as a preferred form. This is a rationalization that takes place at the world level reflecting the authority and influence of epistemic communities of educational and related expertise committed to progress and justice. From their perspective progress and justice require not just greater inclusiveness and expanded enrollments but also greater flexibility regarding the terms of inclusion. What gets taught and learned and what gets investigated should be mostly a matter of individual taste or personal choice rather than firmly anchored in canonical authority buttressed by faculty mandarins (Lenhardt 2003). Curricular innovations, whether approved or disapproved, are more likely when canonical authority declines or was never crystallized in the first place. Broader organizational innovations, whether approved or disapproved, are also more likely when universities are expected to be attuned to their environments and to their students.

Universities: Entrepreneurial and in Ruins?

Higher educational expansion is dramatically evident throughout the world. No salvation outside higher education is increasingly taken for granted in the

West. But the terms of inclusion or salvation are a tad more problematic. For some the ever-more flexible university envisioned by the socially embedded model of the university is an opportunity and potentially a great benefit (Clark 1993). For others this is a vacuous vision, and its triumph marks the demise of the university (Readings 1996). In what follows I briefly contrast the different lenses through which Clark and Readings assess the contemporary university. I do so to highlight differences in sensibilities to university character and change, sensibilities that I contend reflect differences in the historical legacies that informed American and Western European universities.

Both Clark and Readings share the premise that universities in the West increasingly face a problematic environment to which they may adjust by becoming more entrepreneurial. But they sharply differ in how they conceptualize the environment and the adjustment to it. The starting point for Clark is demise in government funding for universities, and the basic problem is how universities continue to be organizationally and fiscally viable. For Clark the university runs the risk of becoming irrelevant, if not obsolete, unless it can reconfigure itself to secure new and multiple sources of funding. With much American optimism, Clark describes the efforts of five European universities to reconfigure themselves. These efforts included revamping the curricula, identifying programs of interest to industry and to the broader community, obtaining multiple sources of funding, and becoming more efficient at managing resources. Clark asserts that all of this was achieved without compromising the academic heartland, and he concludes that these entrepreneurial universities experienced academic revitalization and a greater sense of organizational autonomy. Taken as a whole, the Clark thesis is a celebration of the university cum flexible and adaptive organization, a celebration much in line with the dominant administrative discourse in American universities today (Gumport 2000).

For Readings better management and more resources will not do the trick. That is because the university faces an institutional identity crisis, not solely an organizational survival one. His starting point is that economic globalization has made the nation-state and national culture irrelevant because all sort of activities are geared to and structured by the world market. This undercuts the university because its institutional mission is to preserve national culture. Minus an institutional mission, the centrality of national philosophy in Germany and national literature in England weakens as new subjects (communications, for example) flourish, and national identity becomes more tenuous. Minus an institutional mission, commitment to excellence in administration, counseling, development, and athletics are not much distinguished from commitment to excellence in scholarship and teaching, the core activities of the university qua institution.

To summarize, the problem for Clark is organizational viability, and his entrepreneurial socially embedded university is the answer. For Readings the problem is loss of institutional soul, and there really is no answer. One man's "entrepreneurial university" is the other's "university in ruins." Clark never explicitly acknowledges that his entrepreneurial university looks suspiciously American while Readings proceeds as if the American university could be viewed as European or English "lite." But American universities early on seem to have been less in awe of both "the university" and "canonical authority." The land grant universities introduced practical subjects with a more instrumental and service orientation. Even older and elitist American universities such as the University of Pennsylvania and Harvard played a role in legitimating graduate business education via MBA programs (Moon 2002). More recently universities such as Cornell were influential in promoting nonbusiness-related curricular innovations such as women's studies. The sharp dichotomy between university disciplines and more technical or applied subjects lasts longer in Western Europe, but here too the dividing line is getting blurred. Subjects once taught only in nonuniversity institutes now find their place within universities; note the rise of the study of business in a growing number of European countries.

To be sure, this is more evident in the newer universities, but as the next section will make clear, even venerable bastions of higher learning are not immune to change. The change results in fewer differences in curricular emphasis between older and newer universities as well as between more and less elite ones. The change also results in more similarities between universities situated within different nation-states, as national canons are weakened, and national practices are subjected to rationalization processes, for example, the call for greater transparency in how faculty manage their time, the assessment of student demands for courses, the quantification of research activities and scholarly output, competitive merit raises for faculty, and so on. However, as noted earlier, these increased similarities are more evident at the organizational level and less so with respect to institutionalized charters and identities. The expected differences should be more pronounced when focusing on more elite universities with more distinctive reputations.

From Oxford to Stanford

No two "world-class" universities would appear to look more different from each other than Oxford and Stanford. The former emerged in the twelfth century and is both blessed and burdened by the dignity bequeathed by antiquity; the latter is a late nineteenth-century innovation that barely has a historical legacy in comparison. Think Oxford, and one thinks of excellence in the study of the humanities, elite reproduction via strong links to the nobility and the clergy, public service and government funding, and highly autonomous colleges. Think Stanford, and one thinks of excellence in the study of the natural sciences and engineering, meritocracy, and career orientation, Silicon Valley, and strong university presidential leadership and strong alumni gift-giving ties to the university. Some of these thoughts correctly reflect on-going differences between these universities, but others are derived from a no longer warranted reputational lore. In what follows I first note some changes in the organization of Oxford, changes highlighted by Soares (1999). Next, I identify some crucial elements in the making of Stanford, elements emphasized by Lowen (1997). Last, I reflect on the influence of common models on what constitutes a university on common organizational outcomes, even as differences in historical legacies continue to influence sensibilities regarding, for example, university industry linkages in these two universities. These differences and commonalities invite this preliminary comparison.

Soares (1999) argues that there was a serious disconnect between the popular perception of Oxford as an unchanging and elitist bastion of humanities study and the ongoing modernization of Oxford. Furthermore he asserts that this popular perception was effectively exploited by the Thatcher administration in its attack on Oxford as an antiscience university allegedly responsible for England's industrial woes in the 1970s. Oxford, Soares concludes, was changing before Thatcher and changing to become less elitist and more science oriented.

Proof that Oxford was becoming less elitist is in part reflected in three trends:

1. The percent of Oxford and Cambridge students from hereditary aristocratic families declined from 50 percent before 1944 to 16 percent in the 1976–89.
2. Before World War II Oxford undergraduates were much more likely to have come from independent schools (62 percent) than from the state sector (19 percent). By 1990 parity has almost been achieved with students from independent schools constituting 48 percent and state schoolers 44.5 percent of Oxford undergraduates.
3. Shifting from class to gender as a stratificational principle, one finds that the composition of Oxford has changed in the direction of greater parity, with women moving from 18 percent in 1923 to 38 percent in 1990. By then end of the twentieth century more than four out of ten undergraduates at Oxford were women. Along class and gender lines Oxford admissions has become more egalitarian. (Soares 1999)

Oxford has also become less humanities centered, less a Republic of Letters. On this point the trends are clearly inconsistent with the popular perception, whether one thinks in terms of faculty composition or broad areas of study. Between 1923 and 1974, with respect to faculty, there are increases in both the science and technology faculty, from 27 to 43 percent and in the social studies one, from 3 to 19 percent. During the same period the humanities faculty is nearly cut in half, from 70 to 38 percent. Between 1923 and 1991 a very similar pattern is found when we look at what undergraduates choose to study or read: increases in the social studies (from 0 to 23 percent) and in science and technology (from 20 to 39 percent) and a sharp decline in humanities, from 80 to 38 percent. These trends are similar to the ones reported in figure 8.2; as the world turns, so does Oxford.

But the ascendancy of these fields at Oxford is not without critics, even among scientists. The nature of the criticism highlights distinctions and traditions, which in turn reveal a marked ambivalence about universities and their potential or actual links to industry. Writing in the *Oxford Magazine* (2001, 4) scientist R. J. P. Williams bluntly states:

> First, if I am right that the education of the student in physics and chemistry is now a matter of rote learning and not joint enquiry with a tutor, then the University should look at these sciences again. It should ask, "Are there no intellectual questions related to such science? How should the subject be taught? Should teaching be in an industrial context? The last used to be the area for the polytechnics. . . . There is a solution. We all accept that the University needs money if it is to carry out studies at an intellectual level in many areas. We must get the money ultimately from scientific research. Let us then set up university research centers dedicated to finding useful things and bringing in money, and separate workers in them from intellectual college teaching.

To save Oxford the proposal is to draw a sharp line between the technical work undertaken in medical and engineering laboratories, work possibly having utility and market value, from the authentic pursuit of knowledge for its own sake, work identified with the humanities but also with pure science. Writing in the twenty-first century, Mr. Williams recognizes that his views may mark him an intellectual snob. But his is not an idiosyncratic view in Oxbridge, and of course this is a view quite consistent with the German model of the university, or at least with that part of the model that reserves for the university the pursuit of fundamental knowledge and assumes its applications, if any, belong in some other highly differentiated institutes. The scientization of Oxford continues with more and more science lectures and science reading opportunities emerging. So too is there an increase in linkages with the world of industry and commerce; the Said Business School in Oxford is open for business.

Resistance to change at Oxford does not reactivate yesterday's dual admissions system—one for scholars and another for gentlemen. Resistance raises questions about institutional autonomy and disinterested scholarship and the degree to which an ascendant applied science undercut both. Resistance reaffirms an institutional charter designed to create national leaders without yesterday's class and gender biases. Resistance also counts on the saga of the tutorial as a value-laden pedagogical instrument. Resistance does not so much stop the organizational changes reflected in the several trends earlier identified as it raises questions about the institutional price paid for social embeddedness.

The Stanford experience radically differs from Oxford's. From its inception in the late nineteenth century, Stanford was in several respects a socially embedded university early on: coeducational, secular, research oriented, and with professional schools of engineering and education. Its founding charter called for service to the children of California, and service had an unashamedly practical tone. In her last address to the Board of Trustees in 1904 Jane Stanford proclaimed:

> Let us not be afraid to outgrow old thoughts and ways, and dare to think on new lines as to the future of the work under our care. Let us not be poor copies of other universities. Let us be progressive." (Cited in the Message from the President in the 2001 Annual Report of Stanford University)

This perspective was shared by the first president of the university, who insisted that undergraduates at Stanford would not be cloistered but instead would be exposed to the real world (Veysey 1965). In its first decades of existence the real world for Stanford was addressed by university presidents with backgrounds in engineering, geology, and medicine. This was a world where Stanford could not effectively compete with its more prestigious and better-funded neighbor, the University of California. This was also a world where Stanford was untouched by federal patronage and only lightly brushed by industry moneys.

Lowen (1997) describes and interprets the transformation of Stanford into a "world class" university with extensive public and private funding. The coming of World War II, and subsequently the Cold War, generated a federal government interest in university science and provided university administrators and scientists with patriotic grounds for forging university government ties. In the 1930s Stanford was more at ease with its modest courting of private support than with seeking federal grants. But from 1940 onward the formation and expansion of links with government and with industry would increasingly characterize Stanford and other major American universities. The influential Stanford provost, Frederick Terman, would refer to these ties as a "win-win-win" situation (Lowen 1997). The federal government interest would go beyond the natural sciences and their national defense applications to include the behavioral sciences and their ramifications. Securing funding for research across the university would become a way of life in American universities. It is now a commonplace for professors in many disciplines to cite their funded projects and their funding sources in their curriculum vita. The magnitude of the funding is optional.

Armed with multiple sources of funding the university is able to take care of those disciplines that are least likely to secure external funding. This is the standard response to the query, "But what about the humanities or the arts?" It is also the standard response to those who worry about undergraduate education and whether the teaching function of the university will be overshadowed by its research orientation (Cuban 1999). Moreover, if additional funds are required or sought, campaigns to raise the moneys are also not unusual. A five-year, billion-dollar campaign for undergraduate education at Stanford is well underway. The William and Flora Hewlett Foundation has given $100 million for this campaign and an additional $300 million to the School of Humanities and Sciences.

The standard response is not without critics. While multiple sources of funding may facilitate relative autonomy from any one source, the overall effect of extensive linkages with external funders has been criticized from both the left (Noble 1982) and the right (Nisbet 1971). However, Stanford and other universities are not deterred. There has been an increase in universities with research and development facilities, with patent offices, and with collaborations with industry in knowledge production and product development. The latter is more evident in the United States than in Europe (Powell and Owen-Smith 1998; Krucken 2003), and Stanford is clearly a leader in this development. The organizational changes that illustrate this development at Stanford do not encounter the sort of institutional resistance exhibited at Oxford. There is nothing in the Stanford charter (legally and symbolically) that gets undercut by these changes. There is nothing in the progress-oriented Stanford saga that appears to be out of sync with creating a multidisciplinary Bio-X research center with megabucks from private funds. The European distinction between clean public funds and dirty private monies fares poorly in the United States where private and public universities increasingly seek public and private funding.

HISTORICAL LEGACIES AND COMMON FRAMES

Oxford dons and Stanford experts are emblematic of different historical legacies and organizational developments. Oxford dons reflect an era in a country where the university was a very distinctive knowledge conservation institution, reserved for a few good men chartered to become national leaders. Stanford experts reflect the university as a more rationalized and less differentiated site of knowledge production in the current world. The distinction between knowledge conservation and production goals is a matter of degree, but it is an important distinction. The pristine Oxford saga, that threatened by the influence of the socially embedded university model, has student and tutor engaged in fundamental inquiry by confronting text, that is, by critically reading, thinking, and writing. The fashionable Stanford way is to generate research opportunities for undergraduates to upgrade their learning experiences. To be sure, the latter involves reading, thinking, and writing, but the goal is knowledge production via fieldwork, interviews, surveys, and the like. The knowledge production imagery has a closer fit to the socially embedded university, and the more socially buffered one is more likely to imagine itself as a conservatory of high knowledge.

The modernization of Oxford and the transformation of Stanford make both universities more organizationally similar to each other than they were before World War II. In both cases the threat of war and then war itself made the universities more relevant and gave the universities more opportunities to secure government and private funds. Both universities were in better financial shape by 1960 than beforehand. For Stanford the changes involved a reputational evolution from local to national to world renown, with the sciences and their applications leading the charge. A similar science-driven charge was underway at Oxford, but while Stanford did not have "Stanford" to contend with, Oxford had to deal with a world-renowned "Oxford." The ongoing tensions between organizational modernization and institutional tradition at Oxford do not have an obvious analog at Stanford.

But how should one explain the scientization of universities throughout much of the world? One answer focuses on economic globalization and its demands on all institutions, including universities. This perspective is incomplete and misleading. What has globalized are models of progress in which science and science for individual, organizational, and national development plays a major role. These models privilege a broader rationalization than that implied by most discussions of economic globalization. Under pressure to account for why they teach what they teach, universities undergo curricular changes to satisfy a range of constituencies. This opens the doors to business and engineering subjects but also to interdisciplinary innovations many steps removed from the world economy. The authority of science in society, independent of its impact on wealth creation or military capability, has become a strong rationalizing force in the university (see Drori et al. 2003). Many curricular innovations, educational research, and even teacher training, for example, invoke the authority of science to justify their place in the university. Furthermore, models of justice have also globalized, and these models emphasize equality and equality of opportunity for all individuals. The phenomenal growth of universities and university enrollments cannot be understood without coming to terms with how successful these models have been in their influence. They have led not only to changes in the social class and gender composition of universities but also to curricular changes. It will not do to vastly increase the numbers and the diversity of enrollees without altering what it means to be a university and what university knowledge can and/or cannot be. Much feminist criticism of the university and of science is ironically facilitated by increases in the numbers of women both in the university and in science enrollments therein (Bradley and Ramirez 1996; Ramirez and Wotipka 2001). Rationalized progress via science and rationalized justice via expanded inclusion undercut the mystique of the university.

More socially embedded universities have fewer mystiques to start with and are more likely to aggressively pursue progress. These universities are sanguine with respect to educational innovations, including the forging of university-industry ties: costs can be managed through conflict of interest guidelines, and the opportunities and benefits are limitless. On the contrary, the more socially buffered universities view these ties and many other educational innovations as problematic, even as they move in directions consistent with rationalized progress. Triumphant common frames of progress and justice inform common university models in an increasingly common world-certification society. Their successful articulation by an army of educational management consultants (progress) and by diverse social movements advocates (justice) accounts for why different universities move in similar organizational directions that could not be predicted by their varying institutional legacies. The latter are not irrelevant, though, as they help us understand persisting differences in sensibilities toward similar organizational developments. An optimistic "win-win-win" perspective makes educational innovation more sensible at Stanford; the celebration of "the home of lost causes" at Oxford promotes more pessimistic sensibilities.

To conclude, universities increasingly enact world models of the progressive and egalitarian university. This enactment leads to much organizational change that is difficult to comprehend, independent of the influence of these models and the epistemic communities that articulate and disseminate the blueprints for how to become a socially embedded university. As a result, one can discern cross-national changes in university organization in the direction of greater institutional isomorphism. Much of the ease or difficulty with which change is embraced requires coming to terms with varying legacies. Change is more difficult in academic systems and in universities, which adhered to the socially buffered university model. Absent a sharp reversal of world ideological forces, though, universities will change and change in the direction of becoming more socially useful, organizationally flexible, and broadly inclusive.

REFERENCES

Ben-David, Joseph, and Abraham Zloczower. 1962. Universities and academic systems in modern societies. *European Journal of Sociology* 3: 45–85.

Bradley, Karen, and Francisco O. Ramirez. 1996. World polity and gender parity: Women's share of higher education, 1965–1985. *Research in Sociology of Education and Socialization* 11: 63–91.

Brint, Steven. 1998. *Schools and societies.* Thousand Oaks, CA: Pine Forge.

——. 2002. The rise of the "practical arts." In *The future of the city of intellect: The changing American university*, ed. Steven Brint, 231–59. Stanford, CA: Stanford University Press.

Chabbott, Colette. 2003. *Constructing education for development: International organizations and education for all.* London: Routledge Falmer.

Chabbott, Colete, and Francisco O. Ramirez. 2000. Development and education. In *Handbook of the sociology of education*, ed. Maureen Hallinan, 163–87. New York: Klewer/Plenum.

Clark, Burton. 1993. *Creating entrepreneurial universities: Organizational pathways of transformation.* Surrey: Pergamon.

Collins, Randall. 1979. *The credential society.* New York: Academic.

Cuban, Larry. 1999. *How scholars trumped teachers: Change without reform in university curriculum, teaching, and research, 1890–1990.* New York: Teachers College Press.

Drori, Gili, John W. Meyer, Francisco O. Ramirez, and Evan Schofer. 2003. *Science in the modern world polity: Institutionalization and globalization.* Stanford, CA: Stanford University Press.

Drori, Gili, and Hyeyoung Moon. 2006. The changing nature of tertiary education: Neo-institutional perspective on cross-national trends in disciplinary enrollment, 1965–1995. In *The impact of comparative education research on institutional theory*, ed. David Baker and Alexander Wiseman, vol. 7, International Perspectives on Education and Society. Amsterdam: Elsevier Press.

Flexner, Abraham. 1930. *Universities: American, English, German.* New York: Oxford University Press.

Frank, John David, and Jay Gabler. 2006. Reconstructing the university: Worldwide changes in academic emphases over the 20th century. Stanford: Stanford University Press.

Frank, John David, Suk-Ying Wong, John W. Meyer, and Francisco O. Ramirez. 2000. What counts as history: A cross-national and longitudinal study of university curricula. *Comparative Education Review* 44: 29–53.

Gumport, Patricia. 2000. Academic restructuring organizational change and institutional imperatives. *Higher Education* 39: 67–91.

Krucken, Georg. 2003. Learning the "new, new thing": On the role of path dependency in university structures. *Higher Education* 46: 315–39.

Lenhardt, Gero. 2003. European higher education between universalization and materialist particularism. *European Educational Research Journal* 1(3): 274–89.

Lowen, Rebecca S. 1997. *Creating the cold war university: The transformation of Stanford.* Berkeley: University of California Press.

Meyer, John, John Boli, George Thomas, and Francisco O. Ramirez. 1997. World society and the nation-state. *American Journal of Sociology* 1: 144–81.

Meyer, John W., David Kamens, and Aaron Benavot. 1992. *School knowledge for the masses.* London: Falmer.

Meyer, John, and Francisco O. Ramirez. 2000. The world institutionalization of education. In *Discourse Formation in Comparative Education*, ed. Juergen Schriewer, 111–32.

Meyer, John, Francisco O. Ramirez, Richard Rubinson, and John Boli. 1977. The world educational revolution, 1955–1970. *Sociology of Education* 50: 242–58.

Moon, Hyeyoung. 2002. The globalization of professional management education, 1881–2000: Its rise, expansion, and implications. Doctoral dissertation, Department of Sociology, Stanford University.

Nisbet, Robert. 1971. *The degradation of the American dogma: The university of America*, 1945–1970. Piscataway, NJ: Transaction.

Noble, Daniel. 1982. The selling of the university: MIT-Whitehead merger. *Nation* 234/5: 129 (February).

Powell, Walter, and Jason Owen-Smith. 1998. Universities and the market for intellectual property. *Journal of Policy Analysis and Management* 17(2): 253–77.

Press, Eyal, and Jennifer Washburn. 2000. The kept university. *Atlantic Monthly* 285 (3): 39–54.

Ramirez, Francisco O. 1997. The nation-state, citizenship, and educational change: Institutionalization and globalization. In *International handbook of education and development: Preparing schools, students, and nations for the twenty-first century*, ed. William Cummings and Noel McGinn, 47–62. New York: Garland.

———. 2003. Toward a cultural anthropology of the world? In *Local meanings/global culture: Anthropology and world culture theory*, ed. Kathryn Anderson-Levitt, 239–54. New York: Palgrave.

Ramirez, Francisco O., and Marc Ventresca. 1992. Institutionalizing mass schooling in the modern world. In *The political construction of education: School expansion, the state, and economic change*, ed. Bruce Fuller and Richard Rubinson, 47–60. Westport, CT: Praeger.

Ramirez, Francisco O., and Christine Min Wotipka. 2001. Slowly but surely? The global expansion of women's share of science and engineering fields of study. *Sociology of Education* 74: 231–51.

Readings, Bill. 1996. *The university in ruins*. Cambridge, MA: Harvard University Press.

Riddle, Phyllis. 1989. University and state: Political competition and the rise of universities, 1200–1985. Doctoral dissertation, Department of Sociology, Stanford University.

Shils, Edward. 1971. No salvation outside higher education. *Minerva* 6 (July). 313–21.

Slaughter, Sheila, and Larry Leslie. 1997. *Academic capitalism: Politics, policies, and the entrepreneurial university*. Baltimore: Johns Hopkins.

Soares, Joseph. 1999. *The decline of privilege: The modernization of Oxford University*. Stanford, CA: Stanford University Press.

Stichweh, Richard. 1999. The form of the university. In *Problems of form*, ed. Dirk Baecker, 121–41. Stanford, CA: Stanford University Press.

Stinchcombe, Arthur. 1965. Social structure and organizations. In *Handbook of organizations*, ed. James G. March, 153–93. Chicago: Rand McNally.

Veysey, Lawrence. 1965. *The emergence of the American university*. Chicago: University of Chicago Press.

Weiler, Hans. 2003. Ambivalence and the politics of knowledge: The struggle for change in German higher education. Paper presented at SCANCOR Conference on Universities and the Production of Knowledge. Stanford: Stanford University.

Williams, R. J. P. 2001. Science in the university. *Oxford Magazine* 186: 1–4.

NINE

How Private
Higher Education's Growth
Challenges the
New Institutionalism

DANIEL C. LEVY

ISSUES AND APPROACH

THE "NEW INSTITUTIONALISM" emphasizes and explains the growing and "startling homogeneity of organizational forms and practices" (DiMaggio and Powell 1983, 148). With a following beyond sociology alone, this literature additionally highlights organizations' routine, repetitive, habitual, and unreflective behavior (DiMaggio and Powell 1991, 8–14). It emphasizes how constraints, rules, and norms condition action and contribute to the emulation of established institutions. It argues that such reality cannot be understood according to traditional concepts of purposeful, utilitarian, technically functional, rational action in a context of free choice for diverse organizations operating in a competitive marketplace.

But concepts of diversity and rationality loom large in the expanding literature on private higher education's growth and functioning.[1] We thus confront a contrast between that literature's emphasis on "technical rationality" and the new institutionalism's emphasis on "institutional rationality."[2] Yet more fundamental to our analysis is the contrast between the new institutionalism's emphasis on *isomorphism* and convergence that yields similarities among entities and the private higher education literature's depiction of ample and expanding diversity. In our usage, diversity means interinstitutional differences so that institutions are at least partly distinctive from other institutions. The distinctiveness is wide-ranging, involving missions, size, funding sources, sponsors, governance, curriculum scope and content, and so forth. (Such distinctiveness does not preclude similarities among many organizations on certain organizational characteristics, which may lead to viable conceptions of "subsectors.") Examples of this kind of diversity emerge throughout this chapter as we juxtapose the contrasting portraits of diversity—mostly linked to technical rationality—and isomorphism—mostly linked to institutional rationality.

Of course, no quick summary does justice to the new institutionalism. That literature stresses what it claims has hitherto been missed and does not deny the existence of diversity or technical rationality. Furthermore, the years since its initial formulation have seen clarifications against exaggeration, especially of limited technical rationality.

This chapter's theme is that the new institutionalism does not prepare us for the organizational distinctiveness brought on by the sharp growth of private higher education. Additionally, the growth of private higher education is linked to technically rational competition. More broadly and speculatively, the new institutionalism may likewise need modification in the face of the robust and multifaceted modern privatization and associated rationalization that contributes to considerable institutional diversification in fields beyond higher education alone.

The theme here is not that the new institutionalism is "wrong" or even inapplicable to the private higher education literature. On the contrary, a related piece (Levy 1999) shows where the new institutionalism can *help* the private higher education literature identify the isomorphism it has both underestimated and failed to explore in broad or conceptual terms, including intersectoral and intrasectoral similarities.[3] In this chapter, however, we will see that where the new institutionalism comes up short, it is less because its logic is flawed than because it misses on the empirical side. Further, the new institutionalism predicts the intensification of certain tendencies quite at odds with those that have become strong in fact, such as privatization as opposed to extension of the state. In some instances, then, a revised reading of empirical tendencies allows us to use a revised new institutionalism, rather than reject it wholesale, to predict and understand diversity as well as technically rational forces behind it.

Exploration of the variable balance between isomorphic and diversifying forces obviously will remain a major item for an ongoing research agenda. This chapter does not identify an exact balance at work in private higher education but rather tries to show and understand the limitations of isomorphic forces (and related aspects of the new institutionalism). Moreover, to make the empirical material manageable, the paper limits its foci. First, geographically, three countries get repeated attention: Argentina, China, and Hungary. Each reveals numerous characteristics typical of many countries in its region, including private growth.[4] I also draw on other countries, admittedly more to illustrate points than to build in this one chapter an empirical base that proves the points. Second, I focus on two landmark and much-cited sociological works: DiMaggio and Powell (1983) on isomorphism, supplemented by their edited book (Powell and DiMaggio 1991), which includes their own overview of the new institutionalism (DiMaggio and Powell 1991). Third, the focus is intersectoral, contrasting the private nonprofit sector and the public sector. This means that much of the chapter's attention to distinctiveness concerns private versus public sectors, with related references to the diversity among private institutions (linked often to competition and the sector's lack of a central governing authority). In any event, attention to fast-growing for-profit-sector higher education would challenge the new institutionalism further.[5]

ISOMORPHISM'S TENETS VERSUS
THE PRIVATE HIGHER EDUCATION CASES

The key tenets about isomorphism in the new institutionalism appear within three categories (DiMaggio and Powell 1983, 150–56): coercive, mimetic, and normative. We collapse them into essentially coercive and noncoercive categories (Levy 1999). Coercive forces are largely imposed by actors or forces from outside the organization, whereas other forces involve more voluntary action by the organizations.

The chief coercive force in the new institutionalism is the state. A common legal environment is imposed by the state and a singular financial source, with conditions attached, likewise generally refers to the state. Additionally prominent is imposition by a field's dominant organizations. For higher education this usually means venerable public universities. Their ability to set rules often involves their working through the state.

At the same time, the power of dominant organizations also manifests itself noncoercively as they set the course that other organizations seek or at least claim to copy. Mimetic isomorphism comes as organizations try to minimize uncertainty, especially where their goals are ambiguous, and to legitimize themselves, especially by emulating well-established and (at least in that sense) successful organizations. Normative isomorphism comes mostly from professionalism. Mimetic isomorphism occurs when actors are otherwise unclear on what to do and therefore copy successful organizations, whereas normative isomorphism arises where professionals or others feel capable of mapping their own policy but do so based on their socialization to dominant norms.[6]

Two observations are pertinent about the limited literature specifically considering the new institutionalism and higher education. First, the new institutionalism has drawn less from higher than from primary and secondary education (and until recently none of the education literature on institutionalism drew much upon private education at any level). Second, higher education works that do consider the new institutionalist tenets tend to portray a fit.[7] Yet this contrasts to how the wider higher education literature sees diversity, as ample or expanding or both.[8] (The Ramirez chapter in this volume points to and explains a mix of commonality and diversity.)

In any event, the heralded concept of 'isomorphism' does not prepare us for an increasingly important chunk of higher education, for the burst of distinctive private higher education growth in many nations since the 1980s (Altbach 1999; Levy 2002b; Levy 1986). Consider, for example, the case of China. Since 1982, after three decades without private higher education, China has had a policy of what we might call "one nation, two sectors." Immediately, more than 100 private institutions emerged, and by 2001 there were 1,291 privates. Both the enrollment growth and the number of organizations here challenge the new institutionalism's imagery of isomorphism. Moreover, certain institutions have achieved economic and social importance, some even attaining academic prominence, unusual for the world's new private higher education institutions (Levy 2002a). Successes include attracting students who have other options and luring professors from estimable public places (Law 1995, 332). China is further representative of a set of Asian countries where private enrollments are still modest compared with many regional counterparts but growing quickly. China's private sector reached 12.4 percent of total postsecondary enrollments by 2001. If we look at the figure for just bachelor and subbachelor levels, without including self-study programs (in which students prepare to take the national examination) and jointly run private-public programs, the figure would be only 1.6 percent in 2001, up from 0.2 percent in 1996.[9] By the number of institutions, the public/private ratio shrunk to 1.5:1 by 2001 from 1.9:1 in 1996, due to both private creation and the merging of public institutions.

Hungary is a second case. Hungary's private surge started a bit later, with the fall of communism. Unlike China, however, some private (religious) institutions survived through the Communist era, though with coercive constraints that limited organizational distinctiveness and with church ownership limited de facto to religious pursuits (Nagy-Darvas and Darvas 1999, 173). By 2001, the private sector would account for 15 percent of enrollments and 54 percent of the country's institutions, not including foreign-accredited institutions, such as the Soros-funded Central European University, that add further diversity. Most of the private institutions, including the few private universities, are religious, but the most remarkable enrollment surge has come in the brand new secular "foundation" colleges. They account for the easy majority of new private enrollment.[10] The government has expressed interest in an increased college/university ratio, linked to foundation growth. Already this growth has shown robustness on measures such as job market ties and distinctiveness from public higher education, notwithstanding regulatory constraints. All these points about private distinctiveness appear to be common in the region, beyond just Hungary.

Argentina is our third case. Argentina's private sector dates from 1959, but a recent surge is reflected in figures on organizational birth. After fifteen institutions gained state recognition by 1973, the state generally denied further institutions for a decade and half. But under the Carlos Menem administration (starting in 1989) and its broad policies of international opening, deregulation, and privatization, the number of recognized private institutions quickly doubled. From 1990 to 1994, while the system's total enrollments fell, private enrollments increased by 30 percent (Durham and Sampaio 2000, 24), growing even during the lean years for private institutional birth. A country that had long lagged sister republics in its private/total proportion would by 1994, at 25 percent private, lie close to the Spanish American norm (Levy 1986, 4–5; García Guadilla 1996, 270, 264). In 2000 fifty-two of ninety-three universities were private (including "institutos universitarios," offering only one field of study). For both universities and all higher education, we again see the tendency for privates to be proportionally larger in number of organizations than in number of enrollments, and the number of private institutions more than doubled in the 1990s. And again the private share is striking on the nonuniversity side, 41 percent versus 20 percent of total higher education enrollments. Argentina ("even Argentina," given the country's European traditions and bias for institutional standardization), illustrates the strong Latin American private growth and diversification.

The rest of this chapter fleshes out and interprets such facts against the institutionalist framework. The facts are intended to indicate how the coercive and noncoercive tenets of isomorphism come up short against the private higher education literature's intersectoral evidence.

COERCIVE ISOMORPHISM: BROAD CHANGES

By the new institutionalism, private institutions might come under strong state influence, limiting pluralism in goals and behavior and indeed nearly all aspects of diversity across institutions. But the present private surge represents an important proportional decrease in state activity and control, a fundamental reversal from the postwar decades in our three countries and most others as well. The state rollback in finance is clearer still, but we lack the space to develop it.[11] The broad changes we refer to are manifest in most of both the developing and the developed worlds, under democratic and undemocratic regimes, though of course to varying extents (with more or less aggressive reform agendas and degrees of implementation), and from different starting points.

The new private surge in higher education is hardly isolated. It should be seen in connection with the broad international "crisis of the welfare state" and the shift from state to private or mixed private-public forms, including non-profit private activity (Salamon 1995, 255–56). Much of this push has come "from below," from grassroots movements in the case of NGOs and a huge demand from students, families, businesses, and other actors in the case of higher education; the multiplicity of sources and groups in turn contributes to the diversity across new institutions and certainly to private differences from public-sector norms. Much of the push is part of a blossoming of society, limiting or altering the state, and an organizational response to rather uncontrolled, competitive, and fundamentally rational demands emanating outside the state. In dramatic cases, as with private research organizations that assumed great importance under Latin American military rule, this blossoming was antistate in pointed ways (Levy 1996).

Yet a paradox is that more often the state welcomes and sometimes even promotes the private surge, which reverses traditional statist ideology and behavior. Nearly worldwide, after all, official doctrine is now to seek a slimmer state that gets more fit by getting less fat. The new institutionalism prepares us for public higher education's resistance to the private surge, but it hardly prepares us for either the surge itself or for the state's acquiescence or even championing of it. As we look more closely at our higher education cases we should keep in mind that they fit broader political economic patterns involving shrinking states, privatization, and a heightened emphasis on markets and competition.

Cases

China has for years officially encouraged private higher education development. A further stride comes with 2002 legislation, putting private higher education on a more solid legal footing and in a positive context. Explicit reasons include increased access and also increased competition as an engine to enhanced academic and economic performance. Indeed one is struck by how openly and strongly many East Asian states, democratic and not, favor private growth, more recently joined by several Middle Eastern states. Owing to different political crosscurrents, at least in the earlier decades in which Latin American private growth took off, states there were generally more circumspect in declarations and policy even once they came to welcome the privatization. There too, however, one notes change, as when Argentine officials now participate in inaugural ceremonies at private institutions. Finally, the Hungarian case highlights a qualification valid in all three cases: state officials have been divided on privatization, pro, con, or rather indifferent. There are also shifts over even short time periods. It may well be that Hungary in the mid-1990s, pushed by the World Bank, was keener on deregulation than it is now (Ministry of Culture and Education 1996). But the promoting forces usually have the upper hand, albeit more clearly in Asia than in Eastern and Central Europe. Education ministries tend to display more reluctance while finance ministries, which have the strongest international ties and have gained power, promote privatization.[12] Again we see a common general force internationally, with variation by nation and region.

Whereas the new institutionalism stresses a common and broadening legal framework, a different picture results from both the significantly lesser state controls applied to the private sector (than to the public sector) and from deregulation. Even where the new institutionalists note deregulation (Powell 1991, 200), they do not depict it as a major empirical trend. Internationally, common system-wide legal frameworks have often been limited or shrinking for private higher education, though delayed regulations and accreditation systems sometimes cut the other way.[13] Countries that lack pluralist and market traditions (and of course realities) tend to have heavier state rules or regulations than other countries do. This marks "path dependencies," fitting the idea in Ramirez's chapter in this volume of nationally varied responses to a global tendency. But change is remarkable even where statism has been prominent. With Ramirez, then, we can see broad international tendencies having both common and varying impacts in different places with different starting points, so that the international tendencies do not produce homogenizing convergence.

Through its forty-four-year history, Argentine private higher education has had for the most part greater autonomy than its public counterpart from the state legal environment (though not over some aspects of curriculum and program). Under periods of repressive military rule initiated in 1966 and then again in 1976, though controls over privates increased, the private-public gap was such that private institutions could hire professors purged from public ones (Levy 1986, 239–40). Such private-public gaps show diversity across at least certain institutions within a system.

Recent work shows a common sequence for new or quickly expanding and transforming private sectors (Levy 2002b). They spring up in unanticipated form, often with a distinctiveness from prior public or even private institutions that stuns many and appalls some. They often arise amid a legal vacuum, neither precisely forbidden nor monitored. Such surprise emergence is quite at odds with tenets of the new institutionalism. Only subsequently does the state perhaps compose a clearer legal and policy framework. Sometimes, as in China, this is mostly to facilitate the private growth—including distinctive growth. Sometimes, as in Hungary and other East European countries, the framework is more reflective of coercive isomorphism (largely from public university pressure), though even there we must note both the legacy of limited to negligible regulation and the persistence of intersectoral differences rather than a common legal framework, as with private freedom from laws on public employees.[14]

Whether or not it occurs alongside some increased regulation, deregulation also occurs even in countries that lack legacies of heavy regulation. Like Mexico, Argentina increases the instances in which private institutions can earn their way to a formal autonomous status. This then allows greater latitude for organizational diversity. Also, where states promote a "private is beautiful" ideology, private higher education sees less need to sacrifice autonomy for state regulations that affirm they are not "too different" from traditional public norms.

Furthermore, even where rules protecting existing public university forms from private (or novel public) university alternatives sustain homogeneity within the university terrain, they may nonetheless fuel diversification. This occurs as alternatives, including private ones, arise in *non*university quarters. Hungary's foundation colleges are examples, as are Argentina's short-cycle private higher education institutions (Balán 1990, 16) and some of its specialized institutions, including an array of research centers. Very few of China's private institutions are universities. Only about 3 percent of private institutions can offer their own degrees. Government makes it difficult for many institutions to be called "educational" as opposed to merely "training," and it confines many institutions to specialized vocational rather than academic status. However, as all these forms bloom there is increasing diversity. Again, many countries beyond the three discussed show a preponderance of private organizations in the college as opposed to university domain (Chile, India, Israel, Japan, the Philippines, South Africa). Thus, insistence on university homogeneity, consistent with the new institutionalism, does not preclude an impact of increased diversity for higher education overall.

To be sure, there is generally some encompassing legal framework for the whole higher education system and in certain instances some specifically for the entire private sector. But deregulation in higher education often reduces standard rules while allowing, even encouraging, diverse practices beyond those rules (Neave 1996, 38). Moreover, it is not too much to assert that the main legal "framework" for most private institutions in many countries does not reach much beyond the individual institution itself, which at least allows great diversity among institutions as well as between the private and public sectors. Regarding public law, private institutions tend to have ample autonomy de jure or de facto or both. This usually goes along with centralized governance *within* the institution, with a degree of hierarchy and administrative control that contrasts with public-sector norms, and the norms of the academic profession, and allows individual institutions to set their own distinctive governance profiles (Levy 1992).

The most remarkable of our three cases regarding the autonomy of private institutions is China, given that the Chinese state remains controlling and repressive in so many ways. Again a pattern (e.g., private autonomy) is widespread even though the degree and form vary (e.g., by type of state). Though Chinese private institutions must conform to certain state and local laws and policies, including on minimum size, qualifications of faculty and administrators, facilities, nonprofit status (for the "educational" rather than the "training" institutions), limited foreign ownership, and avoidance of "feudalistic and superstitious activities," they have had the "autonomy to define their own aims, mechanisms and management models" as well as to appoint their personnel (Law 1995, 341; Pan and Wei 1995, 9). Reasonable observers could even argue that regulation of privates has been inadequate (Mok 1997, 275).

In short, whereas DiMaggio and Powell (1983) first wrote at a time when the state had gained enormous power over decades, we live in an era of a shrinking state in certain key aspects of many social fields, with ramifications for state legal and regulatory frameworks (as well as state finance and the dominance of established public organizations). The logic of the new institutionalism, but not the empirical trends it perceived, could thus be reconciled with rising organizational diversity. Similarly, the significant trend from state to market dynamics, a theme in higher education the world over, runs counter to the new institutionalism's depiction of isomorphism through limited technical rationality.

EXAGGERATING NONCOERCIVE ISOMORPHISM: DIMINISHED GOAL DOMINANCE

As on the coercive side, so on the noncoercive side, it is not the logic of the new institutionalism so much as its applicability to the modern context that appears tenuous. Though the new institutionalism works well to help us understand the mimetic and normative isomorphism that does appear between private and public higher education, it falls short for the astonishing growth of private higher education in organizations quite distinct from preexisting public ones. The discussion here centers on goals, with some attention to the interrelated concept of legitimacy.[15]

The new institutionalism astutely shows why isomorphism is often enhanced where goals are ambiguous, as emulation of accepted organizations promotes the legitimacy of the copiers, and where technologies are uncertain, as organizations seek safety (DiMaggio and Powell 1983, 153). Moreover, both ambiguity and uncertain technologies are often associated with both higher education institutions and nonprofit organizations.

We might suggest a countertendency. The new institutionalism seems to assume an essential commonality of goals even where goals are ambiguous. Yet the private higher education literature shows how diverse the goals of various actors and thus organizations can be—and perhaps how uncertainty allows room to defy what has typically been done, since what has typically been done is not clearly the best formula. (This ties to legitimacy since the lack of a clear public-centered source of legitimacy undermines a sense that one packet of goals and practices from that source is the prescribed packet.)

Indeed, private institutions often arise or grow because the public sector is unwilling or slow to recognize the multiple forms of legitimacy available in the environment and the new higher education goals they allow. A key example is where public universities insist on traditional academic standards while privates respond to growing belief in efficient passage into the invigorated market economy. Thus, students seeking an English-language preparation for quick insertion to an internationalizing business arena flock to private higher education institutions in Azerbaijan, Italy, Malaysia, and many other countries.

Alternative Goals

Although the state's central regulations and formal evaluation often claim to employ a singular notion of higher education's proper goal as attainment of the highest levels of academic standing (with the most intellectually adept professors and students, disciplines, methodologies, and so forth), multiple actors have de facto pursued different notions of legitimate goals and views of what is worthwhile. Moreover, as opposed to a new institutionalist notion of minimizing risk by copying the most successful institutions on the academic gold standard, they have undertaken the risks of innovation. Partly they do so out of a realization that they could not perform well on the gold standard anyway. The great majority of Hungary's private institutions, like others in the region, are viewed as nowhere near competing with public universities in institutional stature (Giesecke 1999).

Additionally, many private institutions have a rational investment strategy that pursuit of tasks not well recognized as legitimate by the most established universities or sometimes by the state can produce tangible results and, ultimately, new forms of legitimacy. Chinese private higher education's pursuit of goals has over time gained surer legitimacy. Private Thai institutions that were regarded with great suspicion and even treated as criminal have attracted students and gained legitimacy over time (Kulachol 1995, 113). A similar trajectory is clear in any country where students flock to private institutions that lack full legal or degree-granting status. The trajectory emerges in the majority of cases where students go to private institutions, for the privates lack the traditional legitimacy of the oldest public universities and specialize in the pursuit of largely different studies and goals.

Thus, the most legitimate goals within one sector of a population of organizations may not be enshrined in another sector. Private-sector heterogeneity of goals is one of many points about subsectoral diversity.[16] Additionally, the private sector's responsiveness to multiple goals and views of legitimacy, when it captures demand, places graduates in jobs and attains other successes, often unleashes a competitive dynamic that leads to some organizational diversification of goals and valued pursuits within the public sector as well.

Where private institutions have pursued goals other than the most touted academic ones, they have generally moved away from another central concept of the new institutionalism: professionalism. With only limited exceptions outside the United States, private higher education institutions have usually had a significantly lower percentage of full-time faculty and students than have their public counterparts, particularly their oldest public counterparts. Though this is typically evaluated as a shortcoming, it is often programmatically reasonable, as well as economically rational, for the different and multiple goals of the new private institutions. Hungary's Gabor Denes, like China's Zhitong University, is largely a distance education institution with very few full-time staff. But the specific point about part-timers and the general point about professionalism hold for the great majority of private institutions in those two countries, Argentina, and beyond.[17] So while the new institutionalist hypothesis that greater professionalism makes for greater isomorphism is sound, the applicability even to such a seemingly quintessentially professional field as higher education can easily be exaggerated. Surging privatization signals declining coverage by professional norms.

Among the new private sectors' many and diverse goals other than traditional academic legitimacy and professionalism are profit (legally declared and distributed or not) and a rising ethnic or religious identification that is not only plural but often a balkanizing counterpoint to the homogenizing national identity usually championed by the venerable public universities. But we focus here on the goal of efficient placement of graduates into the job market as the most general private higher educational goal, whether for elite or quite academically undistinguished institutions, often with a claim of out-competing public counterparts on this score—and with a marked hue of reflective, calculated, utilitarian, technically efficient pursuits by both individuals and organizations (demanding and supplying this higher education). Commercial private higher education may often be more isomorphic to businesses (see also Bernasconi in this volume) than to public universities.

Hungary's foundation colleges (which would have grown faster were there fewer public regulations inhibiting responsiveness to the job market) are much quicker than public counterparts into fields linked to the post-Communist economy, great demand, and high salaries. These include management, business administration, advertising, economics, informatics, tourism, and some areas of law, a pattern found also for neighboring Romania and most of Eastern Europe, with similar implications about the rationality of a plunge into waters where demand is high and supply lags (Nagy-Darvas and Darvas

1999, 170; Eisemon et al. 1995, 141). Chinese privates also respond in an economically rational way, in similar fields, to a new market economy. Zhou (1995, 16–17) points out that these fields are all "highly practical," and the demand exceeds the supply of personnel. Yin and White (1994, 217, 226) emphasize the "spontaneous response by institutions to an increasingly commercialized economic environment" and the great variety of new partnerships with industry. Yanjing Huaqiao University illustrates the move into international finance. Though the concentration of private over public institutions in these fields was established long ago in Argentina, in the 1990s the country's new economy of privatization, deregulation, and international openness led to a reinvigoration in business-related fields (Levy 1986, 260–63; García de Fanelli 1997, 31). But the evidence on such field concentrations comes from private sectors globally, including relative latecomers to private higher education, Africa and Australia (Sawyerr 2002; Marginson 1997).

The fields of study that predominate in private higher education and are intertwined with its heavy emphasis on employment goals, crucial to its legitimacy, are part of an international trend immersing higher education in various marketplaces. (In terms of Ramirez's chapter, this shows how higher education is increasingly "embedded.") In a sharp break from isomorphic tenets, we move further from situations linked to an institutionalism where organizations can simply copy and otherwise minimize evaluation and competition based on technical efficiency (Meyer and Rowan 1991). "Performance conditionality" becomes the name of the game (Neave 1996, 36–37), and this on balance moves systems more toward organizational diversity, including through privatization of various sorts. Both the diversification and the technically rational competitive forces that largely propel it clash substantially with what the new institutionalism would postulate for higher education.

CONCLUSION

This chapter has compared evidence on private higher education with the new institutionalism's tenets, and it has identified where the new institutionalism might be amended. Had space allowed, additional sectoral perspectives would reinforce the case. For example, the new institutionalism expects increasing isomorphism within fields as they age, but fresh private sectors and subsectors bring something new within fields, and they bring plural environments (rather than merely a common one). Intrasectoral diversification is ample on the private side.[18]

We are far from asserting that the new institutionalism is impoverished overall or irrelevant for the case of private higher education internationally. On the contrary, the new institutionalism can help us appreciate the isomorphism that is truly associated with higher education privatization (Levy 1999). More broadly, the worthy task in analyzing sets of organizations is not usually to establish that there is basically isomorphism *or* diversity but to identify and understand where, why, and how each is at play. The present piece raises concerns that may warrant modifications of the new institutionalism. In some ways, the modifications limit the new institutionalism, yet in other ways they could enlarge its appropriate applicability.

The most basic concern raised in this chapter is the limited force and reach of isomorphism. Related to that is the presence of ample technical, competitive rationality. The new institutionalism does not prepare us for such a picture. Instead, Bernasconi's chapter in this volume is consistent with our generalizations about rationality.[19]

More generally still, though tentatively because we have examined just one field, we see reason to expect echoes in other subject matter. Isomorphism may be frequently and increasingly weaker than the new institutionalism suggests. Like other useful and novel academic movements, the new institutionalism may have initially over-corrected, in this case against views of diversity and technical rationality in both organizational sociology and economics. Additionally, however, the new institutionalism has proven exaggerated or partly misleading because of the ways the world has been changing in recent decades. Multiple forms of privatization are at play, along with increased pressures for technical efficiency. The new institutionalism needs to come to grips with a modern reshaping of the forces that condition the organizational structure of fields. These include states, professions, and markets. We have seen how a revamped and diminished state, along with invigorated markets and limited professionalism, has contributed to increased organizational diversity linked to technical rationality.

Fields, at least wide and complex ones such as higher education, usually experience isomorphic and anti-isomorphic tendencies simultaneously. As with our focus on sectors, much depends on where we look. What is isomorphic to what? The literature generally assumes that organizations copy within a field or population (Haveman 1993), but an institution may be isomorphic to another institution, a subsector, a sector, private entities outside the field, a public entity other than the state, or an international pattern, any of which may be dominant or not. To be isomorphic to one or another of these entities may be to be quite distinctive from others.

In some circumstances the tools for modifying the new institutionalism may lie in organizational sociology that seemed somewhat outdated or exaggerated to those who formulated the new institutionalism. In other circumstances tools for understanding organizational diversification through technically rational competition appear to lie within the new institutionalism itself, but with a different view of which forces are ascendant.[20] Where the institutions, actors, roles, and structures are aligned and have the (growing) weight that the new institutionalism supposes, isomorphism through organizational rationality is indeed salient—but the alignment and weight are very much in question.

NOTES

This chapter originated as PROPHE (Program for Research on Private Higher Education) working paper no. 3, 2003, http://www.albany.edu/~prophe/.

1. For bibliographic and other information on private higher education, see the web site in the prior endnote.

2. So the ascendant organizational literature finds organizational rationality but rationality oriented to bolstering legitimacy, certainty, survival, power, and so forth.

3. Among other recent works exploring the juxtaposition of isomorphism and diversity involving private higher education, see Bernasconi in this volume, Suspitsin forthcoming, and Tomusk 2003.

4. In fact, most developing countries have seen more extensive private growth than have the three countries we discussed here. On Asia, Wongsothorn and Wang (1995a, 1995b); on Latin America, Levy (1986), Balán and Ana M. García de Fanelli (1993), Durham and Sampaio 2000.

5. Whereas the private higher education literature makes sectoral differences fundamental within "systems," the new institutionalism looks more at "fields," "populations," or "industries" (DiMaggio and Powell 1991, 9, 13–14). When it looks across sectors, it highlights similarities among organizations.

6. Internationalization can be invoked on both the coercive (e.g., strings attached to assistance) and noncoercive (e.g., imported norms) ends.

7. The Powell and DiMaggio volume includes one higher education piece (Brint and Karabel 1991), on community colleges, which notes gaps in the new institutionalism rather than doubts its basic tendencies. Perhaps the best-known book explicitly on U.S. higher education diversity is Birnbaum (1983), who finds a lack of diversification even in the great growth of the 1960s and 1970s. One work that directly challenges isomorphism is Kraatz and Zajac (1996) on curriculum changes.

8. Depiction of grand institutional diversity dominates the mainstream U.S. higher education literature, though the international stage is more complicated (Marginson and Considine 2000, 176). The sole international volume concerned with the theme of isomorphism versus diversity in higher education (Meek et al. 1996) produced mixed evidence (as does Ramirez's chapter in the present volume).

9. In fact, the 12.4 percent figure represents a fall from 16.2 percent in 1996 because the public sector has been growing more rapidly (62 percent in 1996–2001, compared to 17 percent for the privates). The publics' faster growth makes China unusual in comparative perspective, largely because its total enrollments had been so low and its recent enrollment growth has been so great. All figures for 2001 and 1996 are calculated from MOE data www.edu.cn/20011105/3008194.shtml; also see *Educational Statistics Yearbook of China* (1996–2001), Department of Development and Planning, Ministry of Education, PRC, People's Education Press. Earlier data come from Mok 1997 and Zhou 1995).

10. Galasi and Varga (2002); Nagy (1996). I also draw off my own World Bank consultancy in the country in 1996, specifically on public policy for private higher edu-

cation growth. Forty percent of Hungary's total higher education institutions are Catholic.

11. The new institutionalism's logic of isomorphism resulting from dependence on state funds is sensible. Empirically, however, the private surge involves institutions operating mostly on nonstate funds, and even public institutions are less state dependent than decades ago. Further, the private institutions seek private money in ways that reflect technical rationality and spur interorganizational diversity, as seen in our three countries (Balán 1990, 15–17; Min 1991; Nagy-Darvas and Darvas 1999, 176–78).

12. Thus, for example, Hungarian finance officials have feared measures that would undermine the private sector's financial autonomy. However, public universities often line up with those parts of the state that are unfriendly to fresh private distinctiveness.

13. Both Hungary's and Argentina's (www.coneau.gov.ar) accreditation agencies are for both the public and the private sectors, exerting some isomorphic force.

14. Nagy and Darvas (1999, 173–74).

15. The new institutionalism rightly emphasizes the seeking of legitimacy and security through emulation of existing organizations. But the private higher education literature shows that private growth often involves a view of public failure, sometimes finding either the state or the public universities weak in legitimacy. Indeed the private organizations often seek their legitimacy through alternative, nonstate options such as businesses, churches, and foreign institutions.

16. Furthermore, where different subsectors or individual institutions are linked to the goals and legitimacy of different organizations outside higher education, they may at once develop some isomorphism to those organizations and thereby diminish isomorphism within the higher education population. For example, we could put into this perspective the fact that Argentina's Catholic and more business-oriented private higher education institutions differ notably from each other in governance and linkages (Balán 1990, 15) as both also differ from the public-sector norm.

17. However, in Argentina, even more than in most of Latin America, public universities too operate overwhelmingly with part-time faculty, and many teach in both public and private places. Meanwhile, if we look at only full-time students, Hungary's private share of enrollments falls from 15 to 10 percent (Galasi and Varga 2002).

18. Internationalization is a broad isomorphic force, but the international agenda is also one that promotes diversification within systems. If organizational differences decline among Hungary, China, and Argentina—and between all and the trend-setting United States—such decline does not offset, and will not in the near future offset, the increasing organizational diversity within each country.

19. Bernasconi also finds private growth-building diversity among universities. (His chapter highlights more private-public similarities than this chapter does but not more than a combination of this chapter and Levy 1999). Bernasconi finds remarkable technical rational activity as institutions seek their own way in a competitive system that rewards "task-performing" over "order-affiliating" behavior. There is exposure to the market more than institutionalist protection from it. In fact, Chile's "new private

universities" often innovate in ways then emulated by the more established public and private institutions. Admittedly Bernasconi's national case is exceptional for its market vibrancy and innovation.

20. There would be some sense of coming full circle here in that DiMaggio and Powell (1983, 147) argue that the forces that led Weber to see isomorphism based on technically rational competition yielded in the second half of the twentieth century to a different isomorphism; they do not say Weber was basically wrong for his time. Perhaps the contemporary era shows resurgence, as a matter of degree, of technical competition, as reflected in expanding private activity. Rowan ("The New Institutionalism and Educational Organizations," in this volume) finds for U.S. schools that rational technical theory assumes increased validity as the demands for accountable results grow, and the public sector gets delegitimized.

REFERENCES

Altbach, Philip. G., ed. 1999. *Private Prometheus: Private higher education and develop-ment in the twenty-first century*. Westport, CT: Greenwood.

Balán, Jorge. 1990. Private universities within the Argentine higher education system: Trends and prospects. *Higher Education Policy* 3(2): 13–17.

Balán, Jorge, and Ana M. García de Fanelli. 1993. *El sector privado de la educación superior: Políticas públicas y sus resultados recientes en cinco países de América Latina*. Buenos Aires: Centro de Estudios de Estado y Sociedad (CEDES).

Birnbaum, Robert. 1983. *Maintaining diversity in higher education*. San Francisco: Jossey-Bass.

Brint, Steven, and Jerome Karabel. 1991. Institutional origins and transformations: The case of American community colleges." In *The new institutionalism in organizational analysis*, ed. W. Powell and P. DiMaggio, 337–60. Chicago: University of Chicago Press.

Catholic University of Hungary. n.d. Pazmany Peter Katolikus Egyetem. Budapest.

Department of Development and Planning, Ministry of Education, PRC. *Educational statistics yearbook of China (1996–2001)*. Beijing: People's Education Press.

DiMaggio, Paul, and Walter Powell. 1983. The iron cage revisited: Institutional isomorphism and collective rationality in organizational fields. *American Sociological Review* 48: 147–60.

———. 1991. Introduction. In *The new institutionalism in organizational analysis*, ed. W. Powell and Paul DiMaggio. Chicago: University of Chicago Press.

Durham, Eunice, and Maria Helena Sampaio. 2000. La educación privada en América Latina: Estado y mercado. In *Políticas de reforma de la educación superior y la universidad latinoamericana hacia el final del milenio*, ed. J. Balán. UNAM/CESU.

Eisemon, Thomas Owen, Ioan Mihailescu, Lazar Vlasceanu, Catalin Zamfir, John Sheenan, and Charles H. Davis. 1995. Higher education reform in Romania. *Higher Education* 30: 135–52.

Galasi, Péter, and Júlia Varga. 2000. Public and private initiatives in higher education: The case of Hungary.

García de Fanelli, Ana M. 1997. Las nuevas universidades del conurbano bonaerense. Buenos Aires: CEDES working paper no. 117.

———. 2001. La formación de posgrado en las ciencias sociales argentinas. *Education Policy Analysis Archives* 9(29).

García Guadilla, Carmen. 1996. *Situación y principales dinámicas de transformación de la educación superior en América latina.* Caracas: CRESALC/UNESCO.

Giesecke, Hans C. 1999. The rise of private higher education in East Central Europe. *Society and Economy* 21(1).

Hall, Richard H. 1996. *Organizations: Structures, processes, and outcomes*, 6th ed. Englewood Cliffs, NJ: Prentice Hall.

Haveman, Heather. 1993. Follow the leader: Mimetic isomorphism and entry into new markets. *Administrative Science Quarterly* 38: 593–627.

Kraatz, Matthew, and Edward Zajac. 1996. Exploring the limits of the new institutionalism. *American Sociological Review* 61: 812–36.

Kulachol, Thanu. 1995. Private higher education in Thailand. In *Private higher education in Asia and the Pacific: Final report, part 2: seminar papers*, ed. T.-I. Wongsothorn and Y. Wang, 109–27. Bangkok: UNESCO PROAP and SEAMEO RIHED.

Kwong, Julia. 1997. The reemergence of private schools in socialist China. *Comparative Education Review* 41(3): 244–59.

Law, Wing-Wah. 1995. The role of the state in higher education reform: Mainland China and Taiwan. *Comparative Education Review* 39(3): 322–55.

Levy, Daniel C. 1986. *Higher education and the state in Latin America: Private challenges to public dominance.* Chicago: University of Chicago Press.

———. 1992. Private institutions of higher education. In *The encyclopedia of higher education*, ed. B. Clark and G. Neave. New York: Pergamon.

———. 1993. Recent trends in the privatization of Latin American higher education: Solidification, breadth, and vigor. *Higher Education Policy* 6(4).

———. 1996. *Building the third sector: Latin America's private research centers and nonprofit development.* Pittsburgh: University of Pittsburgh Press.

———. 1999. When private higher education does not bring organizational diversity: Argentina, China, Hungary. In *Private Prometheus: Private higher education and development in the twenty-first century*, ed. P. Altbach, 17–50. West Port, CT: Greenwood.

———. 2002a. The emergence of private higher education's roles: International tendencies relevant to recent Chinese reality. Peking University, Higher Education Forum, no. 1, 2002, 89–96; Xiamen University, *International Higher Education* 2, 2002: 1–8.

———. 2002b. Unanticipated development: Perspectives on private higher education's emerging roles. PROPHE Working Paper No.1, April 2002, Program for Research on Private Higher Education (PROPHE), State University of New

160

DANIEL C. LEVY

York at Albany. Available online at http://www.albany.edu/~prophe/publication/paper.html.

Marginson, Simon. 1997. Imagining ivy: Pitfalls in the privatization of higher education in Australia. *Comparative Education Review* 41(4): 460–80.

Marginson, Simon, and Mark Considine. 2000. *The enterprise university: Power, governance, and reinvention in Australia.* Cambridge, UK, New York: Cambridge University Press.

Meek, Lynn, L. Goedegebuue, O. Kivinen, and R. Rinne. 1996. *The mockers and the mocked: Comparative perspectives on differentiation, convergence and diversity in higher education.* Oxford: Pergamon.

Meyer, John, and Brian Rowan. 1991. Institutionalized organizations: Formal structure as myth and ceremony. In Powell and DiMaggio, 108–42.

Min, Weifang. 1991. Higher education finance in China: Current constraints and strategies for the 1990s. *Higher Education* 21: 151–61.

Ministry of Culture and Education. 1996. *Higher education in Hungary: The higher education act.* Budapest.

Mok, Ka-ho. 1997. Retreat of the state: Marketization of education in the Pearl River Delta. *Comparative Education Review* 41(3): 260–76.

Nagy, Judit. 1996. Constraints on development of private higher education in Hungary. Report for the World Bank. November.

Nagy-Darvas, Judit, and Peter Darvas. 1999. Private higher education in Hungary: The market influences the university. In *Private Prometheus: Private higher education and development in the twenty-first century*, ed. P. G. Altbach. Westport, CT: Greenwood.

Neave, Guy. 1996. Homogenization, integration and convergence: The Cheshire cats of higher education analysis. In Meek et al. 26–41.

Pan, Maoyuan, and Yitong Wei. 1995. China: Legislation guarantee for the development of private higher education. In *Private higher education in Asia and the Pacific: Final report, part 2: seminar papers*, ed. T.-I. Wongsothorn and Y. Wang, 9–12. Bangkok: UNESCO PROAP and SEAMEO RIHED.

Powell, Walter. 1991. Expanding the scope of institutional analysis. In Powell and DiMaggio.

Powell, Walter, and Paul DiMaggio, eds. 1991. *The new institutionalism in organizational analysis*, 183–203. Chicago: University of Chicago Press.

Sadlak, Jan. 1994. The emergence of a diversified system: The state/private predicament in transforming higher education in Romania. *European Journal of Education* 29(1).

Salamon, Lester M. 1995. *Partners in public service: Government-nonprofit relations in the modern state.* Baltimore: Johns Hopkins University Press.

Sawyerr, Akilagpa. 2002. *Challenges facing African universities: Association of African universities.* Draft.

Tomusk, Voldemar. 2003. The war of institutions, episode 1: The rise, and the rise private higher education in Eastern Europe. *Higher Education Policy* 16: 213–38.

Wongsothorn, Tong-In, and Yibing Wang, eds. 1995a. *Private higher education in Asia and the Pacific: Final report, part 1: Summary and recommendations.* Bangkok: UNESCO PROAP and SEAMEO RIHED.

Wongsothorn, Tong-In, and Yibing Wang, eds. 1995b. *Private higher education in Asia and the Pacific: Final report, part II: seminar papers.* Bangkok: UNESCO PROAP and SEAMEO RIHED.

Yin, Qiping, and Gordon White. 1994. The marketisation of Chinese higher education: A critical assessment. *Comparative Education* 30(3): 217–37.

Zhou, Nanzhao. 1995. The evolution and policies concerning NGO-sponsored higher education in China. In *Private higher education in Asia and the Pacific: Final report, part 2: seminar papers*, ed. T.-I. Wongsothorn and Y. Wang, 13–24. Bangkok: UNESCO PROAP and SEAMEO RIHED.

TEN

Institutional Change in Education: Evidence from Cross-National Comparisons

DAVID P. BAKER

ON A TREE DIAGRAM of the evolution of theoretical perspectives on society, the trunk and roots from the structural-functional side of the tree would support the new institutionalism limb. Among those roots would be Durkheimian ideas about how institutions are central to a structural description of modern society, as well as the Weberian idea that institution is to sociology what competition is to economics (Durkheim 1901). New institutionalism is essentially a theory-driven, rich description of social institutions as the basic building blocks of society. Resting as it does on components of a functional theory, it has all of the empirical advantages and disadvantages associated with this broad perspective. Functional images of society have advantages in producing accurate description of culture and social order but suffer disadvantages in describing how social change occurs. Analyses of conflict processes play a far greater role in describing the origins of social change than do institutional analyses of society. Yet for new institutionalism to become a fully mature theory it must address the origins and effects of change.

How can we detect when social institutions undergo fundamental change versus long-term deepening of existing institutional patterns? And how can we predict when change in institutions will happen? In its current form, new institutional theory (hence forth NI) is hard pressed to address these questions. And indeed much of the criticism directed toward NI has noted this weakness (Jepperson 2002). These are major questions before the future of NI as a useful theoretical paradigm, but a full exploration of possible answers is beyond the scope of this chapter. Recent observations of complex changes in the consequences of greater institutionalization of formal education worldwide on students, families, and educators, however, yield useful empirical material from which to consider institutional change (e.g., Baker and LeTendre 2005).

This chapter briefly describes ideas about institutional change that run through the literature on NI analysis and shares some notes on how NI could start to think about institutional change, particularly change caused by endogenous processes within institutions. Then, three empirical worldwide educational trends are used to explore these ideas about predicting institutional change.

IDEAS ABOUT INSTITUTIONAL CHANGE

Mixed in among past theoretical and empirical research on NI are some clues about ways to develop a theory of social change that is based in the rhythms and dynamics of institutions. These discussions boil down to three contrasting images of the primary nature of change and social institutions. The first image is that institutional change results primarily from exogenous factors; the second is the exact opposite, in that change is primarily a function of endogenous factors; and the third is that institutions are mostly immutable and experience very little real change.

The thinking about exogenous-induced change primarily focuses on institutional change as a function of influences from other related institutions (Berger and Luckmann 1967). For example, the change in one institution, such as the rise of industrial capitalism across the eighteenth and nineteenth centuries, changes other institutions, such as the demise of feudal production. As one institution is created or gains in institutional force this can reduce, change, or cause death of related institutions. However, views of exogenous factors of change are not limited only to institutional interactions. "Exogenous shocks" can block reproduction of past institutional patterns (Jepperson 1991). For example, noninstitutional exogenous factors such as rapid demographic change brought on by a shock such as an epidemic disease can have an ensuing impact on institutions such as what happened to European institutions after the Black Death in the fourteenth century. Most observers of institutions see the potential for external shocks to cause social change, but what remains to be developed is a reasonable account of slow social change over extended periods of time.

This leads to a consideration of endogenous factors in change, which are harder to identify. In a somewhat tautological fashion, the literature on NI that focused particularly on formal education has tended to offer the image of greater or lesser degrees of *institutionalization* as an engine of change (e.g., Meyer 1977). Institutions change as the models (scripts and schema) take on deeper and more expansive institutionalization. This idea is appealing and has been used to consider how mass education has developed over time, and my analysis of the three educational trends relies on this idea. At the same time, this idea comes dangerously close to tautological problems often associated with general functional ideas about change. In other words, institutions change as a function of greater or lesser institutionalization of particular institutional patterns—something changes because it becomes more of what it is. Institutions and the process of institutionalization end up underdefined and not sufficiently differentiated from one another to see clearly how change in one causes a change in the other.

Ron Jepperson, the NI theorist who has probably studied this issue most, attempts to sort this out by using four notions of institutional change: institutional formation, institutional development, deinstitutionalization, and reinstitutionalization (Jepperson 1991). He thinks about the first as an "exit from social entropy" in the creation of institutions. The second is a process of deeper institutionalization of existing patterns. The third is the opposite process. The final comes closest to the vision of interaction of institutions as change.

Although these ideas are useful in the abstract, they have not been applied much in NI analysis of real empirical trends in education. Probably the best set of theoretical ideas and hypotheses on institutionalization of education comes from John Meyer's seminal 1977 paper on the effects of education on society as an institution, in which he lays out a number of far-reaching consequences from the increasing incorporation of formal mass schooling as an institution in modern society. The brilliance of the argument is the identification of far-reaching and transforming functions of education as an institution. From this observation, a whole research literature was born documenting the basic process of growth of institutionalization of schooling—said simply, the rise of mass enrollments, mass curricula, and mass school systems over time and across the world (e.g., Fuller and Rubinson 1992). As useful as this literature has been, it has not tended to address variation in the institutional process itself, variation that many new institutionalists predict will explain institutional changes.

Part of the problem is finding effective perspective on institutionalization. It is obvious that the longer the perspective in terms of historical time the better, but often this is hard to achieve in actual research. Working with material across multiple centuries, Durkheim has an advantage in describing the prefeudal Catholic Church as the institutional transformer of education for special talents in antiquity to education of the entire soul that in turn developed into education of the entire child en route to modern education (Durkheim 1901). Compared to institutional analysis of the relatively brief development of modern state-sponsored mass schooling of only about a century and a half, Durkheim is afforded the opportunity to examine long-term trends that reflect institutionalization more clearly. Even the 150-year perspective on the rise of mass public schooling looks good in comparison to the cross-sectional cross-national analyses I try in this chapter. Can NI develop techniques to examine more contemporary and faster moving change and at the same time distinguish between substantial and trivial institutional change? Unless we want to admit that institutions, while not completely immutable, change at only a glacierlike pace and that indications of faster change are not important, we must be able to model and predict more immediate endogenous institutionalization effects on change. Otherwise as sociologists we become a sort of abstract historian without much impact on the understanding of the immediate institutional world and the relatively rapid fundamental change that occurs all around us.

An emerging new institutionalism in political science and economics relies heavily on evolutionary models applied to institution change (e.g. Burlamqui, Castro, and Chang 2000). Biological evolution is the model used in these versions of NI with obvious connections to population ecology models commonly applied to the demography of formal organizations. Small, maybe even random, events can catch on and lead to innovation that changes institutional structures. Related to this are a wealth of anthropological studies that document the ways in which globalized institutions are modified by local cultures, producing a steady stream of unique qualities floating around any institution as large and global as is mass education (e.g. Anderson-Levitt 1987; Ben-Peretz and Halkes 1987; Flinn 1992; Wolcott 1967). These presumably can provide the initial fodder for innovation and evolutionary change. While appealing as a model of change, an evolutionary perspective on institutions has not yet worked out the real process of change. Competition for environmental niches and genetic mutations provide specific causal processes behind biological evolution, but similar mechanisms for evolutionary institutional change are less clear.

EDUCATIONAL PHENOMENA AND
ENDOGENOUS INSTITUTIONAL CHANGE

I examine three educational phenomena discovered through recent analyses of cross-national data on schooling found in the Third International Mathematics and Science Study (TIMSS) (Baker and LeTendre 2005). Of each case I ask three questions: (1) Does this represent real institutional change? (2)

What might be the cause of the phenomenon from an institutional perspective? and (3) Could we have predicted this type of change? These are big and complicated questions, so I provide more speculation than definitive answers. But in doing so, I hope to raise a number of the relevant issues about institutional change in education as well about interpreting empirical observations in light of NI theory.

THE INSTITUTIONAL PARADOX OF THE WORLDWIDE GROWTH OF SHADOW EDUCATION

The Facts

Supplemental private educational activities consumed by families with public-school students with the expressed purpose of helping their children in schools are spreading throughout the world. Large-scale use of structured, supervised outside-school learning in the form of tutoring, review sessions, proprietary cram schools, and related practices to help in the mastery of academic subjects in school are found in substantial numbers in most educational systems worldwide. While activities such as tutoring have been around for centuries, their endurance and growth in light of a century and a half of worldwide expansion of public mass schooling is an interesting phenomenon to consider from a NI perspective. Further, there is evidence to suggest that the use of these private outside-school educational activities has intensified over time and that they are rapidly becoming normative components of education in this era of highly legitimated public mass schooling.

In 1992, while researching how social status was reproduced in the reputed highly meritocratic Japanese selection to university process, the late David Stevenson and I coined the term *shadow education* to describe these kinds of educational activities (Stevenson and Baker 1992). Shadow education conveys the image of outside-school learning activities paralleling features of formal schooling used by students to increase their own educational opportunities (see also Bray 1999; George 1992; LeTendre 1994; Tsukada 1991). These activities go well beyond routinely assigned homework; instead they are organized, structured learning opportunities that take on schoollike processes. And most important they *shadow* the requirements of the public school that the child attends. The after-hours cram schools found in some Asian countries, such as *juku* in Japan and *hakwon* in Korea, are the most extreme in mimicking in-school forms. But there are a wide variety of activities that share a similar logic, such as correspondence courses, one-on-one private tutoring, examination preparatory courses, and full-scale preparatory examination schools (e.g., Japanese *yobiko*). For example, systems of tutoring are extensive in Hong Kong, Singapore, Taiwan, South Korea, Greece, and Turkey. This phenomenon has become so widespread that in 1999 UNESCO commissioned Mark Bray, a comparativist of educational systems, to chronicle and document these activities worldwide. Using national case information, his report, *The Shadow Education System: Private Tutoring and Its Implications for Planners*, shows both the growth of these kinds of activities and the spread across nations. (See also the chapter by Davies et al. on private shadow schooling in Toronto in this volume.)

In an analysis of students' use of shadow education in some forty national systems in the mid 1990s from the TIMSS data, my colleagues and I find some astonishing trends about the use of these activities (Baker, Akiba, LeTendre, and Wiseman 2001). If we make the reasonable assumption that the nations participating in TIMSS represent what is occurring in most educational systems worldwide, shadow education is a large worldwide phenomenon. For example, almost four out of ten seventh and eighth graders weekly participate in tutoring sessions, cram schools, or other forms of shadow education activity worldwide. While most weekly participation consists of one hour or less, one-fifth of the students in these nations who use shadow education activities do so for two or more hours per week. In some nations the use of shadow education appears to be heading toward near universal use among public-school students. For instance, more than three-fourths of the seventh and eighth graders in nations such as South Korea, Japan, South Africa, the Philippines, and Colombia weekly participate in shadow education activities. In Japan it has been noted that one of the main reasons students give for participating extensively in shadow education after the idea of improving their academic performance in school is that so many of their friends participate that they want to attend for social reasons as well. Keep in mind that these are activities purchased from private sources by families of public-school students.

At the same time it is clear that this phenomenon has not equally penetrated education systems everywhere. Figure 10.1 shows the range of shadow education use by nation. Although there are no nations without shadow education, in some nations such as England, Norway, and Germany fewer than 20 percent participate.

In addition to the large use of shadow education, we also found that by far the modal use of these activities was for students with poorer performance in mathematics, not for the elevated enhancement of successful mathematics students. Even though use of the Japanese *juku* has the image of a place where good students get better for strategic advantage on high-stakes examinations, shadow education in most places is largely a remedial operation (although a share of this could also be for examination performance). In nations with substantial amounts of shadow education such as Cyprus, Israel, and Belgium two to over three times as many students with poor mathematics abilities are using shadow education than those with high abilities. In other countries the remedial strategy is less dominant, but it is still substantial. For example, in the

FIGURE 10.1
Shadow Education by Nation, Eighth-Grade Mathematics

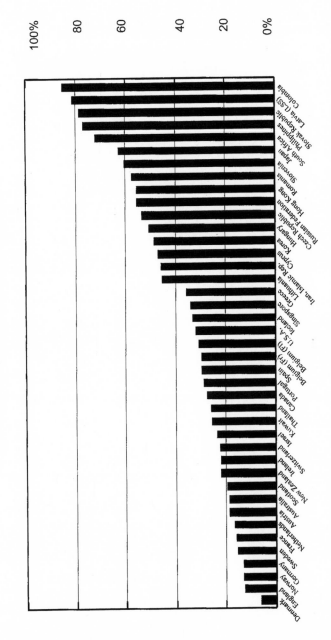

Source: Baker, D. P., Akiba, M., Letendre, G. K., and Wiseman, A. W. (2001). "Worldwide Shadow Education: Outside-School Learning, Institutional Quality of Schooling, and Cross-national Mathematics Achievement." Education, Evaluation, and Policy Analysis.

United States, Germany, and Kuwait about 30 percent more mathematically challenged students use shadow education. Three-fourths of the forty nations in the study have extensive shadow education that is primarily remedial in its use. In only three nations is there a primarily enhancement strategy behind most shadow education.

Given this then, what should we make of the phenomenon of shadow education institutionally? An analysis of the cross-national differences shed some light on this. Although data across both time and space are best to get glimpses of institutional changes, cross-sectional, cross-national data can provide some suggestions of ways to think about this institutionally. In the original article, multivariate analyses found three results that shed some light on institutional change. First, as might be expected with the predominant remedial nature of shadow education in most nations, extensive use is not a function of preparing for high-stakes examinations. While this is clearly not the case in nations such as Japan and South Korea, where shadow education is in part driven by high-stakes exams, it is true across the full sample of nations. Second, lower public expenditures and lower gross enrollment rates are related to more national levels of use of shadow education. Taken together, these two factors account for 25 to 40 percent of the cross-national variation in some indicators of national use of shadow education. Last, cross-national variation in use of shadow education is not related to national achievement levels in mathematics.

Interpretation

Does this phenomenon, and its correlates, mean a change in the institution of education as we currently know it, or is this a relatively meaningless by-product of institutional forces already in place? Is the increased presence of supplemental private educational activities geared to public school requirements a sign of institutional weakening of state-supported mass education, or is it the opposite? Finally, could we have predicted the growth of shadow education from the current institutional configuration of modern schooling?

The widespread prevalence of shadow education and intensity of its use in the schooling processes of students and families dramatically underscores the degree to which state-supported, mass schooling expanded both across the population and life-courses. It dominates child socialization and the ability of families to place children in adult roles and statuses. Instead of seeing the rise of private supplemental activities as a sign of institutional decline or major shift in institutional configuration, it is more in line with this empirical case to think of shadow education as a likely consequence of a greater institutionalized education system within nations. As schooling becomes the primary institution for the generation and transmission of knowledge to generations of children in the form of achievement, one may expect the continued growth in outside-school activities that are specially aimed at children's performance within schools. Homework and the assumption of extensive parental involvement in academics are now common features of the formal educational institution; shadow education takes this same process a step further.

What is interesting here is that shadow education growth is not a simple mechanical outcome of high-stakes tests in systems that have limited avenues for family SES advantage to be played out. Rather, the data indicate that underfunded and underenrolled national systems of education produce more shadow education, and a large portion of this is remedial (this may also happen in underfunded parts of overall well-funded national systems, as in the United States). As mass public education expands and intensifies as an institution, families in less-funded and less-enrolled (probably representing issues of access) systems use shadow education. Shadow education augments the formal public system, which can be an extensive augmentation.

Perhaps then the best interpretation of this phenomenon is to think of it as institutional change, but change more along the lines of evolutionary change as a function of greater institutionalization of preexisting institutional configuration. Mass public schooling sets the stage for the increasing importance of education as an institution and, to the degree that this process creates greater demand for quality schooling than is supplied, augmentation through shadow education is likely. Keep in mind, too, that no country lacked some measurable level of shadow education, and that many economically well-funded education systems also have extensive shadow education. As mass schooling as a world norm continues to intensify the importance of schooling, shadow education itself becomes an institutionalized component of mass education that grows and expands. The process is one in which institutionally, schooling articulates more and more with social and economic allocation, hence increasing its own institutional power over meaning and behavior. It would be expected then from this interpretation that shadow education activities would eventually take on nonacademic rationales for participation. TIMSS case study data from Japan, for example, shows adolescents participating in shadow education in part as a social connection to their peers; therefore, it is a vehicle for socializing as well as for study (Baker and LeTendre 2005; OERI 1998).

Theory about institutions does not offer much help in predicting the kind of deepening evolution of preexisting institutional configurations that produce, in the case of education, the conditions needed to generate high levels of shadow education. The key to developing such a theoretical understanding is to see how mass schooling, greater legitimization of academic achievement, and a heightened sense of demand for quality schooling come together in systems to produce large-scale shadow education. As shadow education loosens the boundaries between public control of education and private educational activities, there are theoretical lessons to be taken away from this case.

Although private educational activities predate the creation of modern public schooling, mass public schooling ironically produces a logic and demand for mass (and mostly private) shadow education in many countries. Furthermore, NI theorists of education should appreciate the ability of widespread shadow education to add a significant nonpublic component to the process without the production of full-scale private schools. Furthermore, this has the potential to change the governance structure of education by introducing private services to a wider host of families and students, hence merging families and private educational resources into new institutional arrangements.

THE PARADOX OF FAMILY AS A WEAKENED INSTITUTION YET WITH INCREASED EFFECTS ON EDUCATION ACHIEVEMENT WORLDWIDE

The Facts

In a recent cross-national analysis comparing the effects of family resources and school factors on mathematics and science achievement, my colleagues and I found that the "Heyneman-Loxley effect" has vanished in a large sample of nations (Baker, Goesling, and LeTendre 2002). In other words, in the late 1970s it was the case that the relative contribution of family effects versus school effects to students' achievement were conditioned by the economic development level of a nation. In poorer nations there were larger school effects and smaller family effects, while in wealthier nations the opposite was true. By the mid-1990s this had vanished and a uniform dominant family effect was in evidence in all of these nations. Because of a lack of data, we cannot assess what the current situation is in extremely poor nations; nevertheless, this is an interesting historical shift.

By the late 1960s, the main dimensions of the impact of family socioeconomic status (SES) on academic achievement were clearly quantified in both American and British societies (Coleman et al. 1966; Plowden 1967; Peaker 1971). Since then a host of studies have described how family SES and schooling interactively reproduce social status through achievement and educational attainment of children (Shavit and Blossfeld 1993; Lareau 1987; Schneider and Coleman 1993; Epstein 1998). Twenty years after the finding that family effects on achievement were very common, two widely cited papers, by Stephen Heyneman and William Loxley, added important findings, namely, that the economic development level of a country (i.e., GNP) conditions the relative strength of this association—between family SES and achievement (1982; 1983). The Heyneman-Loxley effect (hereafter "HL effect") challenged what had previously been thought of as a uniform pattern across both associations, namely, a smaller association between school factors and achievement compared to a larger association between family SES and achievement. The HL effect in developing nations, which shows substantial variation in school quality in the early 1970s, illustrates the strength of schooling as a mechanism to distribute human capital. But what should we make of the fact that by the mid-1990s the HL pattern had vanished, and family effects are now larger than school effects in all tested nations across a range of economic development?

The Interpretation

In the twenty-five years since the HL effect was reported the world has seen intensified institutionalization of mass schooling particularly evidenced by increased political and economic investment in access to education and in organizational quality. The accompanying political logic of human capital development as a nationally planned and funded project has clearly been promoted throughout developing nations through many mechanisms, including investment strategies of multilateral development agencies (Black 1996; Chabbott 1998, Mundy 1998). As shown in figures 10.2 and 10.3, over the past three decades a long-term trend in the expansion of mass education has intensified, in terms of both enrollment rates and public expenditures, throughout less-developed nations, although developed nations are clearly ahead in this trend (Tsang 1995). This has resulted in three interconnected changes in the development of formal schooling in these nations that are often cited as empirical evidence of greater institutionalization of mass public schooling: (1) greater enrollment coverage among youth populations; (2) longer average school careers; and (3) greater expenditure by the state on education (Baker and Holsinger 1996). Could our finding of a vanishing HL effect be caused by this greater institutionalization of mass schooling, and what does it suggest for our understanding of how the institutions of family and school articulate over time?

Probably one of the most common of truisms taken from thirty years of research on the ability of schools to reproduce social status is that "family background has a large effect on achievement levels of students." Meaning that even though meritocratic learning and outcomes are central institutional values within modern mass schooling, empirically family resources, in a number of forms, often have nonmeritocratic influence on achievement levels. Higher levels of family resources, including plain old-fashioned capital and all newly "discovered" forms, including social, cultural, and intellectual, cause higher achievement after controlling for anything else about the student and school that researchers can think up. Modern school systems are porous when it comes to family resource effects even though they value meritocratic processes, and in some cases such as South Korea, have extensive policies aimed precisely at eradicating family effects. As an institutional value, meritocractic is both a

FIGURE 10.2
Growth in Secondary Enrollment Ratios: 1970–1995

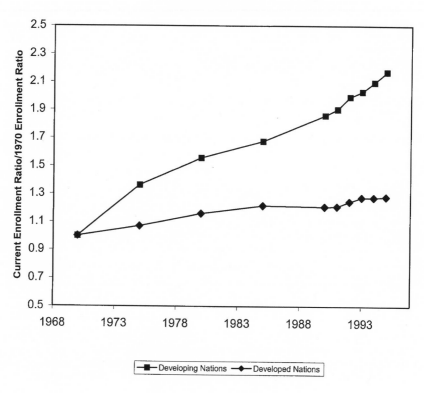

Source: UNESCO (1999).

social justice value and an efficient and fair way to sort people into social and economic status.

The HL effect in the late 1970s puts another twist on this image, and now we have cross-national data at two historical points during which considerable institutionalization of mass schooling occurred worldwide. Investment in mass schooling by nation-states and multilateral agencies, backed by an ideology of providing some minimum level of school quality throughout the nation, has shifted the potential toward greater direct family SES effects in the social stratification process. The macroprocess of institutionalizing mass schooling across a large part of the world may have achieved a resource threshold in the quality of schooling. This is one very plausible explanation for a shifting HL effect over time. As mass schooling has become institutionalized around the world, the mechanics of schooling in terms of curriculum, teaching, and perhaps other resources become more standardized at minimal levels (Benavot et al. 1991).

FIGURE 10.3
Growth in Public Expenditure on Education: 1980–1993

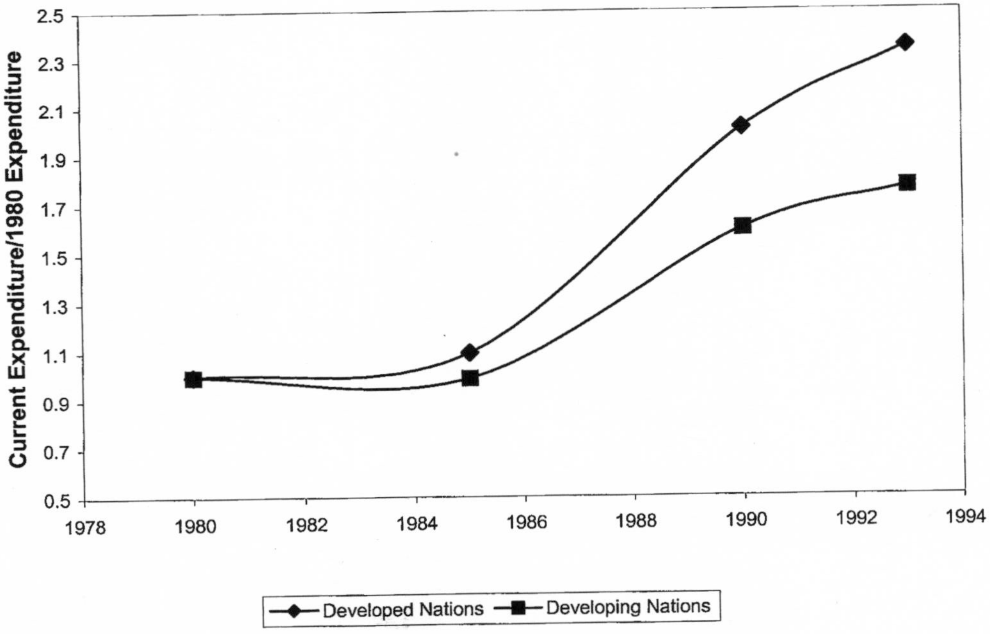

Source: UNESCO (1995).

The full ramifications of this process have only recently reached a significant portion of the Third World. For example, just since the late 1970s there has been widespread increase in basic secondary education in a majority of less-developed nations. The same is true for the importance of schooling and motivation issues among students and families as schooling becomes a normalized part of the life course, as well as a possible increase in the rate of return for individual investment in education (Cohn and Addison 1998; Pallas 2000). This does not mean that within-nation school quality differences do not continue, but family inputs can take on larger effects as schooling quality reaches a threshold throughout a nation. This process has cut down on the large differences in school resource quality within less wealthy nations and made family resources more salient in educational stratification worldwide. In a mass system of schools, quality differences perhaps do not have a monotonic effect on achievement differences; rather there may be larger school effects early in the development of the system when there is still a significant number of schools operating below basic threshold levels of resources.

Family effects on educational outcomes are often considered from a sociological point of view as an institutional failure or at the very least a latent institutional feature in the social reproductive nature of modern schooling. While it is true that one clear and important institutional function of schooling is to allocate people to opportunity, and this is a very manifest and legitimated process, nonmeritocratic allocation appears to cause some problems for an institutional account of schooling. According to those who see schools as highly reproductive, there are two culprits. One is the school, observers of which find evidence of intentional and unintentional social class bias. The other, of course, is the family with its constant motivation to mix intimate relationships with children with mobility (or reproductive) strategies for life chances. Turning this on its head, we can think of spreading family effects on achievement as paradoxically an outcome of a weakening family institution and a strengthening education institution (Baker and LeTendre 2005). There are two related processes here.

As schooling and the formal labor market take on more of the allocative power in modern society, and take away such power from the family as an institution, families are relegated to use mobility strategies through these dominant institutional configurations. Considered from a long historical perspective, the family has lost considerable power in the public spheres of society. Organized now as mostly a mixture of intimate refuge, a consumptive unit, and center of intensive childrearing, the family as an institution has no *direct* power in allocation processes and only *indirectly* influences status attainment of offspring. Conversely, the premodern family, along with similar social units such as the clan, had significant legitimated reproductive public functions in a direct fashion (e.g., direct family inheritance, clan status, family-based apprenticeships, and inherited sinecures). At precisely the same epoch during which family, along with religion, lost institutional power, both the rise of industrial capitalism (rationality and individualism in general, too) and, not long after, the spread of mass schooling sealed the family's "institutional fate" in modern society. In their book *The Homeless Mind*, a significant impact on thinking about institutional processes in modern society, Berger, Berger, and Keller (1974) correctly argue that the modern family has become "underinstitutionalized" as consequence of the greater institutional power of other modern institutions, particularly formal education.

But what then to make of increasing family effects on educational outcomes, if the family has actually gotten weaker as an allocative institution? The answer is found in understanding what creates the situation for family effects in the first place. And here the historical shift away from the HL effect is informative. If we are right in our speculation that the recent decline of nations with significantly underfunded (read less institutionalized) systems of education is the reason why large between-school differences have vanished, then we need to think about what has caused that. In short, as education becomes more institutionalized worldwide, the minimal level of acceptable educational quality in all nations rises. While there continues to be variation in school quality within all nations, it is quite likely that greater institutionalization tends to reduce variation at the bottom of the school quality scale. Therefore school quality is spread more evenly and is less related to national economic development (at least among the semipoor nations). This creates a situation where any influence that family resources have on achievement (i.e., parenting of cognitive development, purchase of outside help, influence on school selection, etc.) will rise in prominence when compared to the greater homogeneity among school quality within nations. So spreading family effects on achievement do not represent increasing domination of family as an institution; rather they represent the increasing institutionalization of mass school and its tendency to reduce inequality of school resources (Baker and LeTendre 2005).

Could we have predicted this trend in say the early 1980s when Heyneman and Loxley and others came out with their findings? To do so would have meant that we are able to project paths of variation in institutionalization and then be able to reasonably identify likely consequences of this. In many ways the pieces to this puzzle were already there. The clear effect of family resources was evident in some of the wealthiest nations at the time, and there is some evidence to suggest that the general contours of the implementation of mass schooling have moved through wealthier nations first over the past century. However, this is by no means a tight association. In a sense then, we could play the game of taking what we think to be the best case (i.e., a nation at a specific time) of the deepest institutionalization and project out from there. But theoretically this is not the most satisfying of games, instead one would prefer a more theoretically grounded approach. But herein is a central challenge before NI—the lack of theory that suggests how and when greater or lesser institutionalization will make significant institutional change versus relatively small incremental change. Or further, how would we begin to develop a general theory of the long-term interaction (competition too) between institutions?

EDUCATIONAL EQUALITY
VERSUS ECONOMIC INEQUALITY

The Facts

There are three interesting cross-national trends about education and economic inequality. First, that there is significant unequal distribution (i.e. between-school) of educational resources within all nations for which we can estimate this. Second, there is also cross-national variation in national levels of education resource inequality. And third, compared to significantly large world levels of within-nation income inequality, education inequality is not as great.

We analyzed educational inequality for the within-nation distribution of seventeen essential educational resources for schooling in fifty-two nations (TIMSS94 nations plus new TIMSS99 nations). All nations had some degree of educational resource inequality. Meaning, for example, that across seventeen basic educational resources, such as instructional materials, teacher quality, and physical plant resources, there are detectable differences between schools within a nation. Larger estimates mean more between-school differences in resources in a nation. Although some differences may be an intentional operational procedure (e.g., special high-quality teachers being assigned to schools with difficult students), additional analysis suggested that most inequalities are by-products of other political and economic processes. Each of the fifty-two nations falls into one of three categories of resource inequality, with about a third of the nations in each. Nations such as South Africa, Turkey, and Latvia are in the category with the larger levels of resource inequality within their systems. Nations such as the United States, Israel, and Korea are among the nations with middle levels of inequality. Nations such as Sweden, Germany, and Cyprus are among those with the least inequality.

Compared to income inequality across many of these nations, educational resource inequality is much lower. There is substantial within-national inequality, and there is additional evidence that this trend is growing, while there is some evidence to suggest that income inequality between nations is decreasing (Firebaugh 2002). The unprecedented wealth generation and concentration from the economic boom of the 1990s has played a major role in these inequality trends. But how do the two institutional sectors—education and labor market—compare in levels of inequality?

Figure 10.4 displays a comparison of education and income inequality across nations. Even though this is a preliminary table in that there are more nations in the education analysis than in the income analysis, it is suggestive. Across these nations educational resource inequality is half the size of income inequality. Similarly, the lowest level of income inequality is higher than the average level of educational resource inequality. Additionally, there is about double the variation in income inequality across nations than in education resource inequality (even though there are more nations in the education analysis). Last, while there is a positive correlation between the two types of inequalities, it is only modest in size.

The Interpretation

Do these trends represent institutional change or at least new knowledge about the institution? It has often been assumed that the institutional arrangements of national education systems greatly shape the structure of social and economic inequalities in modern society. This idea has been a central tenet of social stratification research at least since Sorokin first wrote about education systems and social mobility in the late 1920s. It is also a foundational idea in the sociology of education. Education systems matter for stratification according to sociologists, because they sort cohorts of children into later adult statuses. There is assumed to be an isomorphism between the stratification of

FIGURE 10.4

Distributional Differences between Educational Economic Inequality, Cross-National Gini Coefficients X (Education N=52; Income N=22)

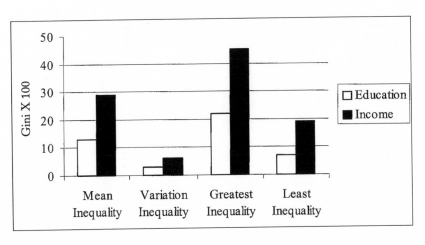

educational opportunities and economic opportunity. Perhaps the best known image of this comes from Turner's (1960) now classic article about the "sponsored" and "contest" mobility systems that differentiate the education systems between England and the United States.

If this is true, then should not educational inequality in resources mirror economic inequality? In point of fact, we find with a limited number of nations only a modest association between within-nation inequalities in these two sectors. Further, many observers of schools (often primarily American schools) assume that there is substantial resource inequality in national systems. Yet it appears to be the case that the implementation of mass schooling in most nations does not produce large between-school inequalities in terms of the actual materials needed to carry out schooling. Certainly what inequality exits is far less than inequalities among income distributions. (It should be noted that the United States has the largest educational resource inequality among wealthy nations, see Baker 2002).

Of course, education and its necessary resources are publicly provided, and it is difficult to hoard or accumulate inordinate amounts of them. The opposite is true for income. Perhaps the best place to look for educational inequalities is in the purchase of private schooling (and shadow education) by a growing wealthy sector of the population. But another way to look at this is to consider the relatively equitable levels of between-school resources in most nations as a clear outcome of a central institutional value about mass schooling. In a world where material inequality is tolerated and even celebrated in some quarters, the notion of grossly unequal school quality is not nearly so evident. Anyone can in a matter of minutes dream up a far more *efficient, elite-serving* inequitable education system than is actually operating in most places in the world today. Indeed there is historical evidence that while many nations had constructed schooling with intentional resources inequalities built in, from the early part of the nineteenth century on they have been systematically dismantled (e.g., Rubinson 1986). Our results show the current ramifications of this trend.

All in all, these inequality trends probably represent less of an institutional change than a long-term consequence of the initial institutionalized ideas behind mass schooling and national development that are at the heart of some much implemented educational policy worldwide. Unlike the cases of shadow education and a vanishing HL effect, for which a stronger case of institutional change can be made, lowering educational inequality is more a trajectory path of mass schooling. Given this, it is perhaps more predictable than other educational phenomena that we can observe with cross-national data.

CONCLUDING THOUGHTS ON INSTITUTIONAL CHANGE

The observation that the rise of global or transnational institutions shapes all parts of culture is central to the NI perspective (Dimaggio and Powell 1991).

Global institutions transcend and shape local, regional, or national versions of institutions such as schooling. The role of global institutional forces in the isomorphic spread of formal education has been the subject of intense study from a NI perspective. In the current world system, the global institution of education greatly shapes individual national cultures of schooling (e.g., Baker and LeTendre 2005; Meyer 1977; Ramirez and Boli 1987). A major insight of NI is that institutionalization is essentially a cultural product and thus is heavily supported by the power of culture. Modern society is constructed out of the transforming power of a dynamic "world culture" that for better or worse evolved out of Western-style rationality and purposeful action (e.g. Berger, Berger, and Kellner 1974). Rationality as a pervasive cultural product of the historical rise of the Western ideas serves to bureaucratize, marketize, individuate, and homogenize the institutions of the world (Finnemore 1996). These engaging principles form consistent norms of behavior across a range of modern institutions, thus tying institutions such as the modern nation state and formal education together in tight political spheres.

Given the degree to which the modern institution of schooling penetrates nations, similar educational processes are repeated in varying degrees around the world creating considerable international isomorphism in schooling. For example, institutional studies of schooling have shown that curricula across most nations have become very similar in content and intent over the past one hundred years; attendance in public schooling for ten to twelve years has become the norm in most nations; national governments typically assume a link between mass schooling and national human capital formation; and trends in school administration have become isomorphic globally (Baker and Holsinger 1996; Benavot et al. 1991; Fuller and Rubinson 1992; Ramirez and Boli 1987). Rationality, along with its offshoots of marketization, individualization, bureaucratization, and homogenization, plays the tune that all modern global institutions march to, but it itself is a cultural product and acts as such throughout the social system.

Given NI's powerful theoretical perspective on social structure and cultural processes (and hence cognitive processes of actors in institutions), the real hurdle is to develop a theory of more immediate institutional change. Showing the effects of isomorphic institutional development across national systems of education is not difficult, but deciding on when a change or innovation is a real institutional change is difficult (e.g., Tyack and Cuban).

The cases examined here—shadow education, increasing family effects on outcomes, and low, but persistent, education resource inequalities—are hardly revolutionary events worldwide. They are not due to some major external shock to the world system; rather they are, at least in hindsight, more or less predictable consequences of existing institutional trajectories of mass education. The real question is will these kinds of phenomena change the institution from within?

Of the three, mass shadow education appears to have the qualities to produce change in mass schooling. In nations such as Japan and South Korea there is already evidence of penetration of this innovation into the everyday operation of schooling. For example, Japanese teachers come to rely on certain types of materials being covered in shadow education, so they alter their presentation in class. A further indication of shadow education's potential institutional power is reflected in the attempts by the South Korean government to closely monitor the growth of use of these activities because in their view they are a threat to educational equity in the nation.

Last, I should note that my interpretation of all three cases has tended to be mostly sympathetic to a general NI framework with the explicit image of the greater institutionalization of mass schooling (Meyer 1977). As Heinz-Dieter Meyer, one of the editors of this volume rightly points out, an alternative interpretation can be proposed, namely, that public mass schooling weakens as forms of private inequality continue to seep into the system. For example, some will surely see shadow education as a private response to an underdeveloped, and maybe underinstitutionalized, public system.

This takes us to sorting out the difference between institutionalization versus organizational implementation within an institutional sector. There is overwhelming evidence that schooling, of any kind, has increased its allocative power and perhaps also its functional power to teach thinking over the past one hundred years (e.g., Martinez 2000, Blair, Gamson, Thorne, and Baker 2005). When both nation-states and individual families spend large sums of money on this process, does that mean less institutionalization? Rather the opposite is true. But clearly the contested terrain of schooling and its governance has changed, and a simple argument about greater institutionalization of education might miss this. It would have been hard to predict thirty years ago as the education (i.e., enrollment) revolution was underway around the world, that a shift to more privatized processes would be so evident today. Does a certain crisis of confidence in public schooling and public administration of it also mean institutional crisis, or is it more likely as fluctuating organizational crisis (Astiz, Wiseman, and Baker 2002)? This is the image that the political right uses in various nations to launch ideas about charter schools, private schooling choice programs, and so forth. Political expedience aside, theory-wise it is a valid question that needs further analysis.

In thinking across all three cases, we return to the notion of institutional change born out of intensification of institutionalization itself. This is a central idea, but one that is hard to empirically test. In particular, the second case, the shifting relationship between family and school influence on achievement, is a clear example of the consequences of greater institutionalization of one institution—mass public schooling—in bringing about change (perhaps weaker institutionalization) in another institution—the family. But we do not have many such demonstrations of shifting institutional processes. In a robust theoretical framework, NI informs us how education continues to be institutionalized. Whether or not we can predict the dynamics of institutionalization from this framework remains to be seen.

NOTE

I am indebted to Charles Bidwell and his chapter in this volume for expanding my perspective on Durkheim's contributions to institutional analysis of education.

REFERENCES

Anderson-Levitt, K. 1987. National culture and teaching culture. *Anthropology and Education Quarterly* 18: 33–37.

Astiz, F., A. Wiseman, and D. Baker. 2002. Slouching towards decentralization: Consequences of globalization for curricular control in national education systems. *Comparative Education Review* 46: 66–88.

Baker, D. 2002. Should we be more like them? American high school achievement in cross-national comparison. *Brookings Papers on Education Policy*. Washington, DC: Brookings Institute Press.

Baker, D., B. Goesling, and G. LeTendre. 2002. Socio-economic status, school quality, and national economic development: A cross-national analysis of the "Heyneman-Loxley Effect" on mathematics and sience achievement. *Comparative Education Review* 46(3): 291–312.

Baker, D., and D. Holsinger. 1996. Human capital formation and school expansion in Asia. *International Journal of Comparative Sociology* 37: 1–2, 159–73.

Baker, D., and G. LeTendre. 2000. Comparative sociology of classroom processes, school organization, and achievement. In *Handbook of the Sociology of Education*, ed. M. Hallinan, 345–64. New York: Plenum.

———. 2005. *National differences, global similarities: World culture and the future of schooling.* Stanford, CA: Stanford University Press.

Baker, D. P., M. Akiba, G. K. Letendre, and A. W. Wiseman. 2001. Worldwide shadow education: Outside-school learning, institutional quality of schooling, and cross-national mathematics achievement. *Education, Evaluation, and Policy Analysis* 23(1): 1–17.

Benavot, Aaron, Yun-Kyung Cha, David Kamens, John W. Meyer, and Suk-Ying Wong. 1991. Knowledge for the masses: World models and national curricula, 1920–1986. *American Sociological Review* 56(1): 85–101.

Ben-Peretz, M., and R. Halkes. 1987. How teachers know their classrooms: A cross-cultural study of teachers' understandings of classroom situations. *Anthropology and Education Quarterly* 18: 17–32.

Berger, Peter, Brigitte Berger, and Hansfried Kellner. 1974. *The homeless mind: Modernization and consciousness.* New York: Vintage.

Black, M. 1996. *Children first: The story of UNICEF, past and present.* New York: Oxford University Press.

Blair, C., D. Gamson, S. Thorne, and D. Baker. 2005. Rising mean IQ: Cognitive demand of mathematics education for young children, population exposure to formal schooling, and the neurobiology of the prefrontal cortex. *Intelligence* 33: 93–106.

Bray, M. 1999. *The shadow education system: Private tutoring and its implications for planners.* Paris: UNESCO, International Institute for Educational Planning.

Burlamaqui, L., A. Castro, and H. Chang. 2000. *Institutions and the role of the state.* Northampton, UK: Elgar.

Chabbott, C. 1998. Constructing educational consensus: International development professionals and the world conference on education for all. *International Journal of Education Development* 18(3): 207–18.

Cohn, Elchanan, and John T. Addison. 1998. The economic returns to lifelong learning in OECD countries. *Education Economics* 6(3): 253–307.

Coleman, J., E. Campbell, C. Hobson, J. McPartland, A. Mood, F. Weinfall, and R. York. 1966. *Equality of educational opportunity.* Washington DC: Government Printing Office.

Durkheim, E. 1901. *The rules of sociological method.* Glencoe, IL: Free Press.

Epstein, J. 1998. *School, family, and community partnerships: Preparing educators and improving schools.* Boulder, CO: Westview.

Finnemore, M. 1996. Norms, culture, and world politics: Insights from sociology's institutionalism. *International Organization* 50(2): 325–47.

Firebaugh, G. 2002. *The new geography of global income inequality.* Cambridge, MA: Harvard University Press.

Flinn, J. 1992. Transmitting traditional values in new schools: Elementary education of Pulap Atoll. *Anthropology and Education Quarterly* 23: 44–58.

Fuller, B., and R. Rubinson, eds. 1992. *The political construction of education: The state, school expansion, and economic change.* New York: Praeger.

George, C. 1992. Time to come out of the shadows. *Straits Times* (Singapore), April 4.

Heyneman, S., and W. Loxley. 1983a. Influences on academic achievement across high and low income countries: A re-analysis of IEA data. *Sociology of Education* 55(1): 13–21.

———. 1983b. The effect of primary-school quality on academic achievement across twenty-nine high- and low-income countries. *American Journal of Sociology* 88(6): 1162–94.

Jepperson, R. 1991. Institutions, institutional effects, and institutionalism. In *The new institutionalism in organizational analysis,* ed. W. Powell and P. DiMaggio. Chicago: University of Chicago Press.

———. 2002. The development and application of sociological neoinstitutionalism. In *New directions in contemporary sociological theory,* ed. J. Berger and M. Zelditich. New York: Rowman and Littlefield.

Lareau, A. 1987. Social class differences in family-school relationships: The importance of cultural capital. *Sociology of Education* 60(2): 73–85.

LeTendre, G. 1994. Distribution tables and private tests: The failure of middle school reform in Japan. *International Journal of Educational Reform* 3(2): 126–36.

Martinez, M. 2000. *Education as the cultivation of intelligence.* Mahwah, NJ: Erlbaum.

Meyer, J. 1977. The effects of education as an institution. *American Journal of Sociology* 83(1): 55–77.

Mundy, K. 1998. Educational multilateralism and world (dis)order. *Comparative Education Review* 42(4): 448–78.

Office of Educational Research and Improvement (OERI). 1998. *The educational system in Japan: Case study findings.* Washington, DC: U.S. Department of Education.

Pallas, A. 2000. The effects of schooling on individual lives. In *Handbook of Sociology of Education,* ed. Maureen T. Hallinan. New York: Kluwer.

Peaker, G. 1971. *The Plowden children four years later.* London: National Foundation for Educational Research in England and Wales.

Plowden, B. 1967. *Children and their primary schools.* London: Her Majesty's Stationary Office.

Powell, W., and P. DiMaggio, eds. 1991. *The new institutionlism in oganizational analysis.* Chicago: University of Chicago Press.

Ramirez, F., and J. Boli. 1987. Global patterns of educational institutionalization. In *Institutional structure: Constituting state, society, and the individual,* ed. G. Thomas, J. Meyer, F. Ramirez, and J. Boli, 150–72. Beverly Hills: Sage.

Rubinson, R. 1986. Class formation, political organization, and institutional structures: The case of schooling in the United States. *American Journal of Sociology* 92: 519–48.

Schiller, K., K. Valdmir, and X. Wang. 2002. Economic development and the effects of family characteristics on mathematics achievement. *Journal of Marriage and the Family* 64(3): 730–42.

Schneider, B., and J. Coleman. 1993. *Parents, their children, and schools.* Boulder, CO: Westview.

Shavit, Y., and H. Blossfeld, eds. 1993. *Persistent inequality: Changing educational attainment in thirteen countries.* Boulder, CO: Westview.

Stevenson, D., and D. Baker. 1992. Shadow education and allocation in formal schooling: Transition to university in Japan. *American Journal of Sociology* 97(6): 1639–57.

Turner, R. 1960. Sponsored and contest mobility and the school system. *American Sociological Review* 25: 855–67.

Tsang, M. 1995. Public and private costs of education in developing countries. In *International Encyclopedia of Economics of Education,* ed. M. Carnoy. Oxford, UK: Pergamon.

Tsukada, M. 1991. *Yobiko life: A study of the legitimation process of social stratification in Japan.* Berkeley: University of California.

Wolcott, H. 1967. *A Kwakiutl village and school.* Prospect Heights, IL: Waveland.

ELEVEN

Breaking the Institutional Mold: Faculty in the Transformation of Chilean Higher Education from State to Market

ANDRÉS BERNASCONI

CHILE'S HIGHER EDUCATION: A STUDY IN INSTITUTIONAL CHANGE

Market forces are transforming higher education. The knowledge-based economy provides universities with unprecedented moneymaking opportunities (Bok 2003), while the new global political economy based on free market institutions together with the state's retreat from its position as preeminent funder of higher education affect structures, values, and practices in universities worldwide. As funding sources diversify, greater power accrues to management, new partnerships are forged with business and industry, competition for students grows more intense, and incentives for faculty are reoriented toward entrepreneurial endeavors (Clark 1998; Ruch 2001; Slaughter and Leslie 1997; Zemsky, Shaman, and Shapiro 2001). 'Marketization' has gained wide currency as a concept apt to describe these developments of the last two decades.

This chapter offers a case study on how the higher education societal sector receives, processes, and is transformed by the inflow of the economic rationality criteria associated with free markets, ample competition, private provision of public services, and a shrinking role for the state. This is a case, in other words, of institutional change. Examining how institutional inertia in higher education was broken in this case has great theoretical interest, because we do not understand the mechanisms of institutional change very well (see, for one Brian Rowan's contribution in this book). It has also practical import, for nowadays many systems of higher education worldwide are moving from state dominance to privatization and market competition.

The setting for my analysis of these issues is Chile, a country that has been both an early example and a patent case of a transition from a predominantly public to a primarily private, market-coordinated, system of higher education, a shift induced by changes in the state and the economy as a whole during the military dictatorship of Gen. Augusto Pinochet (1973–1990). Beginning in the late seventies, a sweeping privatization and deregulation program of Chile's state-owned companies, capital markets, financial institutions, labor regulations, social security, health, and education was introduced, the pace and depth of which can hardly find a match anywhere in the world. After several years of painful adjustment to a new political economy where the engine of growth was no longer the State, but the private sector, Chile's economy took off in the mideighties, beginning what fifteen years later is widely regarded as one of the most spectacular recent periods of steep and sustained economic growth of a developing country anywhere outside of Asia. The size of the Chilean economy tripled, purchasing-power-adjusted per capita income reached close to ten thousand U.S. dollars, poverty was cut by half, and extreme poverty was reduced to the low single digits. The return to democracy in 1990 brought freedom and political stability, while leaving the legacy of economic reforms largely untouched. As a rare combination of democracy and prosperity, Chile began to be touted by the "Washington consensus" of multilateral financial institutions, think tanks, and economists in academia, as the model country for Latin America.

Chilean higher education took the same path: the system was privatized and deregulated, and competition was imposed upon its institutions as the only possible strategy for survival. Numerous new private institutions emerged in the eighties. Public universities were required to charge tuition and engage in other revenue-generating endeavors as their level of public funding plummeted. What remained of public funding began increasingly to be made available to universities on a competitive basis.

Twenty years after Chilean higher education was reformed, "privateness" has come to be its dominant feature, in both enrollments and funding, and Chile stands among the world's leaders in the extent of private participation in tertiary education. Chilean higher education has been extolled as a model, especially by the World Bank, and not only for Latin America, but for the tertiary education sectors around the world.

Focusing on the evolution of the Chilean academic profession during this period of transformations, this chapter will first describe the background, key components, and main results of the Pinochet regime's higher education policy and its continuation after the return of democracy in 1990. It will then move to a consideration of how the new realities in higher education structure and funding have affected the contours of the academic profession and the societal sector in which universities operate. Next, the theme of institutional transformation will be broached, with the aid of the case material previously laid out.

I will argue that the uncontestable power of a dictatorial regime is not sufficient explanation for institutional change of this scale and depth. The vast reach of the Pinochet-era reforms, their shared ideological foundations, the economic success of the new model, and the preservation of the core of the reform program under democratic rule all contributed to a cultural shift from statist to market orientation that permeated most segments of society, not just the elites, and most sectors, not just education. In this environment, universities forged the organizational forms that the new conditions demanded, in a process in which isomorphic dissemination was a significant factor. As a result, new grounds for organizational legitimacy, centered around values such as efficiency, effectiveness, and accountability, appropriate to the new social order, arose.

Primary data for this study were collected from twelve universities, representing the thirty-eight fully licensed universities operating in Chile in 2001. The selection of universities in the study included four public universities, three "old" private universities (founded prior to the 1981 higher education reform), and five "new" private universities (established under the provisions of that reform). The method used was primarily qualitative in nature, relying on archival material and interviews of senior university administrators (rectors, vice rectors, provosts, and deans). Site visits were conducted between October 2001 and January 2002.

FROM STATE DOMINANCE TO PRIVATIZATION

As Levy has shown (1986, 66–76) since the creation in 1842 of the University of Chile higher education in Chile was dominated by the State, even after six private universities emerged between the end of the nineteenth century and the 1950s. The concept of the 'teaching State' encapsulates the notion, largely unchallenged until the last part of the twentieth century, that education was the state's responsibility and that private entities engaged in education were just collaborators in the educational mission of the state.

The higher education reforms of 1981 did away with this concept, and higher education experienced a transformation in many ways parallel to that of the entire country. Intent on expanding enrollments, differentiating the higher education system, and bolstering competition, and inspired in its "neoliberal" economic agenda, the military regime authorized the creation of new private universities and nonuniversity tertiary-level institutions. In what many saw as an effort not only to achieve the aforementioned goals, but also to reduce and control the potential for political activism of the two public universities, their regional colleges were transformed into fourteen small, independent public universities.

As of 2000, there were in Chile sixty-four universities and 176 nonuniversity, postsecondary institutions. A measure of the degree of privatization is the fact that 75 percent of all universities are private, as is 100 percent of the nonuniversity tertiary sector.[1] Enrollments follow a similar pattern. Not only did they rise significantly in the 1985–2000 period, but also the private sector came to be dominant, with 71 percent of the overall enrollments and 59 percent of university enrollments.[2] To put these figures in international perspective, it is worth noting that Chile is one of the world leaders in the private share of enrollments, and first in Latin America (World Bank 2000, 30).

Between 1981 and 1990 public funding to higher education decreased by 40 percent in real terms, and some 30 percent of the remaining public subsidy was made available to universities on a competitive basis. Subsidized public and old private universities were required to recuperate part of their costs by collecting tuition at levels as close as possible to actual unit cost, and a subsidized public loans program was created to assist those unable to make the tuition payments. Research began to be funded separately, through the National Fund for Scientific and Technological Research set up in 1982 to distribute research grants on a competitive, peer-review basis. New private universities were to be funded entirely through tuition revenues. Their students did not have access to the public loans program, but private universities were allowed since 1989 to compete for a portion of the public subsidy and to submit research proposals to the government research fund.

Although public funding to higher education started to climb immediately with the advent of democracy in 1990, only in 2000 did it recover its 1981 level.[3] Even with its upturn in the 1990s, public funding represents only one-fourth of Chile's expenditures in higher education. As table 11.1 shows, Chile ranks among the nations with the highest share of private spending over total expenditures in higher education, while tuition revenues as a proportion of current expenses in Chilean public universities reach one of the world's top levels.

To sum up: both in terms of type of institutions and their enrollments, and in terms of funding structure, Chile exhibits one of the most private higher education systems in the world. This is not to say that public universities are irrelevant to the higher education endeavor. Quite to the contrary, the University of Chile, a public institution, continues to produce about half of the

TABLE 11.1
Private Expenditures as Percent of Total Higher Education Spending, 1998,
and Tuition Revenues as a Proportion of Current Expenditures
in Public Universities, 1995

	Private Exp. as % H. Ed. spending, 1998 (a)	Tuition as % of exp. in public universities, 1995
Korea	83.3	46
Jordan	n.a.	40
Chile	75.8	36
Jamaica	n.a.	24
Ecuador	n.a.	23
Singapore	n.a.	19.8
Costa Rica	n.a.	15.6
Thailand	67.5	6.7
Japan	58.3	3.8
Indonesia	56.7 (c)	12.6
Peru	55.4	n.a.
Philippines	54.3 (c)	9.7
Vietnam	54	22
United States	53.2	25.3
Australia	43.9	n.a.
Canada	43.4	n.a.
Israel	40.6	n.a.
U. Kingdom	37.3	n.a.
Spain	27.9	19.8
Ireland	27.4	30.3
Argentina	25.7	n.a.
Italy	25.3	n.a.
Hungary	23.4	2.1
France	14.5	1.3
México	12.1	n.a.
Germany	7.9	n.a.
Turkey	5.8	14.7

(a) Source: World Bank's EdStats database, Thematic Data, Private Education Expenditures, at http://devdata.worldbank.org/edstats/ThematicDataOnEducation/PrivateEducationExpenditure/tab23.xls.
(b) Source: Salmi and Alcalá, 1998:10, 11.
(c) Year 1995

research originating in Chile and together with some other public institutions enjoys a high measure of social esteem and academic prestige. The point here is, rather, to convey the exposure of Chilean universities, public and private, to the forces of the market, as one of the dominant, if not the most significant dimensions, of Chilean universities' institutional environment. This is the context in which the academic profession has developed since the early 1980s.

Traditionally, faculty positions in Latin American universities have been served by successful practitioners of the professions who teach part-time and do not carry out any research (Schwartzman 1993; Altbach 2000, 2002). The notion of the full-time academic with a doctoral degree and a research agenda is relatively new and still exceptional in the region as a whole, although a few universities exist, mostly in Argentina, Brazil, Chile, Colombia, and Mexico, where full-time researchers can be found in critical mass numbers. Despite the impulse given to research in Chile in the late sixties, it continued to be a minority occupation for the next two decades, and then mostly in the natural sciences. Estimates derived from Schiefelbein (1996, 291) and Chile's National Council for Scientific and Technological Research put the proportion of faculty actively engaged in research at 13 to 15 percent of the total academic staff of Chilean universities.[4]

Although the university research community is small, it represents a considerable upgrade of Chile's capacities since the 1980s. Researchers in universities doubled their number between 1981 and 2000. Faculty with full-time or half-time appointments represented some 35 percent of faculty positions in 2000,[5] up from single-digit figures two decades earlier. The proportion of faculty with graduate degrees (masters and doctorates) climbed to 30 percent in 2000, from 18 percent in 1991 (Schiefelbein 1996, 286). Productivity increased as well: In 1981, 2,668 full-time equivalent (FTE) researchers produced 673 publications indexed by the Institute for Scientific Information (ISI). In 1995, 4,702 FTE researchers published 1,376 indexed articles.[6] In 2000, some 5,600 FTE researchers generated 1,816 ISI publications.[7] Moreover, Chilean researchers are more productive than their Latin American peers. While it takes an average 4 Chilean researchers to produce an article in a year, 5 are needed in Venezuela, and 10 in Mexico.[8]

Although the majority of Chilean faculty are still far from the kind of training and research orientation that defines the academic profession in developed countries, progress has been notable, and the cultural influence of the models of the scholar as a scientist and of the U.S. research university have become overwhelming, as shall be explained later in this chapter.

THE CONTEMPORARY
CHILEAN ACADEMIC PROFESSION

The notion of higher education as market dominates the outlooks of university administrators interviewed for this study. Frequently expressed were the concepts of 'education as an industry' and 'students as clients.' A related concept is that of undergraduate higher education becoming increasingly commodified, and universities finding themselves hard pressed to differentiate themselves from others through a recognizable institutional hallmark or brand name. Competition is the prevalent form of relationship between institutions. A vice-rector at a public university explains, "Now every institution puts out its best resources to compete for the best students, research projects . . . because this is a competition, this is the reflection of the economy of our country, its economic model, which is of wild competition. The government says 'here are the resources, compete, and let the best win.'"

University administrators react to the market with varying degrees of enthusiasm. While new private university officials find themselves in their element (after all, it is that open market for higher education that made new private universities possible), administrators in public and old private universities take it with a mix of annoyance at its philosophical implications, resignation at its inevitability, and muffled excitement at the opportunities it offers. But regardless of the attitude toward the market of higher education, no one seems to ignore it. There was also a consensus among my interviewees that the academic profession has changed dramatically since the reform of the 1980s took hold nearly a decade earlier, and there is wide agreement that the fundamental elements of those changes point to a professionalization of academic jobs, the emergence of a new profile of the full-time academic, and the development of a labor market for professors.

The last decade has seen a sizable expansion of the number of people with doctorates in all disciplines and in the professions, from biology to mathematics, from law to journalism. Requirements for joining academe have inched upward as the quality of applicants rises. Other respondents mention increased interest in graduate studies among young people and more interest in academe among people who are better qualified both in terms of work experience and graduate degrees.

Full-time academic work, long the only form of academic work in the natural sciences in Chile, is permeating such traditional redoubts of part-time teaching by successful practitioners as the schools of law and engineering.

Not only have present day professors increasingly been trained as academics; they can make a living out of their academic work, a possibility that was not largely available twenty years ago. In one old private university, for instance, expenditures in academic personnel increased by 50 percent between 1998 and 2001. In another, the same proportion of increase took place between 1992 and 2001. All but two of the universities in my sample offer significant monetary incentives for good performance. Productive faculty can certainly do well by doing good these days. In one old private university, the variable part of the salary of a productive professor who reaps the benefits of the several incentive programs at her disposal can reach 50 percent, while in one public university, productivity bonuses can reach 60 to 70 percent of the base salary. Possibly as a result of the rise in qualifications in academic personnel, and a commensurate improvement of salaries, the prestige associated with the job has increased. Even teaching part time has acquired more prestige among people in the private sector, who see it as a form of personal fulfillment, as well as value added to their professional resumes.

A new actor has emerged in the Chilean academic profession: the "entrepreneurial" professor, a highly competent, productive, dedicated researcher and teacher, who manages to make good science and a good living out of doing things professors did not do fifteen years ago, such as obtaining and managing large research grants, serving on boards of private companies, advising the government, writing consulting reports in matters of his or her expertise, and charging for conferences. A dean in a biology department puts it thus:

> Fifteen, twenty years ago an academic was an isolated intellectual, working quietly in seclusion, with a low salary. Nowadays researchers are like CEOs of their research lines. They actively mingle socially, they talk with businesses types—previously this was regarded as exposing oneself to contamination—, they give opinion, they provide consulting services, they appear in hearings before Congress. We have to get our own money to do research. In the past, the university would give us a little money. Now it gives us nothing unless we bring money [. . .]. Then you have to manage money, have an accounting system, deal with banks, requests for proposals. It is not as calm as it once was, it is more stressful, you face evaluations [. . .]. You have to be good at computers, organizing events, leading people . . . and if you are good, you do well.

Although entrepreneurial faculty constitute a minority nationwide, and within any given university, I found examples of them in many settings, not just in the natural sciences: in a public school of engineering, in an old private business school, in many departments of economics, and in a new private law school, among others.

Over the past ten years a labor market has evolved, where the monetary value of the services of professors of different backgrounds and fields can be readily ascertained and invoked to shape compensation policy. As a result of the development of "prices," greater mobility of human resources ensued. The need to deal with other job opportunities an academic may have, inside or outside academia, appears increasingly more pressing. Universities where the pay scale ignores this notion are permanently struggling to recruit and maintain qualified faculty in high-income fields.

COMPONENTS OF THE NEW INSTITUTIONAL
ENVIRONMENT OF HIGHER EDUCATION

As a higher education market developed, and is increasingly understood as such by the actors of the system, as a vibrant market develops too in the academic profession, as entrepreneurial faculty appear in the scenario, and old private and public universities increasingly come not only to accept the legitimacy of new privates, but even to adopt some of their formerly contested managerial features, the societal sector changes, and a new legitimacy results. New values emerge, such as productivity, efficiency, or merit pay; novel actors take center stage (the entrepreneurial professor, the professional administrator, peer reviewers, members of accrediting agencies), and a new rewards and punishments system develops, consisting, for example, of bonuses for published articles, variable salary, and accreditation decisions. The institutional environment thus elevates rational adaptation to market competition to a position of paramount importance for organizational legitimacy—what is legitimate is being a rational actor—but without totally suppressing, as we will note, the shared beliefs that shaped the academic profession in the past. Elements of the displaced institutional environment remain as balancing forces, limiting administrators' maneuvering room. Such is the case with the entrenched beliefs of senior faculty about, for instance, equal pay for equal rank, the separation of the university and the marketplace, and professional autonomy.

More Salary in Exchange for More Work (and Less Stability)

Traditionally, the compensation for low salaries in academia was the laid back nature of the job. People did not make much, but they led stress-free lives and had guaranteed employment. That is changing, to the chagrin of many a faculty member who would much rather have a low salary, outside work, and stability, than a higher pay and greater accountability. No wonder, then, that none of the new private universities offer tenure, and the two universities in my selection, one public and one old private, where tenure can be revoked in case of poor academic performance, are known to have the highest salary levels.

Where the weight of stability has proven to be too heavy to lift, even with the lever of salary improvements, the favorite administrative tool for getting more mileage out of professors has been a combination of incentives and variable salary, which has the advantage of forcing no one to work harder who does not want to, while reaching with better economic compensation only those who work for it.

Although ranking of professors seems like a taken-for-granted part of their identity as academics, new private universities in my study do not offer tenure. Three of the seven institutions where tenure exists have made it a regular practice to appoint faculty to nontenure-track, nonranked positions to prevent young PhDs from turning down an appointment to a junior post because of the low salaries associated with it. To retain them, universities offer nontenure-track positions with higher salaries.

Organizational Models Inside and Outside Academia

Public universities generally look up to the University of Chile, but they also find inspiration in private universities' aggressive outsourcing of services and use of part-time teachers. An imitative trend is explicitly acknowledged with respect to new privates. A public university official says of the new privates: "You become like them or they'll eat you up. . . . The drama of a public university is that it either modernizes itself, or it'll die, like the public school died thirty years ago. . . . Public universities will be like public high schools, for poor people, with low scores. Second rate."

Reference points can also be found outside the university sector. For some managers at new privates, running a university is not that different from running a business. One administrator explains: "[M]y job is to ensure the quality of the university's production process. We therefore develop the bases for generating production processes under standards of quality." This means, he adds, ensuring consistency in graduates. Faculty need to teach the curriculum because that is what leads to the desired professional profile. Interestingly, in one public university, whose leaders want it to be the model university of the public sector, this means being modern, comfortable in a global world, efficient, agile, and sensitive to its setting. By having attributes normally associated with private institutions, this university seeks to break the prejudice that says that public is wasteful and low quality. But it sticks to the values of tolerance, pluralism, and nondiscrimination, lest it becomes, as someone there said, "too private."

A Redefined Notion of the Profile of an Academic

The idea of an academic as a successful practitioner in a profession who teaches part time has been effectively replaced by a new gold standard: an academic is a researcher with a doctorate, a full-time commitment to her university, and a demonstrated capability to obtain research grants and publish in the international mainstream literature. By rewarding this profile, public policy has been a key contributor to the development of the new standard.

Since the late eighties, the government allocates part of its funding to public and old private universities on the basis of performance indicators rewarding faculty with graduate degrees, externally funded research projects, and ISI-indexed publications. Playing to the indicators is a highly profitable skill, as attested, for instance, by the following statement, heard at public university: "Research awards are not meant to increase salaries, because they reach a small proportion of faculty. They are intended to improve our indicators. If we improve indicators, we increase our revenues, and we can give better service to our students."

A second area of higher education public policy with heavy impact on faculty is the accreditation of graduate programs by a public accrediting agency. It too requires faculty with doctorates, indexed publications, and projects from the government research fund. As with the indicators, the relatively narrow scope of accreditation has expanded its reach so as to permeate the whole system with its standards of good practice.

If these governmental messages were not enough, both the official guide of universities and programs for higher education applicants and the unofficial rankings prepared for massive consumption by a newsmagazine count and publish the numbers of faculty with graduate degrees, faculty who are full time, numbers of indexed publications, and grants from the government research fund.

One old private university started in the midnineties to pay monetary bonuses to its faculty for ISI-indexed publications, a radical approach to boosting indexed publications, and one that was widely copied by other universities.

Publication in journals indexed by ISI is increasingly becoming the only legitimate way to publish, and not only in institutions whose funding depends on it. As with full-time faculty, externally funded competitive research, and graduate degrees, ISI publications have become institutionalized as markers of academic rigor and success throughout the university system. What started as a set of standards imposed by the funding policies of the government, to which old private and public universities adjusted as much as they could out of rational-instrumental behavior, has become a system-wide institutional norm, the proper way of doing things.

The Persistence of an Academic Culture

The ISI publication standard has not been free of challenge. Faculty in humanities, social sciences, arts, or engineering, all of which have little tradition in Chile of ISI publications, complain about publication requirements that stress mainstream outlets.

Salary differentiation has also seen faculty resistance. There is a culture of "same function, same salary" across faculty who came of age in the sixties. In the words of an administrator at an old private university:

> We have a culture of academic of the sixties here, where there is no evaluation, the professor is master of his tasks, his time, his research. . . . [W]e have trouble understanding the modern way of managing human resources. . . . [T]here are still people who complain about the requirement that people spend their time in the university. . . . [T]here is lots of pressure to measure productivity, of which there was none then. Today, if we want to measure productivity, they say "what do you mean 'productivity'? I teach course x in the doctoral program!"

The issue is greater than salary. A vice-rector at a public university explains it thus:

> There is nostalgia for a university that no longer exists. Nostalgics are faculty over 50, in the two highest ranks, who won't assume the reality of private growth, won't assume that students are clients. Concepts of planning, performance measurements, pay for results, goals based performance, are resisted among nostalgic faculty. It's a new model of the university.

Seemingly, "nostalgic" faculty enjoy the slow pace and austere comfort of an academic life of lecturing and no accountability, where work is independent from money, and money comes from the government. He may have lost the university-wide salary equalization battle, but he has found a new battle ground at the level of the school. Earning differentials may be a fact of life across different schools, or a perverse but unavoidable intrusion of the market in the university, but within a school, all academics ought to be equal, they maintain.

The power of these cultural elements has not been strong enough to prevent change, but it is a force reform-minded administrators must contend with. A vice-rector at an old private university explains: "The goal is to break the civil service mentality, whereby at the end of the month, regardless of quality and productivity of work, the paycheck would be the same for all. It's been hard to change that, but we have made good progress. It was hard to assume, but now it's quite internalized." Indeed, the pace of adaptation of the universities in my sample to the new institutional environment can be quite closely correlated with the cultural make-up of its faculty: universities with large numbers of professors who began their careers in the eighties or later tend to adapt more rapidly than those whose faculty staff were formed in the sixties and seventies.

INSTITUTIONAL CHANGE AND THE
DEVELOPMENT OF A NEW LEGITIMACY

In the new institutionalism, the institutional environment is the main source of legitimacy (DiMaggio and Powell 1983, 148; Meyer and Rowan 1977; Scott and Meyer 1991). For the past twenty years Chilean universities have struggled to become more responsive to a new higher education environment. They have done it not from the shadows, since they find sufficient legitimacy in the institutional environment to carry on with their program in the open. Students as clients, performance measurements, pay for results, goals based performance, efficiency, and productivity have become the dominant values in the system. The logic of the "nostalgic" academia is receding, replaced by those new concepts.

In this sense, and challenging the prevalent ideas about educational organizations (Cohen and March 1974; Meyer 1977; Meyer and Rowan 1977; Weick 1976), Chilean universities have come to acquire both the discourse and many of the practices associated with "task-performing" (technical) organizations, while their "order-affirming" (or institutional) features recede to the background. Their competence on task performance, far from being glossed over, is at the center of the concerns of the organization, as one of the key elements on which its legitimacy and success are predicated.

At the basis of this transformation are the reforms of the late seventies and early eighties, a sharp change in the rules of the game that redefined completely not just the institutional environment of higher education but also the fundamental structure of the Chilean economy. In a fashion unlikely to have developed under democratic rule, both for its bluntness and its ideological zeal, first a new constitutional and statutory legal framework was imposed and then society was ordered to adapt to it. This was social engineering at its most ambitious. Most elements of the welfare state that had been built in Chile since the fifties were dismantled, allowing few departures from the "neoliberal" orthodoxy. Had the military dictatorship's economic program not been upheld in the nineties by the democratic governments that followed, it is unlikely that the values and norms of the marketplace would have taken such a strong command on the behavior of actors in higher education. This continuity represented, for universities betting on a policy reversal, a watershed moment of realization that there would be no going back to the statist environment of the sixties and seventies.

It is not only the unchecked power of a dictatorship that explains how such profound social change could be completed in just two decades. Nor is it enough to point at the centralist tradition of Chilean politics and governance, where capturing the seed of power in Santiago entails control over the whole country, or to invoke the remarkable social homogeneity of the nation's population, free of ethnic, religious, regional, or any cleavages other than class: probably as important was the all-encompassing nature of the Pinochet-era reforms. The foundations were overturned of every major institutional sphere, from labor to health care, from banking to education, from government to social security, under the aegis of the same social organizational principles, within the span from 1978 to 1981. In other words, reform was massive, swift, and thoroughly consistent.

Therefore, it was not just universities who had to struggle to reinvent themselves or perish in a new environment of privatization, unregulated markets, unfettered competition, and a vanishing presence of the state, but almost every societal sector found itself in the same predicament. That lent the new political economy overwhelming force, boundless penetration, and the immunity to challenge that comes from the spread of the idea that resistance is futile. Then economic success gave it ironclad political support. Thus, it is not difficult to see how the constituting elements of the market economy would have been assumed, not just by the Chicago school economists who led the reforms, but now by the common citizen as well, as "natural" principles of social organization. In taking markets for granted as the adequate, rational, and necessary mechanism for the allocation of resources of every kind, individuals and organizations came to institutionalize a new model of social order and new criteria for organizational legitimacy.

CONCLUSIONS: FROM INSTITUTIONAL TRANSFORMATION TO ORGANIZATIONAL CHANGE

If one takes the evolution of the academic profession in the last three decades as evidence, Chilean universities seem to have adapted quite successfully to the new institutional environment: there are now more and better qualified academics than twenty years ago, with increased dedication and better pay, which translates into more mainstream research, and a more active engagement with society at large.

Public policy has undoubtedly played a key role in jump-starting and sustaining this drive. Public subsidies are connected to graduate degrees and research performance, and so is accreditation of graduate programs. Public funding for research has quadrupled since 1990, and it now stands at a sizable 15 percent of all public funding to higher education. Universities have reacted as expected to the available incentives.

Public policy is not alone in pushing for organizational change. As shown here, other key pressures have been the isomorphic spread of private organizational forms that resulted from the "packing" of the institutional landscape with private universities, the leadership of the public and old private universities who first figured out how to adapt to the new rules, the role modeling of research faculty and "entrepreneurial" professors, and, finally, the influence of the U.S. research university, which grew stronger as the United States increasingly became the favorite destination for Chilean graduate studies in the period considered here.

The U.S. definition of a professor as someone with a doctoral degree, who works full time and with exclusive dedication in one university, who wins competitive research grants, and publishes the results of his research in ISI-indexed journals has become so dominant as to displace to a subordinate role the previously commanding figure of the successful practitioner of a profession who teaches part-time. The research professor is the measure of legitimacy, distinction, and success throughout the Chilean higher education system.

The "experimental" quality of much of what has happened in Chile in the last decades has, together with the drawback of its exceptionalism, the advantage of the clarity of its results. In the experience of Chile, a deep and lasting change from dominant state to dominant market institutions was possible over a relatively short span as a result of an almost simultaneous overhaul of the structure and ordering principles of every major societal sector, imposed with tight consistency across the board. The large scale of the reforms, together with their success in promoting economic growth, crystallized a new social order.

Organizations in the higher education sector adapted to the new environment by developing norms, roles, values, and a rationale compatible with the new order. Isomorphic patterns can be detected throughout this process of transformation, both with regard to private-sector organizations generally, the U.S. research university, and the trail left by successful early adopters of the new rationality.

NOTES

1. Consejo Superior de Educación, *Indices* database, 2000.

2. Ministry of Education, Chile. Compendio de la Educación Superior: www.mineduc.cl.

3. Ministry of Education, Chile. Compendio de la Educación Superior: www.mineduc.cl.

4. Comisión Nacional de Investigatión Científicay Technológica (CONICYT): Science and Technology Indicators, at http://www.conicyt.cl/bases/indicadores/2001/capituloIII.

5. Consejo Superior de Educación, *Indices* database, 2000.

6. Data source for number of researchers: CONICYT: Science and Technology Indicators http://www.conicyt.cl/bases/indicadores/2001/capituloIII/T3–14.htm. Data source for publications: World Bank, 2000:124.

7. CONICYT: Science and Technology Indicators, at http://www.conicyt.cl/bases/indicadores/2001/capituloIV/T4–8.htm.

8. CONICYT: Science and Technology Indicators, at http://www.conicyt.cl/bases/indicadores/2001/capituloIV/T4–12.htm.

REFERENCES

Altbach, Philip G., ed. 2000. *The changing academic workplace: Comparative perspectives.* Westport: Greenwood.

——— . 2002. *The decline of the guru: The academic profession in developing and middle-income countries.* Chestnut Hill, MA: Center for International Higher Education, Boston College.

Bok, Derek. 2003. *Universities in the marketplace: The commercialization of higher education.* Princeton: Princeton University Press.

Clark, Burton R. 1998. *Creating entrepreneurial universities: Organizational pathways of transformation: Issues in Higher Education.* Oxford: Pergamon.

Cohen, Michael D., and James G. March. 1974. *Leadership and ambiguity: The American college president.* New York: McGraw-Hill.

DiMaggio, Paul J., and Walter W. Powell. 1983. The iron cage revisited: Institutional isomorphism and collective rationality in organizational fields. *American Sociological Review* 48(2): 147–60.

Levy, Daniel C. 1986. *Higher education and the state in Latin America: Private challenges to public dominance.* Chicago: University of Chicago Press.

Meyer, John W. 1977. The effects of education as an institution. *American Journal of Sociology* 83(1): 55–77.

Meyer, John W., and Brian Rowan. 1977. Institutionalized organizations: Formal structures as myth and ceremony. *American Journal of Sociology* 83(2): 340–63.

Ruch, Richard S. 2001. *Higher ed, inc. The rise of the for profit university.* Baltimore: Johns Hopkins University Press.

Salmi, Jamil, and Gabrielena Alcalá. 1998. *Opciones para reformar el financiamiento de la enseñanza superior.* LCSHD Paper Series no. 35. Washington, DC: Human Development Department, World Bank.

Schiefelbein, Ernesto. 1996. The Chilean academic profession: Six policy issues. In *The international academic profession: Portraits of fourteen countries,* ed. Philip G. Altbach. Princeton, NJ: Carnegie Foundation for the Advancement of Teaching.

Schwartzman, Simon. 1993. Policies for higher education in Latin America: The context. *Higher Education 25.*

Scott, W. Richard, and John W. Meyer. 1991. The organization of societal sectors: Propositions and early evidence. In *The new institutionalism in organizational analysis,* ed. Walter W. Powell and Paul J. DiMaggio. Chicago: University of Chicago Press.

Slaughter, Sheila, and Larry L. Leslie. 1997. *Academic capitalism: Politics, policies and the entrepreneural university.* Baltimore: Johns Hopkins University Press.

Weick, Karl E. 1976. Educational organizations as loosely coupled systems. *Administrative Science Quarterly* 21(1): 1–19.

World Bank, Task Force on Higher Education and Society. 2000. *Higher education in developing countries: Peril and promise.* Washington, DC: World Bank.

Zemsky, Robert, Susan Shaman, and Daniel B. Shapiro. 2001. *Higher education as competitive enterprise: When markets matters.* New Directions for Institutional Research, No. 111 Fall. San Francisco: Jossey-Bass.

TWELVE

Lessons Learned and Future Directions

BRIAN ROWAN

THE CHAPTERS IN THIS BOOK discussed the "new" institutionalism as it developed in the field of education from the late 1970s onward. One purpose of these chapters was to reflect critically on this orienting perspective for the study of education; another was to chart some new directions for how this perspective can be used to study education in the near future. The editors of this book saw these tasks as needed in light of contemporary trends in education. As we have seen, the new institutionalism of the 1970s and 1980s was widely heralded for its portrayal of schools as loosely coupled organizations subject to strong government regulation, but now there is an increasing government press for accountability, a tighter coupling of educational organizations, and the emergence of a dynamic private sector in education around the world. A major goal of this book has been to inquire about how a new institutionalism might be used to analyze these trends and thus continue to be relevant to the study of education.

THE NEW INSTITUTIONALISM IN EDUCATION: INITIAL FORMULATIONS

In the introduction to this volume, we noted that a new institutionalism has emerged in the broader social sciences over the past three decades. Importantly, the origins of this movement can be traced (in part) to scholarly developments in the field of education, especially the work of John W. Meyer and colleagues during the late 1970s and early 1980s. Among the best known strands of this work are the influential papers by Meyer and Rowan (1977, 1978) on schools as institutionalized organizations, the collection of essays by Meyer and Scott (1983) using institutional theory to analyze the structure and operations of the U.S. education sector, and a subsequent line of work on the rapid diffusion of a "world" model of basic schooling from its origins in European nations to nations around the world (e.g., Meyer, Ramirez and Soysal 1992; Meyer, Kamens, and Benavot 1992).

In the broader social sciences, this work constitutes a distinctive current within the new institutionalism. In particular, the analysis of education developed by John Meyer and colleagues was built around a view of institutions as taken-for-granted, rulelike schemata that shape and explain social behavior. Like older forms of institutional analysis in the field of education, this new institutionalism was developed in order to explain why a particular form of state-sponsored, mass schooling arose in Western European and North American nations and then spread rapidly to most other nations of the world. However, rather than arguing that mass schooling arose as a consequence of the functional requirements of industrial societies for more highly educated workers, or that mass schooling was simply the institutional means that capitalists chose to reproduce class inequalities in the industrial division of labor, Meyer and colleagues saw the rise of a uniform pattern of state-sponsored, mass schooling as a consequence of the institutionalization and subsequent diffusion of "rulelike" understandings about the appropriate nature of educational organization in modern nation states. In this view, mass schooling—as an institution in society—had its origins in European ideologies of the state, the role of citizenship, and the rights and responsibilities of individuals, all of which converged to bring about a theory of mass education for societal development. As developed, this ideology included most of the familiar "grammar" of modern schooling. It was constituted by a set of deeply institutionalized assumptions about the positive role of schooling in societal development, about the "rights" and responsibilities of citizens with respect to schooling, and about the uniform structure that basic schooling should take, including standardized types of teachers, students, schools, curricula, and so on.

When *education* scholars talk about the new institutionalism, they are often referring to this particular brand of institutional theory and to the innovative ideas it launched. More narrowly, education scholars often frame their understanding of the new institutionalism around a single paper: J. W. Meyer and B. Rowan's (1978) influential discussion of American schools as institutionalized organizations. This paper and others by J. W. Meyer and colleagues have given rise to several ideas critically examined in this book.

One idea examined in this book is that schools (as institutionalized organizations) mobilize resources and ensure their survival by conforming to institutionalized rules, not by performing efficiently in a marketplace for education goods and services. This argument derives from a view of schooling as a state-sponsored and nonmarket activity, and the associated assumption that absent market pressures, schools are shaped more by normative, cognitive, and regulatory forces than by materialist forces.

Another idea that comes under scrutiny in this book is the principle of isomorphism, the proposition that schools in the same institutional environment develop similar structures and functions. In Meyer and Rowan's (1978) analysis, the principle of isomorphism was seen to result from the homogenizing influence of state rules. However, the principle of isomorphism was later extended to the field of higher education by Levy (1999, following DiMaggio and Powell 1983) and then to analyses of the rapid diffusion of basic education institutions to societies around the world (J. W. Meyer, Ramirze, and Soysal 1992; J.W. Meyer, Kamens, and Benavot 1992).

Yet another distinctive idea examined here is that educational organizations are loosely coupled systems. Meyer and Rowan (1978) saw loose coupling as the result of two peculiar features of American education: the multilayered and pluralistic political governance of schooling, and the uncertain technology of instruction. Both features of American schooling were seen to encourage schools to decouple structural units from one another and from technical activities.

As we have seen, most of the chapters in this book were written in reaction to these ideas. So, as a concluding statement of what this book accomplished, let us now signal what we think the main points are that were made by the authors in reaction to these ideas.

Multiple Perspectives on Institutions

One contribution of this book has been to argue that the pioneering work of Meyer and colleagues is but one of several possible ways of orienting institutional theory to the study of education. In fact, this book describes several other orienting perspectives that have emerged under the heading of the new institutionalism and explores how these perspectives can be used to examine current trends in education.

Broadening the Scope of Institutional Theory

A second contribution of this book has been to probe the empirical limits of institutional theory as developed in the 1970s and 1980s. As we have seen, the new institutionalism of Meyer and colleagues was developed to explain a particular phenomenon—the expansion of mass education systems around the world. An important question asked by several authors in this book, however, is whether the central tenets of this form of institutional analysis can be extended beyond its original targets of explanation. For example, can this form of institutional analysis be applied not only to the study of basic (i.e., K–12) schooling but also to higher education? Moreover, can we use institutional theory to study the rise and functioning of more than state-sponsored schooling, for example, private education? Also, can institutional theory explain not only the emergence of loose coupling but also tight coupling within organized systems?

Examining the Process of Institutional Change

A final contribution of this book has been to ask whether the new institutionalism, at least as developed in the field of education, adequately describes processes of institutional change. As we shall see, several authors in this book point to shortcomings in the prevailing approach to the study of institutional change and suggest some new avenues for analysis.

MULTIPLE PERSPECTIVES ON INSTITUTIONS

Let us begin this epilogue with a discussion of the multiple theoretical perspectives that exist on the nature and functioning of institutions. An interesting scheme for classifying these perspectives was developed by Campbell and Pedersen (2001), who identified four relatively distinctive "orienting perspectives" to institutional theory: rational choice institutionalism, historical institutionalism, cognitive institutionalism, and discursive institutionalism. At least three of these perspectives are illustrated by one or more chapters of this book.

A model that is *not* explored in this book is *rational choice* institutionalism. In the broader social sciences, this perspective has been used extensively by the new institutional economists (e.g., Williamson 1975) and is perhaps best known for its explanation of the rise of alternative forms of corporate governance. But rational choice models also appear in other social science disciplines with increasing frequency. (For a sketch of this body of work, see Rowan and Miskel 1999, 360 and *passim*). At the core of this perspective is the assumption that social actors are strongly motivated to realize their own self-interests and, as a result, seek to impose (or at least advocate for) those institutional arrangements that give them the most benefit. In the field of education, rational institutionalism appears in a few discussions of principal-agent relationships in educational organization (for a review, see Rowan and Miskel 1999) and in House's (1996) discussion of institutional choice in education.

The author who comes closest to advocating for a rational choice theory of institutions in this book is Charles Bidwell. Bidwell criticizes the new institutionalism as it developed in education for focusing too much on the taken-for-granted aspects of educational institutions and thus for neglecting how educational institutions are shaped by conflict, bargaining, and power arrangements. However, Bidwell's argument is grounded less in a pure form of rational choice institutionalism than it is in a closely related form of analysis that Campbell and Pedersen (2001) call "historical institutionalism." In this view, the institution-building activities of self-interested parties are intrinsically embedded in a nexus of already existing institutional arrangements that not only shape actors' desires and beliefs but also constrain possible courses of action. As a result, institutional change is often "path dependent" in the sense that interest-based conflict unfolds in an already structured environment that affects the likelihood that powerful interests can and will succeed in their institution-building efforts.

An illustration of how this explanatory paradigm can be used to explain contemporary events in education appears in Rowan's brief examination (chapter 2 of this volume) of why accountability systems emerged in the K–12 education sector in the United States, but not in the U.S. higher education sector. Rowan notes that interest groups pressing for test-based accountability are present in both the K–12 and higher education sectors in the United States but that such accountability systems have been institutionalized *only* in the K–12 education sector. Rowan's explanation for this development is that, for a variety of historical reasons, the K–12 sector has developed a more uniform architecture of performance assessment and is more centralized than the higher education sector. He argues that these differences in preexisting institutional arrangements have made it easier for accountability interests in the K–12 sector to succeed in their reform agenda than in the higher education arena.

Bidwell's advocacy (in this volume) for historical institutionalism was written in reaction to a third approach to institutional analysis—the perspective that Campbell and Pedersen (2001) call "cognitive institutionalism." This, of course, is the form of institutional analysis developed by Meyer and colleagues, and the one that underlies much of the new institutionalism in education. In this book, the chapters by Spillane and Burch and Bernasconi illustrate how cognitive institutionalism can be used to explain emerging trends in education. The guiding idea in these chapters is that educational institutions exist as taken-for-granted schemata that shape people's understandings of the world and provide scripts to guide people's thinking and activities. Interestingly, however, both Spillane and Burch and Bernasconi use cognitive institutionalism to explain the rise of tight couplings within education sectors.

A final model of institutional analysis appearing in this book has been called "discursive institutionalism" by Campbell and Pedersen (2001). This perspective holds that social actors use language and other symbols to actively construct meaning within institutionalized settings. In this view, then, institutional change is driven and constrained, not just by interest groups and existing institutional arrangements alone, or by cognitive schemata, but also by the discourse processes used to give institutions definition and meaning. Put differently, new institutional arrangements require new symbolic interpretations built up by new narratives and discourse. These new narratives can arise in a variety of ways, including processes of symbolic bricolage, displacement, translation, or direct confrontation across discourse communities. The main point, however, is that interpretive processes both suggest *and* limit possibilities for social action, framing problems in particular ways, suggesting thinkable courses of action, providing acceptable vocabularies of motive, and so on. In this book, the chapter by H. D. Meyer on the waxing and waning of the myth of common schooling represents a particularly creative application of this perspective.

BROADENING THE SCOPE
OF INSTITUTIONAL ANALYSIS

The chapters presented here do more than illustrate the diversity of orienting perspectives constituting the new institutionalism, however. They also illustrate how these perspectives can be used to revise and extend institutional theory to new contexts.

Institutional Theory and Higher Education

One contribution of this book, for example, has been the deliberate inclusion of scholars whose work focuses on higher education institutions. Three chapters in this book discussed this institutional sector (Ramirez, Bernasconi, and Levy). Ramirez and Bernasconi translated institutional theory to the higher education sector with apparent ease; Levy was more cautious.

Consider how Ramirez uses institutional theory to study higher education. For several years, Ramirez has been arguing that a "world model" of higher education exists and is diffusing to nations around the world, much as a "world model" of basic schooling diffused to societies in the world system after World War II. In this volume, Ramirez emphasizes the ways in which this world model calls for a "socially-engaged" university and examines how that ideology is impacting two prestigious universities in very different national environments (Stanford, in the United States, and Oxford, in England). One important point about Ramirez's analysis is that he is seeking to generalize the diffusion model of institutional change from its original intent of explaining events in basic education to a new context where it now also explains events in higher education. But in this volume, Ramirez introduces a new twist to this argument by stating that unique national contexts affect the ease with which different universities adopt this world model. In the language adopted by Ramirez, for example, the unique national histories of England and the United States, as well as the unique organizational histories of Oxford and Stanford, represent "path dependencies" that produce unique adaptations of standard world models, in particular national societies, affecting the timing and ease with which such models get adopted by particular universities. Thus, the approach developed by Ramirez blends both cognitive institutionalism and historical institutionalism.

Another straightforward adaptation of institutional analysis to the field of higher education is provided by Bernasconi. Here, the principle of isomorphism so central to cognitive institutionalism is used to explain the progressive adoption by Chilean higher education institutions of new institutional forms. What is ironic and distinctive about Bernasconi's analysis, however, is that he is using institutional theory to explain the increased use of highly rationalized operational criteria in an increasingly deregulated, privatized, and market-driven education sector. Thus, Bernasconi's analysis suggests that cognitive institutionalism—with its special emphasis on the legitimation of new organizational schemata, and the subsequent diffusion of such schemata through the principle of isomorphism—can be extended not only to explain events in higher education but also to explain the diffusion of highly rationalized forms of management.

A chapter by Levy (in this volume) was far more cautious in its appraisal of the relevance of institutional theory to the study of higher education. Levy's point of departure is the observation that private-sector higher education organizations do not appear to be following the canonical form of organization found in the more established and prestigious public sector. Instead, they appear to be much more diverse and distinctive in organizational form and much more subject to market criteria of performance. This raises questions in Levy's mind about the extent to which the institutional theory—with its dominant image of state-regulated supply of education, pressures for institutional conformity as opposed to technical efficiency, and tendency toward organizational isomorphism—applies to the study of higher education.

Institutional Theory and Markets

Levy's chapter brings us to the second way in which this volume tested the reach of institutional theory, for as it turns out, not only Levy, but also Rowan (chapter 2 and 5) and Davies, Quirke, and Aruni addressed the issue of how to apply institutional theory to the study of market settings. This problem is important because the early focus of institutional theory was on state-sponsored schooling, and because observations of that context generated institutional theory's major insights about organizational isomorphism, loose coupling, and the role of legitimacy as opposed to technical efficiency in enhancing organizational success. Indeed, in the early work of Meyer and colleagues, the reach of institutional theory was explicitly limited to the case of organizations operating in "institutional" environments (i.e., institutional sectors subject to strong regulatory and/or normative pressures but lacking market pressures). Moreover, these environments were explicitly contrasted with "technical" environments (which were defined as more market-driven and technically certain).

Over the years, the distinction between "technical" and "institutional" environments has been questioned. For example, institutional theorists of various stripes now view markets as *institutionalized* arrangements and therefore argue that an important problem for institutional theory is to understand how markets arise and function (e.g., Williamson 1975; Dobbin 1995). In this book, Rowan (chapter 2) follows this line of argument. In particular, he urges institutional theorists in education to follow the lead of Dobbin (1995), who adapted cognitive institutionalism to the study of market institutions by examining how shifting ideologies shape the way markets are organized in societies and how organizations operating within these new market arrangements develop new strategies to succeed. Rowan urges a similar form of analysis in education, first in order to account for the rise of market-provided schooling in the United States and around the world, second to chart the varying ways markets are organized in different education sectors, and finally to examine how schools in market-organized environments operate.

Like Rowan, Davies, Quirke, and Aurini (chapter 7 in this volume) also want to see if institutional theory can be applied to the analysis of market settings in education. But these authors make a distinction between what they call "market theory" and institutional theory. In their view, market theory is not a theory of how organizations act when confronted with market institutions—and thus not a branch of institutional theory. Instead, they see market theory as an alternative theoretical perspective that can be contrasted with institutional theory. The importance of Davies and colleagues' contribution to this volume is their empirical analysis of the structure and functioning of four kinds of private educational organizations in Toronto, Canada. In this study, each group of organizations was found to be operating in a uniquely configured institutional environment, which Davies and colleagues describe in terms of the mix of market competition and regulatory pressures. The key finding of the study is that these varying mixes of pressures lead organizations to develop quite different structures and operations. In particular, Davies and colleagues report that diverse organizational forms arise in market environments with weak regulatory guidance and a lack of performance monitoring. But they also find that when education markets are more highly regulated and subject to stronger performance criteria, there tends to be a greater degree of homogenization of organizational forms. Thus, Davies and colleagues point to a simple principle of institutional analysis—that organizational dynamics are deeply affected by the complex configuration of institutional environments, and insofar as these institutional environments contain varying mixes of market and governance arrangements, no single pattern of educational organization is to be expected across different institutional environments.

Institutional Theory and Tightly Coupled Organizations

A final way this book tested the limits of institutional theory was to see if this theoretical perspective provides analysts with the conceptual tools needed to explain both loose and *tight* coupling in educational organizations. This question is related to the study of markets just mentioned, for in its earliest incarnation, institutional theory in education tended to equate the presence of institutionalized controls with nonrational action (e.g., a logic of conformity) while technical and market environments were seen as producing more rationalized action (e.g., a logic of efficiency).

However, in the years since institutional theory first emerged, many analysts have argued that rational action is itself a deeply institutionalized cognitive schemata, and more to the point, that the presence of this schemata and its legitimacy as a mode of action depends on the presence of particular institutional arrangements (e.g., Dobbin 1995; Powell 1988; Scott 1995) This theoretical stance is important, for as Rowan and Bernasconi point out, it allows institutional theorists interested in studying education to study how institutions can in fact be developed to promote technical rationality and reward technical performance.

The ways in which institutions affect the technical core of schooling are discussed in two chapters in this volume. The first is Charles E. Bidwell's critique of cognitive institutionalism as it has developed in the field of education. Bidwell faults the "loose coupling" version of institutional theory for neglecting to study how work activities are de facto controlled in the absence of externally-institutionalized work rules. Bidwell suggests that when institutional environments provide only vague guidance about technical activities inside educational organizations, "faculty work culture" tends to fill in the void. This proposition makes a great deal of sense. For example, in higher educational organizations, which are weakly regulated by the state, faculty work culture is a central means by which issues of curriculum and instruction are handled. Moreover, as Bidwell points out in this volume, there is a growing research literature on faculty work cultures in schools, much of it pointing to how these cultures affect curriculum, instruction, and professional learning.

James Spillane and Patricia Burch (in this volume) take this argument one step further. Like Bidwell, they are concerned with the role of faculty work culture in enacting institutionalized rules, although more so than Bidwell, Spillane and Burch emphasize the role of *discipline-specific* work cultures in K–12 schools (an emphasis that again corresponds to research on faculty work in higher education). Spillane and Burch note that the external regulation of instruction varies substantially across the various subjects taught in American elementary schooling so that in each discipline, faculty are provided with more or less external guidance about particular dimensions of instruction, work with different instructional tools and artifacts such as tests and texts, and develop different relational networks cutting across system levels. This, of course, leads to many different forms of coupling, some loose, some tight, some tangled (Rowan 2002).

NEW MODELS OF INSTITUTIONAL CHANGE

A final contribution of this book has been to discuss the problem of institutional change. One of the major contributions of the new institutionalism that emerged in the 1970s and 1980s in education was to conceptualize this problem in terms of a model of diffusion. For example, Meyer, Ramirez, and Soysal (1992) examined the expansion of mass education systems throughout the world using a statistical model of diffusion from a central source, where the number of societies adopting mass schooling over time followed the classic S-shaped curve of diffusion research. Even earlier, Rowan (1982) used a similar concept of diffusion to study when California school districts adopted new structural positions. In this volume, Ramirez implicitly uses a model of diffusion in his discussion of world models of higher education. More generally, the notion of structural forms diffusing throughout institutional sectors serves as one of the central models of institutional change, not only in research on education but also in research on other sectors (for a review of studies in this genre, see Scott 1995).

Several authors in this volume address some of the problems this approach to modeling institutional change faces. One problem, for example, is to explain institutional *origins*, that is, how the ideology of mass schooling that disseminated around the world arose in the first place. In this book, Bidwell's analysis suggests that institutional origins occur as interest-group dynamics get played out within existing institutional configurations. Existing institutions both shape existing interests and affect an interest group's likelihood of putting new institutional arrangements in place. Along with Bidwell, we think there is much room for this kind of analysis in institutional theory, not so much to rehash older debates about the origins of mass schooling in the modern world but rather to better understand emerging events in education. For example, as Rowan (chapter 2) notes, there is a pressing need for institutional theorists to explain such contemporary trends in education as the rise of accountability systems or the development of education markets. Questions of institutional origins thus have immediate significance to institutional theory.

David P. Baker also addresses issues of institutional change in this volume. Baker agrees that a uniform "world" model of basic schooling has diffused to nations around the world. But he argues that, after initial adoption of this model, the institutionalization of basic schooling "intensifies" within societies. That is, once adopted, mass schooling gradually comes to enroll more children, for longer periods of time, consuming more societal resources, and making life chances more and more dependent on school performance. The question Baker asks is whether this process of intensification unleashes a predictable pattern of additional changes in the development of mass schooling. Baker is thus searching for what he calls "endogenous" processes of institutional change, that is, patterns of change that can be predicted from the internal logic and operations of state-sponsored, mass education systems.

Baker's data suggest at least some predictable patterns of change. For example, the universalistic norms governing "world models" of schooling encourage a leveling of school quality (as education spending comes to be more evenly distributed across schools within the same nation). This, in turn, results in an increase in the relative importance of family effects on cognitive achievement (i.e., as schools themselves become more alike in their effects on learning, family differences become per force the main factor differentiating achievement levels among students). But as this occurs, the meritocratic norms of mass schooling unleash a further change—the increased tendency for individuals, regardless of income, to purchase additional education through shadow education agencies as a means of securing their children's advantage in this universalistic system. Thus, pressures and counterpressures inside the system lead to endogenous patterns of change in the institution.

We think the "internal" logic of mass schooling might be leading not only to the developments Baker describes but also to other trends, especially the movement toward tighter forms of education accountability and/or the spreading of market-based forms of basic education services. Roger Benjamin (1980), for example, argued that once nation-states solve the problem of access to publicly provided services such as education, the progressive rationalization of societies worldwide inevitably leads to calls for increased accountability in the public provision of goods and services. Thus, we might assume that as nation-states expand access to basic education, calls for accountability inevitably increase. A similar internal logic might lead to expansion of education markets, again as a means for more powerful parents to secure advantages for their children in a meritocratic system in which the public sector has been "leveled" in terms of quality.

A final problem in the study of educational change is suggested by Heinz-Dieter Meyer's discussion of the waxing and waning of the "master myth" of common schooling in the United States. Meyer's account of this process begins in a period of great institutional uncertainty in American education, a time when multiple models of schooling existed, none of which were endorsed by powerful centers (Katz 1971). He then describes how leaders of the common school movement developed an appealing narrative to justify the rise of a more centralized and bureaucratized school system, framing this narrative in ways that appealed to many different factions. Over time, Meyer argues that this narrative experienced a process of symbolic bricolage—the addition and reframing of different narrative elements in response to various historical events. He concludes that this narrative is no longer as appealing as it once was and that this loss of rhetorical relevance and power is now working to erode the legitimating power of the common school ideal in American society. Meyer's chapter is a very creative illustration of a form of analysis that Campbell and Pedersen (2001) called "institutional constructivism." It highlights not only the dramatic and rhetorical processes involved in institutional change but also how institutions are both contingent and contested, not only at their points of origin but also after institutionalization. In addition, this idea supplements the other approaches to institutional change just discussed, opening the field to some innovative forms of analysis little used in educational institutionalism to date.

CONCLUSION

In summary, perhaps the most important contribution of this book is its demonstration of how to expand the scope of new institutionalist analyses in the field of education. Whereas the new institutionalism was originally developed in the field of education to study the spread of state-sponsored, basic schooling around the world and to explain the loosely coupled nature of America's K–12 education system, the perspective is now being used to study events in other education sectors and new patterns of organization and governance within education systems. This book shows that in expanding the scope of institutional analysis, education researchers are making several contributions: they are bringing to bear a broader number of theoretical perspectives on education as an institution, looking at both public- and market-sector developments, explaining both loose and tight couplings in the system, and formulating new models of institutional change. All of this bodes well for the continuing relevance of institutional theory to the study of contemporary events in education and for enriching our understanding of the seemingly ever-growing number of institutional arrangements through which basic and postsecondary education are now provided around the world.

REFERENCES

Benjamin, Roger. 1980. *The limits of politics: Collective goods and political change in postindustrial societies.* Chicago: University of Chicago Press.

Campbell, John L., and Ove K. Pedersen. 2001. The second movement in institutional analysis. In *The Rise of Neoliberalism and Institutional Analysis*, ed. John L. Campbell and Ove K. Pedersen, 249–82. Princeton, NJ: Princeton University Press.

DiMaggio, Paul J., and Walter W. Powell. 1983. The iron cage revisited: Institutional isomorphism and collective rationality in organizational fields. *American Sociological Review* 48: 147–60.

Dobbin, Frank R. 1995. *Forging industrial policy: The United States, Britain, and France in the railway age.* New York: Cambridge University Press.

House, Earnest R. 1996. *Schools for sale: Why free market policies won't save America's schools and what will.* New York: Teachers College Press.

Katz, Michael. 1968/2001. *The irony of early school reform: Educational innovation in mid-nineteenth century Massachusetts.* New York: Teachers College Press.

Levy, Daniel C. 1999. When private higher education does not bring organizational diversity: Argentina, China, Hungary. In *Private Prometheus: Private higher education and development in the twenty-first century,* ed. P. Altbach, 17–50. West Port, CT: Greenwood.

Meyer, John W., David Kamens, and Aaron Benavot. 1992. *School knowledge for the masses: World models and national primary curriculum categories in the twentieth century.* London: Falmer.

Meyer, John W., and Brian Rowan. 1977. Institutionalized organizations: Formal structure as myth and ceremony. *American Journal of Sociology* 83: 340–63.

———. 1978. The structure of educational organizations. In *Environments and Organizations,* ed. Marshall W. Meyer, 78–109. San Francisco: Jossey-Bass.

Meyer, John W., and W. Richard Scott. 1983. *Organizational environments: Ritual and rationality.* Beverly Hills, CA: Sage.

Rowan, Brian. 1982. Organizational structure and the institutional environment: The case of public schools. *Administrative Science Quarterly* 27: 259–79.

———. 2002. Rationality and reality in organizational management: Using the coupling metaphor to understand educational (and other) organizations—a concluding comment. *Journal of Educational Administration* 40: 604–11.

Rowan, Brian, and Cecil G. Miskel. 1999. Institutional theory and the study of educational organizations." In *Handbook of Research on Educational Administration,* ed. Joseph Murphy and Karen Seashore-Louis. 2nd edition. San Francisco: Jossey-Bass.

Scott, W. Richard. 1995. *Institutions and organizations.* Thousand Oaks, CA: Sage.

Williamson, Oliver E. 1975. *Markets and hierarchies: Analysis and antitrust implications.* New York: Free Press.

THIRTEEN

Gauging the Prospects for Change

HEINZ-DIETER MEYER

INSTITUTIONS CHANGE for the most part with glacial speed. More radical transitions are usually limited to rare and singular moments in history. At the end of a book whose chapters describe new institutional developments across historic, sectoral, and national boundaries, one inevitably wonders if the diverse observations presented here might give us a clue whether we are observing a mere increment in the glacier's downward skid or the opening of a crack that could result in a landslide.

TRICKLE OUT: INCREMENTAL CHANGES
ALONG THE INSTITUTIONAL PERIPHERY

One of the recurrent themes we encountered throughout the book was a growing institutional diversity that often trumped the tendency for institutional isomorphism that institutional research in past decades found to be so prevalent. In many cases the departures from entrenched models of schools and universities are limited, taking place on the periphery of the established institutions. For example, growing commercial tutoring services for students in K–12 do not pose a threat to core institutions of public education. But, in the aggregate, they provide a kind of "shadow education" that is grafted onto the established forms. Other movements on the periphery include marked increases in private for-profit and nonprofit organizations offering K–12 and higher education, public-private partnerships among schools, colleges, and other private or voluntary organizations, a rising interest in home schooling, cyber-education, and so on. Where new institutional models of private schools and universities have sprung up, they defy some of the rules and norms institutionalized in the dominant models. Countries that never knew any other institutional forms of education outside the government sector have become home for educational entrepreneurs who effectively address unmet educational needs. As the boundary between public and private forms of schooling and education is redrawn, the change occasionally spills back over into the public sector whose leaders feel new competitive pressures from which public institutions have hitherto been excluded. In some cases this means the retreat of central government control in favor of greater autonomy for local units. In others government bureaucracies are trying to force greater accountability and standardization on the large majority of schools that remain in the public domain.

None of these developments readily conforms to any of the grand narratives of social change—neither to the secular trend of rationalization Weber diagnosed nor to the rise of unaccountable and uncontrolled powers of institutions that is part of the stock diagnosis of postmodernists. But this must not blind us to the fact that the changes we are witnessing go well beyond the merely cosmetic or residual. Rather, we are observing a "softening" of the traditional configuration in which government is the taken-for-granted supplier of education (Meyer 2001). At the same time we find a growing acceptance for education whose legitimacy does not derive from the state. Even if for now most of these changes occur on the periphery of the entrenched core institutions of education, a small but dynamic alternative institutional sector can under certain circumstances become the take-off point for more massive metamorphoses.

WHY LARGE-SCALE LOSS OF LEGITIMACY IS UNLIKELY: THE LOGIC OF INSTITUTIONS AND ORGANIZATIONS

Legitimacy erodes as more people take practical steps toward organizations based on new types of legitimacy. Unlike most organizations, which exist in the service of more narrow and clearly defined purposes, educational organizations are deeply anchored in a society's finely spun web of norms and expectations, tied down by myriads of constituents holding myriads of expectations. Schools are expected to turn out qualified workers, responsible citizens, individuals who are appreciative of their own and respectful of other cultures, loyal believers in the nation's dominant secular or religious faith, as well as versatile cosmopolitans ready to engage a global world. They are held to mold hetero-geneous groups of young people into a cohesive community of shared beliefs and to reproduce the nation's identity. Furthermore, they are expected to maintain a large and diverse student body in a state of order and control, sub-ject to the approval of the reigning parent generation who remember their own education and use it unwittingly as *the* standard for the schools of their children. Education is the most "upstream" of all social endeavors, closest to the point at which a nation's cultural and institutional orthodoxies originate. Their upstream location makes educational institutions perhaps the most change resistant among the large-scale public institutions, simply because they are supported by the deepest sentiments of tradition, habit, and identity held by the largest number of people. The same reason makes any sudden, wide-spread disenchantment with our schools unlikely—no matter how well or poorly they serve our perceived or real needs. As has been pointed out many times throughout this book: insulating an institution's legitimacy from its technical efficiency is precisely the effect of institutionalization. Unlike non-institutionalized organizations that will be judged by their effectiveness and efficiency, the support of institutionalized organizations is guaranteed almost independent of their performance and despite the availability of demonstra-bly superior models. The difference between the logics of institutions and organizations helps explain this oft-posed puzzle of institutional inertia. Insti-tutions are not judged by how well they facilitate the attainment of specific goals but rather by how much they contribute to social order and stability. Thus the question, "Why are less-than-optimal arrangements sustained, even in the face of opposition?" (Powell 1991, 190) is largely beside the point when it comes to institutions. Those who ask it operate on the mistaken assumption that institutions are like organizations, operating in the service of specific goals. In that view, the more evidence there is for the "poor performance" of an institution the sooner it may break its inertia. This, however, is demonstra-bly not the case.

Another explanation why institutions remain unfazed by performance-based critiques is given by economists and sociologists who often refer to the ideas of "lock-in" and "vested interests" to explain institutional inertia. According to economists lock-in occurs whenever a particular social practice or technology is sufficiently entrenched so as to make switching to an avail-able superior practice prohibitively costly. The vested-interest thesis refers to the fact that the negative impact of an institution's demise on the interests of its supporters is often greater than the opposite impact on its potential radi-cal opponents.

> Practices and structures often endure through the active efforts of those who benefit from them. . . . It is clear that elite intervention may play a critical role in institutional formation. And once established and in place, practices

and programs are supported and promulgated by those organizations that benefit from prevailing conventions. In this way, elites may be both the architects and products of the rules and expectations they have helped to devise. (Powell 1991, 190–91)

Both the lock-in idea and the vested-interest thesis base their explanation of inertia-in-the-face-of-superior-solutions on the assumption that a rational constituency will prefer more over less efficient institutions. Neither of these explanations refers to the social, emotional, and cognitive supports that people derive from the continuity of their key institutions. While organizations answer to metrics of effectiveness and efficiency, the standard for the effectiveness of institutions is not their technical performance but their ability to maintain order and stability and to be viewed as legitimate. When organizations become inefficient, they either die or reinvent themselves. Institutions, however, only change when they produce instability instead of order.

Legitimacy and efficiency are thus incompatible standards. When we assert our beliefs and values we do so *regardless* of efficiency concerns. This means that institutions are not easily shaken by arguments about "suboptimality" or "inefficiency" because their first and foremost mission is to represent and enact our beliefs and values.

Institutional inertia is the flipside of "social stability." It is a crucial prerequisite for a stable society. Institutions are the answer to the question: what makes social order possible (in the face of selfishly rational human beings). Their inertia is simply the price we pay for the possibility to live life under reasonably predictable, ordered conditions. But while mere discontent with the performance of public education will not lead to an erosion of its legitimacy, the gradual trickle-out observed above may well do so. As people recognize the feasibility of schooling outside the old order, their ability to act on their feelings will increase. This is especially so as additional causes hasten the pressure for change.

A LOOK AHEAD

No probe of the changing educational landscape is complete without considering what may be the two most powerful change agents: the pressures emanating from the "knowledge economy" leading to growing demands for knowledge professionals and the World Wide Web and its power to revolutionize education.

As many observers have pointed out, one effect of the knowledge economy is to alter the power balance between knowledge workers and owners (Drucker 1998). Unlike industrial workers, knowledge workers carry their "means of production" in their head, making them less susceptible to the whims of bosses and owners. Teachers are a key segment of knowledge workers. They need to master complex skills and knowledge, yet they continue in subaltern positions that leave them with less rather than more autonomy and discretion over their work (Smith 1998). As historians and sociologists of education have amply documented, this "teacher-as-shop-floor-worker" model is deeply entrenched in the American tradition of a "one best" model for public education (Callahan 1962; Tyack and Cuban 1995). It also forms the basis for the teacher unions' commitment to collective bargaining as opposed to educational professionalism (Meyer 2005). While school administrators were able to carve out "executive" roles for themselves (thus making sure they would profit from the high esteem in which American culture holds business executives) teaching became institutionalized as a kind of guidance to rote learning.

The idea of schools as mechanistic organizations organized around a simple task—the diffusion of literacy—stands in sharp contrast to the possibility of decentralized, flexible organic organizations that could prepare young people for the knowledge society (Brian, Rowan, Stephen W. Raudenbush, and Yuk Fai. Cheong 1993). Toward that end, today's students need far more than the ability to read, write, and do arithmetic. They need to learn how to become leaders in teaching, learning, and self-management. This requires that teachers themselves have achieved mastery on that level, rather than a narrow contents expertise limited to one subject and one grade level. Like with many of their knowledge peers, teachers' long-term productivity will more critically depend on their ability (and that of higher education) to create a new institutional model of teaching and learning that will bolster their competence and increase their autonomy.

Meanwhile, higher education, too, is coming under even stronger pressures to change. A number of experts have testified that higher education's center of gravity is slowly shifting from liberal arts undergraduate education to returning adult professional education (Brint 2002; Duderstadt and Womack 2003; Lanham 2002). Declining birth rates and increasing life expectancy mean that more adults will return for more academic "refueling stops" over a longer life span. That suggests a growing demand for job-related courses such as management, education, health sciences, and applied technology. It also means that an increasing number of adult students will be interested in "just-in-time" learning experiences rather than the traditional four-year degrees.

Just as the late Middle Ages supplanted the oral discourse—then the main form of academic communication—with the printed word, so it seems that late modernity may enrich the spoken and written text with cyber-space communication. Universities would have to operate with equal ease in traditional as well as virtual learning environments, and in local as well as global contexts. Face-to-face and online learning are already becoming equal and complementary ways of learning, as newspaper and television have become complementary media of information. By putting their courses online, universities open their classrooms to a global audience of students.

An even sharper acceleration of competitive dynamics between the new for-profit entrepreneurs and the established higher education is, according to some, likely to follow a segmented, selective competitive strategy of educational entrepreneurs who wish to exploit the full effect of the World Wide Web. Instead of competing with core institutions on the latter's turf, the entrepreneurs may (and some do already) concentrate on those parts of higher education where they can deliver high quality at competitive prices. The comprehensive university is thus coming under pressure from higher education niche players—entrepreneurs who target the low-cost, high-revenue slices of the smorgasboard offered by the comprehensive universities.

The entrepreneurs try to exploit the fact that a university's many different activities—undergraduate, graduate, professional, doctoral, and certificate education in market-proximate and market-distant fields—have different cost and revenue structures. There are the "cash-cows" (e.g., business or teacher education) and the sinkholes (e.g., doctoral training in the sciences). By focusing on the former, the entrepreneurs can operate on the principle that excellence and efficiency in a narrow field beat comprehensive mediocrity. As higher education entrepreneurs are getting established in the returning adult, corporate, and international market, they are positioning themselves to become highly competitive players for a wider range of domestic higher education "products." All this may leave the reform-minded cautiously optimistic. As the trickle-out to new and modified institutions continues, as the knowledge economy and the ubiquity of the World Wide Web add to the mounting pressures for change, more people will avail themselves of the option for partial and full exit from the established system. The institutional periphery may well become an experiment for the feasibility of alternative models of legitimate education. As that happens, the current trickle may ultimately produce sizeable streams.

REFERENCES

Brint, Steven G., ed. 2002. *The future of the city of intellect.* Stanford, CA: Stanford University Press.

Callahan, Raymond. 1962. *Education and the cult of efficiency.* Chicago: University of Chicago Press.

Drucker, Peter. 1998. From capitalism to knowledge society. In *The Knowledge Economy,* ed. Dale Neef, 15–34. Woburn, MA: Butterworth Heinemann.

Duderstadt, James J., and Farris W. Womack. 2003. *The future of the public university in America: Beyond the crossroads.* Baltimore: Johns Hopkins University Press.

Lanham, Richard A. 2002. The audit of virtuality: Universities in the attention economy. In *The future of the city of intellect,* ed. Steven G. Brint, 159–180. Stanford, CA: Stanford University Press.

Meyer, Heinz-Dieter. 2005. Trade, profession, or entrepreneurs? The market-faithful raise important questions about the future of teacher unions. *American Journal of Education* 112, November, 107–14.

————. 2001. Civil society and education: The return of an idea. In *Education between state, markets, and civil society: Comparative perspectives*, ed. Heinz-Dieter Meyer and William L. Boyd, 13–33. Mahwah, NJ: Erlbaum.

Powell, Walter. 1991. Expanding the scope of institutional analysis. In *The New Institutionalism in Organizational Analysis*, ed. Walter W. Powell and Paul J. DiMaggio, 183–203. Chicago: Chicago University Press.

Rowan, Brian, Stephen W. Raudenbush, and Yuk Fai Cheong. 1993. Teaching as a non-routine task: Implications for the management of schools. *Educational Administration Quarterly* 29: 479–500.

Smith, Hedrick. High-school—The neglected majority: Whose mid-kids are on track for the global economy? In *The Knowledge Economy*, ed. Dale Neef, 219–40. Woburn, MA: Butterworth Heinemann.

Tyack, David, and Larry Cuban. 1995. *Tinkering toward utopia: A century of public school reform.* Cambridge, MA: Harvard University Press.

Contributors

JANICE AURINI is a post-doctoral fellow in the Department of Sociology at Harvard University. Her dissertation examines the emergence of private education businesses in Ontario, and their implication for new institutional theory.

DAVID P. BAKER is currently the Harry and Marion Eberly professor of education and sociology at Pennsylvania State University. His scholarship focuses on the comparative study of the institutional impact of education on modern society. His most recent publications include *National Differences, Global Similarities: World Culture and the Future of Schooling* (Stanford CA: Stanford University Press [with G. LeTendre]); and "Rising Mean IQ: Cognitive Demand of Mathematics Education for Young Children, Population Exposure to formal Schooling, and the Neurobiology of the Prefrontal Cortex," *Intelligence* 33, 93–106 (with C. Blair, D. Gamson, and S. Throne).

ANDRÉS BERNASCONI is a professor at the Institute of Political Studies, Universidad Andres Bello, Chile. His research interests are the academic profession in Latin America, the private sector of higher education internationally, and comparative higher education law. He is currently a collaborating scholar in the Program for Research on Private Higher Education, headquartered at the State University of New York, Albany. A lawyer by training, he holds a master's degree in public policy from Harvard University and a PhD in sociology of organizations from Boston University.

CHARLES E. BIDWELL is the William Claude Reavis professor of sociology, emeritus at the University of Chicago. He is author of "Schools as Formal Organizations," in *Handbook of Organizations*, ed. James March (1965), an early paper that pioneered institutional analysis in education. His current research is focused on the social organization of education and schooling and the life course. His recent publications include "Analyzing Schools as Organizations: Long-Term Permanence and Short-Term Change," in *Sociology of Education* (2001) and "The Problem of Classroom Goodwill," in *Stability and Change in American Education* (2003). An essay on the comparative analysis of public and private education in the United States, written with Robert Dreeben, will appear in 2006.

PATRICIA BURCH is an assistant professor at the University of Wisconsin, Madison in the Department of Educational Policy Studies. Burch draws on theories of organizational learning and change to examine the implementation of K–12 educational reform. Her current research focuses on the role and influence of profit organizations and public-sector middle management in educational policy implementation.

SCOTT DAVIES is professor of sociology at McMaster University. He has published widely on sociology of education in American, British, and Canadian journals and is currently interested in the impact of market forces on education.

DANIEL C. LEVY is distinguished professor at the State University of New York, Albany. He teaches courses in the social analysis of education. Levy's main research interest is how educational institutions fit into civil society. His eight books and numerous articles deal mostly with higher education policy. As scholar and consultant, he has lectured at almost all the leading U.S. universities and on six continents. Levy is the recipient of grants from leading foundations and of awards from academic associations.

HEINZ-DIETER MEYER is currently associate professor at the State University of New York, Albany. His main interests concern institutional and organizational effects on organizational change and the implications for management and policy. Recent publications in English include "Education between State, Markets, and Civil Society: Comparative Perspectives" (Lawrence Erlbaum), and "Tocqueville's Cultural Institutionalism" in the *Journal of Classical Sociology* (2003). Meyer teaches courses in organization theory, social theory, and education management. Prior to joining the State University of New York at Albany, he taught at the University of Goettingen, Germany, and at INSEAD, Fontainebleau, France.

FRANCISCO O. RAMIREZ is professor of education and (by courtesy) sociology at Stanford. He is the coauthor of "Science in the Modern World Polity: Globalization and Institutionalization" and of "Student Achievement and

National Economic Growth," *American Journal of Education* (2006). His current research interests include human rights and human rights education, rethinking education as incorporation, the rationalization of universities, and the impact of these developments on women and their role in fostering these developments.

BRIAN ROWAN has written extensively on institutions and education. He has authored several influential early papers in the field. His current scholarly interests lie at the intersection of organization theory and school effectiveness research and include a large-scale, longitudinal study of the design, implementation, and effectiveness of three of America's largest comprehensive school reform initiatives. Prior to joining the education faculty at the University of Michigan in 1991, Rowan was a senior research director at Far West Laboratory for Educational Research and Development and chairperson of the Departmet of Educational Administration at Michigan State University.

JAMES P. SPILLANE is the Spencer T. and Ann W. Olin professor in learning and organizational change at Northwestern University where he teaches in the learning sciences and human development and social policy graduate programs. He is also a faculty fellow at the Institute for Policy Research. Spillane's work explores the policy implementation process at the state, school district, school, and classroom levels and school leadership and management. He is author of "Standards Deviation: How Local Schools Miss-Understand Policy" (Harvard University Press, 2004) and "Distributed Leadership" (Jossey-Bass, 2006).

LINDA QUIRKE is a faculty member at Wilfrid Laurier University's Brantford campus, in sociology and organizational leadership. Her research interests center on schools' responses to their institutional environments. Her PhD dissertation explores how deviant or "rogue" Toronto private schools resist isomorphic pressures and secure legitimacy by appealing to alternative sources of support. She has recently copublished work on Toronto private schools in the *American Journal of Education* and in a chapter in a forthcoming book edited by Maureen Hallinan.

Index